VIVALDI'S
VENICE

VIVALDI'S VENICE

Music and celebration in the baroque era

PATRICK BARBIER

Translated from the French by
Margaret Crosland

Souvenir Press

First published 2002 by Editions Grasset et Fasquelle

Copyright © 2002 Editions Grasset et Fasquelle

English translation Copyright © 2003 by Souvenir Press and Margaret Crosland

This translation published 2003 by
Souvenir Press Ltd,
43 Great Russell Street, London WC1B 3PD

ISBN 0 285 63670 7

Typeset by Avocet Typeset, Chilton, Aylesbury, Bucks

Printed in Great Britain by
Creative Print and Design Group (Wales), Ebbw Vale

To Pierre-Emmanuel
and Coralie

Acknowledgements

The author wishes to express his heartfelt thanks to all the people who, from near and far, in Venice and in France, gave him encouragement and help in his research, especially Professor Giuseppe Ellero of the Istituto Ricovero ed Educazione, specialist in the former Ospedali of Venice, for his great kindness, his enthusiasm and availability; Dr Franco Casini, of the Istituto per le Lettre ed il Melodramma at the Fondazione Giorgio Cini; Professor Gino Benzoni of the Istituto per la Società Veneziana at the Fondazione Giorgio Cini; the conservators of the Biblioteca Marciana and the Fondazione Querini Stampalia; Stepan Kechichian of the Collegio Armeniano (Cà Zenobio), the conservators of the archives of the Ministère des Affaires Etrangères, in Paris and Nantes. Also Dominique Fernandez, Olivier Echappé, Laura Clerfeuille, Marie-Liesse Barbier, Patrick Favre-Tissot-Bonvoisin.

Contents

Acknowledgements   vi
List of illustrations   xii

CHAPTER 1: **A city, its people, and music**   *page* 1
Music and society in Venice: a few preliminaries   2
Omnipresence of music in Venice. Supremacy over
Naples. Aims of this book
Music everywhere and at every moment   3
Music, art of the people. Astonishment of foreigners at the
extent of its practice. The barcarolles. A people who
expressed themselves in music
Can we really know Vivaldi?   08
Lack of documentation on Vivaldi. Family origins and
ecclesiastical career. Impossibility of practising the
priesthood. His personality, his portraits. Vivaldi as seen
by his contemporaries

CHAPTER 2: **Discovering Venice in Vivaldi's day**   17
Portrait of a city and its people   19
Demography of Venice in the time of Vivaldi. The different
social classes and their hierarchy. The nobility and the doge.
Interactions between the social classes
On some Venetian lifestyles   25
The arrival of an outsider in Venice, his feelings of
strangeness (urbanism, calendar, times of day). The
gondoliers, women and courtesans. Difficult contacts

Contents

*between the nobility, ordinary people and foreign visitors.
Licentiousness and gambling*

Feast days and ritual as guarantees of stability   36
*A plethora of ritual feast days. Their division into three
categories: immoveable feasts (Christmas, etc.) moveable
feasts (Ascension and the marriage with the sea) and
'extraordinary' feast days (coronation of a doge,
enthronement of a patriarch)*

Carnival, quintessence of the Venetian spirit   45
*Six months of carnival in three periods. The taste for
wearing masks. The games on Carnival Thursday, the
bulls on Carnival Sunday, the madness of Shrove Tuesday*

Summary of the 38 immovable religious feast days
in Venice   51

CHAPTER 3: **The Ospedali, or musical fame for the
poorest of people**   54

The four Ospedali: orphanages and conservatoires   54
*Remote origins of the four Ospedali. Their place in the
city and what remains of them today. The aims of these
institutions*

Organisation and social life in the Ospedali   58
*Admission of poor children and orphan girls. Population
of these institutions. Management, 'choir' girls and
'working class' girls. Discipline and outings*

An international musical reputation   62
*Fame of the young girls. Admiration of foreign visitors.
Concerts, masses, oratorios. Contribution to Venice and to
the Ospedali. Improved social status for the girls but a
ban from practising music on leaving. The love of one
boarder for the painter Tiepolo*

Vivaldi and La Pietà   70

Contents

Individual characteristics of La Pietà. Specialisation of this Ospedale in instrumental music. Performance and distribution of the voices. Role of Vivaldi and of the various maestri. The oratorio Juditha triumphans. *The concertos composed for La Pietà and the contribution of the Red Priest. His influence on the whole of Europe. The decline of the Ospedali at the end of the eighteenth century*

CHAPTER 4: **Sacred music and religious festivals**   83
The religious organisation of the city   84
*The patriarch and the primicerio of St Mark's.
Relationships between the Church and the State.
Ordained and lay clergy*
Ordinary people in the great Venetian ceremonies   86
*Highly individual Venetian religious practices.
Magnificent processions and sacred or 'republican'
celebrations. The burial of a doge. Relaxation of morals
in the eighteenth century.*
Music at St Mark's and its performers   93
*Originality of the services at St Mark's. The chapel
master, the singers and the musicians. Intensity of
religious life at St Mark's and the organisation of the
ceremonies. Splendour of the processions in the Piazza or
during Holy Week*
Musical and social life in the convents   100
*Freedom of morals in the convents. Casanova's
adventures with a nun. Masked visitors in the parlour.
Ceremonial festivities in some convents. Balls and operas
in the parlour*

Contents

CHAPTER 5: **Venetian opera and its public**   108

Venice, opera capital of the seventeenth century   109
*Venetian opera in the seventeenth century and the
opening of the first theatres to the general public.
Exceptional role of Monteverdi and Cavalli. Spirit of
these operas and astonishment of foreign visitors*

The theatre audience   113
*The Italian-style auditorium and the mingling of social
classes. The groundlings. The theatre boxes, real private
salons. Life in the boxes and the multiple pleasures offered
by the theatres. An evening at the opera. Behaviour of the
lower classes and the habit of spitting down from the
boxes*

The mechanics of opera production

Family owners and impresarios   120
Décor and production   126
Castrati and women singers   129
Farinelli in Venice   132
Satire on behaviour in the theatres   139
Vivaldi's operas in their context   144
*Spread of his influence abroad. Vivaldi's débuts in opera.
Vivaldi's dependence on second-class theatres. The singer
Anna Girò and her relationship with the Red Priest.
Vivaldi's journeys. Vivaldi and the satire of Benedetto
Marcello. Genius and weaknesses of Vivaldi's operatic
repertoire*

CHAPTER 6: **Musical splendour of the private
palazzi**   155

The 'academies' or music at home   155
*Different meanings of the word 'academy'. Societies for
musicians, the Philharmonic Academy, the Society of*

Contents

*Saint Cecilia, the social protection of musicians. The
'amateur' concerts according to different social classes.
Parties and balls on special occasions*
A party with the Contarini family   163
*The villa and the theatre at Piazzola. The magnificent
fêtes of 1679–80. The operas, their productions and
lighting illuminations*
Ceremonies and receptions at the embassies   165
*Arrivals of the ambassadors. Luxurious life in the
embassies and formal ceremonies. An evening at the French
Embassy*
The art of the 'serenade'   169
*An allegorical mini-opera. The ambassadors' commissions
and the entertainments linked to dynastic events. Vivaldi
and the French Embassy*

Epilogue: Death in . . . Vienna   174
*Vivaldi's death certificate. Reasons for his departure from
Venice. Assessment of his work. Solitude and poverty of
Vivaldi in Vienna. Subsequent neglect. Rediscovery of his
music in the twentieth century*

Notes   178
Bibliography and archive sources   184
Index   192

List of Illustrations

Frontispiece: Portrait of Vivaldi (Museo Civico, Bologna; courtesy Scala)

Between pages 82 and 83:

1. The Ospedaletto church, showing the grilles behind which the girls sang
2. Girls' Concert (given at the Philharmonic Society, 1782), painting by Gabriele Bella (courtesy, Museo Civico Correr, Venice)

3. The Mendicanti, Venice, as it is today (photo, Patrick Barbier)
4. The Nuns' Parlour, painting by Francesco Guardi, based on the nuns' parlour at the convent of San Zaccaria (courtesy, Ca' Rezzonico, Venice)

5. Interior of the Teatro San Benedetto, engraving by Antonio Baratti (courtesy, Museo Civico Correr, Venice)
6. The Ridotto, or Gambling Room, painting by Francesco Guardi (courtesy, Ca' Rezzonico, Venice)

7. Carnival Scene, Painting by Domenico Tiepolo (courtesy, Musée du Louvre, Paris)
8. Masked Conversation, painting by Pietro Longhi (courtesy Ca' Rezzonico, Venice)

CHAPTER 1

A city, its people, and music

Argos is said to have had an hundred eyes . . . in
this place one wishes to be all *ears* for music . . .
Dr Burney

Venice has always fascinated and disconcerted travellers. Even today, you only have to see the enthusiasm of people ready to absorb the splendour of the palazzi and the churches, the strikingly picturesque canals, the bridges and the campi, the atmosphere that has apparently remained unchanged for centuries, while others find it hard to accept the swarms of tourists, the decaying façades and the foul smells from the same canals. Everything for and against has been said for centuries about the same places. Simply consider the remarks made about the Grand Canal from the time of Commynes in the fifteenth century ('I believe it the most beautiful avenue in the world') to Régis Debray ('The only sewer in the world which makes the onlooker as intoxicated as if he were casting off in the Marquesas Islands').

There was just as much contradiction among the seventeenth- and eighteenth-century visitors. They were fascinated by the strange way in which Venice was built along the lagoon but they realised how inconvenient it could be. They envied the apparent freedom of the Venetian lifestyle, the keen love of festivity and all forms of pleasure, without entirely approving the laxity of these people who believed neither in God nor in reason, made light of everything, and turned everything into a joke, past, present and future. They admired the stability of this patrician Republic, apparently strong and unchanging, but they were suspicious of the omnipresent police, denunciations and secret executions. For everyone, Venice remained a delight and a mystery: geographical, political and artistic.

Music and society in Venice: a few preliminaries

Throughout all the pages written about Venice in the baroque era, music remained one of the principal subjects of interest and – must it be said? – of amazement. Music, much more than the other arts, and on an equal footing with political and religious life in La Serenissima, as the Republic was known, never ceased to attract the attention of travellers, even those least interested in it. The fact is that throughout the seventeenth century Venice had become a beacon for the whole of Europe through the reputation of its operatic theatres, the first open to the general public as from 1637, then, at the start of the eighteenth century, through the astonishing development of its instrumental music. But even more than the repertoire it was the mingling of musical life with social life, rare in Europe, that fascinated visitors of all kinds. Few cities associated a branch of the arts, such as music, so closely with the entire social set-up, from the most humble of gondoliers to the most cultivated Venetians. Music was everywhere, in the religious ceremonies and festivals, so numerous at that time, in the theatre, in the charitable institutions, in private concerts and especially in the street, where many foreigners maintained it was there that they found the best musicians, the best serenades, all impromptu, that could possibly be heard.

Why did Venice occupy such a predominant place on the musical chessboard of Europe? After all, according to Baretti, was not the whole of Italy, 'the land of Europe most favourable to music?' The Neapolitans could claim a similar position, for, according to some observers such as the Abbé Coyer, they lived 'more through their hearing than through other senses? Naples was indeed another musical capital, through the fame of its four conservatoires and the celebrated musicians that it had trained and 'exported'. But the musical rise of Naples dates from the first decades of the eighteenth century and owed much more to the development of *opera seria* and the birth of *opera buffa*. The Venetian school was already far ahead. Its golden age was even well in advance of Vivaldi's era: from the arrival of the Flemish Adrian Willaert in 1527, which was to make the chapel of St Mark's into one of the most brilliant in Europe, until the death of Monteverdi in 1643, Venice flourished. Then, with its role of operatic capital during the seventeenth century and the brilliant productions of Marcello, Albinoni and Vivaldi at the start of the eighteenth, the art of music and the people of Venice continued to fuse together in a surprising alchemy which perplexed passing foreigners. 'The nation's enthusiasm for this art is incomprehensible,' Charles de Brosses noted.

This is why it is interesting to describe now what daily life, musical and ceremonial, was like in Venice during the seventeenth and eighteenth centuries. It can be evoked through many archive documents, traveller's recollections, letters from Venetians or foreigners, essays on the seventeenth and eighteenth centuries and the many links which existed between music and Venetian society.

The chosen period is that of Antonio Vivaldi, born, it should be remembered, in 1678 and dying in 1741. A new biography of the maestro would certainly be valuable for a better understanding of the man and his period. But it is well known that documents about the composer are rare: accounts that mention him are few in number while only thirteen of his letters, limited to the period 1736–9, are known today. This explains the small number of monographs that have been written to date about the composer of *The Four Seasons*. That said, the Vivaldi period, from every point of view, is fascinating: his youth was conditioned by the peak years of the Venetian opera, a highly popular genre, but protected and developed by the great patrician families; the first half of the eighteenth century was the period of fame for the *ospedali*, which produced the best female musicians and singers of Italy; it was also the period when Venice triumphed in the area of instrumental music, notably with the famous concertos of Vivaldi which Europe adopted very quickly. During this time the frantic whirlwind of festivities and carnival grew more powerful, sweeping La Serenissima up, half a century before its final collapse.

Music everywhere and at every moment

Few people have expressed themselves through music as much as the Venetians. 'They sing in the squares, in the streets and along the canals,' wrote Goldoni; 'the shopkeepers sing as they sell their goods, the workers sing as they leave their work, the gondoliers sing while waiting for their masters[1].'* Shopkeepers and gondoliers represented a small fraction of a society entirely preoccupied with the pleasure of words and music: in the Republic of Venice, from the highest class of the nobility to the orphan girls in the *ospedali* and the humble fishermen, from the Bucintoro to the most modest craft, men, women and children lived and expressed themselves in music.

All over the city and along the lagoon, in every aspect of life, this daily practice continually impressed travellers in the seventeenth and eighteenth centuries. It was difficult for them to admit that a street musician could play like a virtuoso, that a half-naked urchin could trill like a nightingale, while fishermen returning in the evening called out to their wives on shore by singing. Music seemed a natural requirement, everyone loved it spontaneously, without question, just as anyone might notice a pretty woman or admire a sunset.

The omnipresence of water, the continual journeys by boat and all that life round the lagoons which passed with a slowness unknown to other nations, favoured the abundance and richness of gondolier songs (*canzoni da battello*) which earned the admiration of all visitors. From the fifteenth century in fact, lyrical poetry in music, of a popular nature, had flourished. It was called *Justiniana*, taking its name from a noble Venetian, Leonardo Giustinian, who was a poet, musician and statesman, belonging also to one of the oldest families of the city. The great vogue for his work was to launch a long tradition which still endured in the eighteenth century. Jean-Jacques Rousseau, during his stay in Venice, was astonished by this art of the people, so natural, never vulgar ('When I heard the barcarolles, I discovered that I had never heard singing before'[2]); explaining their innate gift by the gondoliers' custom of going to the theatre to listen to music. In his *Dictionnaire de musique* Rousseau defined them as

> songs in the Venetian language sung by the gondoliers in Venice. Although the barcarolle airs are designed for the people and often

*Notes and sources are listed on pp. 178–81.

composed by the gondoliers themselves, they are so melodic and have such a pleasant accent, that there are no musicians anywhere in Italy who are not proud to know and sing them.[3]

Once back in France Rousseau tried to make everyone learning how to sing discover these melodies that he described as 'Italian'; they were in fact the gondoliers' barcarolles for which music-lovers in many countries then developed a great passion. This publication of *Canzoni da battello* dates from 1753 and followed soon after those brought out by the English publisher Walsh. Even in Venice eighteenth-century visitors rushed to buy copies of the lyrics of these songs, just as present-day tourists now buy knick-knacks.

It might be thought at first that these gondola barcarolles, which reached a high level of poetic and musical refinement, expressed the principal qualities of the inhabitants, which might be called the 'Venetian soul', made up of sensitivity, innocence, joie de vivre and a taste for the passions of love. But in fact the lyrics used by the gondoliers were usually verses from fashionable operas adapted into dialect, or more often still poems by Tasso which the gondoliers seemed to know very well without ever having read him:

> Let us not forget, in honour to Tasso, that most of the gondoliers know by heart much of his poem *Gerusalemme liberata*, that several know it in entirety, that they spend summer nights singing it alternately from one boat to another, that Tasso's poem is definitely a fine barcarolle, that before him only Homer had received the honour of being sung in this way, and since then no other epic poem has been used in the same way.[4]

A fine homage, in fact, confirmed by Goethe, who heard stanzas by Tasso sung by the gondoliers in their accomplished way.

The boatmen could be heard singing verses in elegant and serious fashion, then replying to each other from one gondola to the next; then six or twelve of them followed each other and exchanged one line or another between them, going as far as their memory allowed. No Venetian newspaper failed to describe the unique atmosphere that reigned over the canals, epecially during the summer season. 'Every night', ran the *Pallade Veneta*,*

> melodies resonate along the canals in joyous and varied serenades, accompanied, apart from the people standing at their windows, by countless boats following them, taking advantage of the cheerful atmosphere to which the music gives rise[5] . . . During this season carefree dinners take place on the boats along the canals; the ears are charmed by the voices and symphonies which fill the air with very sweet musical melodies[6] . . .

The same praise occurs in the *Guida de' Forestieri* (Guide for Foreigners): 'It is usual to make much music in the boats, but if this happens it is usually in the summer season, after dinner, and the largest number of boats pass each other along the Grand Canal . . .'[7]

As a general rule the songs preserved in the Venetian libraries[8] consist of the melody, by stanzas, and the bass continuo, sometimes the melodic line alone. In order to sing them with accompaniment today they have to be re-arranged. Love remains the central theme of these stanzas in dialect, as shown by the summaries of three songs together with the themes they develop:

The inconsolable farewell: 'I am dying because I must abandon you. I must go away and I will be like a man in chains. I did not think I would ever suffer so much: it would have been better to die young. Farewell for ever, who can stay my tears? Farewell my beauty.'

Cheeky love: 'As a child I lived on milk, and now I'll give you the milk and keep the tits. They are the only ones from which I have never been weaned, I shall never tire of them.'

Hymn to life: 'I'm totally happy, I'm totally free, I enjoy life in the country, in the palazzo or in a gondola; in sunshine or in rain, everything radiates love.'[9]

That is a selection of boat-songs and stanzas which would soon fascinate the Romantic generation and inspire the most beautiful

---

*Pallade Veneta, which will often be quoted in this book, was a broadsheet which appeared in printed form during 1687–8, then in manuscript form until the start of the eighteenth century. It included a rich variety of subjects: theatres, parties, music, religious ceremonies, literature, political events and anecdotes. It could be compared to the French *Mercure Galant*.

barcarolles, vocal and instrumental, from composers such as Mendelssohn and Chopin.

The poetic and musical delight experienced by travellers passing through Venice was also accompanied by a profound admiration for the quality of performance and competence possessed by these humble people who had received no formal musical education. It is possibly in this respect that the memoirs and descriptions of the eighteenth century move us most deeply, particularly when they emphasise the innate feeling for group singing, for two or several voices, simultaneous proof of rare gifts and a totally natural quality which is known today as 'amateur performance'. 'Harmony prevails in every part,' wrote Dr Burney in about 1770.

> If two of the common people walk together arm in arm, they are always singing, and seem to converse in song; if there is company on the water, in a gondola, it is the same; a mere melody, unaccompanied with a second part, is not to be heard in this city . . . Luckily for me, this night a barge, in which there was an excellent band of music, consisting of violins, flutes, horns, basses, and a kettledrum, with a pretty good tenor voice was on the great canal, and stopped very near to the house where I lodged; it was a piece of gallantry, at the expence of an *innamorato*, in order to serenade his lady.[10]

Thirty years earlier Grosley had said the same thing: 'In the piazza, a man of the lowest class, a shoemaker, or a blacksmith in his working clothes, begins an aria; others of his kind join in, singing the aria in several parts with accuracy, precision and taste such as is barely found among the highest society in our northern countries.'[11]

These two accounts, along with one that follows, include an additional expression of astonishment: given the scorn shown by travellers of their rank and quality towards the lower classes, usually insignificant in their eyes, the absolute beauty of what they heard forced them into daring comparisons between these humble *popolani* and their fellow citizens in their own country, who came of a higher class and were better educated. This led to the discrepancy which constantly existed between musical Italy and other countries.

'Music is not limited to sophisticated people', added the Frenchman Ange Goudar:

> it has penetrated as far as the world of beggars; poor people sing as they ask for alms . . . I am sorry that you are not here, my lord, for I would arrange a great concert for you in the middle of the Piazza San Marco performed by fifty musicians, beggars by profession, who together would produce as much sound as the Paris Opéra. You must not imagine that these virtuosi read music at sight for most of them are blind.[12]

Now it was precisely among the ordinary people of the San Marco district, between the basilica and the nearby alleys of San Giovanni in Bragora that the Vivaldi family appeared, all of them totally fascinated by music.

Can we really know Vivaldi?

Vivaldi, the vital thread of this study, will appear here and there, among the girls at the Pietà, at the opera or at various secular and religious events. Few cities during the seventeenth or eighteenth centuries have been so closely associated with a composer. Certainly one could cite Mozart and Salzburg, but it is known that the composer of *Don Giovanni* had no love for his native city and even less for the authorities on whom he depended. He should be associated more closely with Prague, as much for his affection for that city as for the successes he achieved there. The other example, closer to our time, is Bach and Leipzig. The Cantor spent twenty-seven years there and it was there that he produced the major part of his work; there is no doubt about his attachment to that city, even if he did not obtain any more recognition and gratitude from the authorities than Vivaldi found in Venice. But as we know, Bach was not a man of one city only: in his life as in his work was there not also the Bach of Weimar or the Bach of Köthen?

The composer of *The Four Seasons* is certainly a somewhat rare example of total fusion between a city, a man and his work. In the first place, because he was born there and spent his life there, with the exception of the sad, painful attempt to move to Vienna during the last months of his existence. Also, and especially, because everything in his instrumental and vocal work reflects the cheerful style, the colours, sometimes sparkling, sometimes misty, the liquid, transparent atmosphere of Venice, Vivaldi and Venice make one together.

But can we really know the composer in any other way except through analysis of his work, rich with 750 scores so far available to us? Can we draw in a few lines the portrait of the man who seems to hover over the city and his time, yet still harbours a vast amount of mystery? As I have said, his letters are insignificant, apart from a single one in which he confides something of himself and describes his difficulty in exercising the priesthood to which he was destined. There is little more to be gained from the accounts by his contemporaries which are rare and brief; a few travellers mention rather than describe him, for the emotional shock they sustained from the city of Venice, with its institutions and lifestyle unlike that of any other, leads them to write commentaries that are more collective than individual. Many grey areas remain therefore and unless new documents come to light here and there it will always be difficult to write a biography of the 'Red Priest' without recounting known events or fairly general characteristics. Even if we encounter Vivaldi again in various contexts, immersed in the musical society of his period, we must be content for the time being with a few indispensable reminders, notably concerning his early years and his religious studies, before he entered the Pietà.

His red hair seems in fact to have been a family trait. The man whom all Venice was to call 'the Red Priest' was the son of a violinist who played at St Mark's, Giovanni Battista Vivaldi, already employed in the orchestra of the basilica under the name 'Giovanni Battista Rosso' (red). This father was surely one of the very good violinists of his time since he was later taken on as 'master of instruments' at the Ospedale dei Mendicanti in 1689 before being cited along with his son among the eminent Venetian violinists listed in the *Guida de' Forestieri* of 1713.

Antonio Lucio was the eldest of the six children of Giovanni Battista and Camilla: he was born on 4 March 1678 (his precise date of birth was only found in 1962) and was baptised at home the same day because of his poor health, which could already explain his future difficulties: the birth certificate even refers to 'danger of death'. A more official baptism took place on 6 May following at San Giovanni in Bragora, his parish church. A plaque on the façade of the building recalls the event for the visitor of today who is delighted by the calm, almost village-like atmosphere of the small square which Antonio walked across so often.

Music was certainly at the centre of family life and it was his father who gave Antonio his first violin and harpsichord lessons. But what of his real studies, his other music teachers? This is the first grey area in Antonio's life; many musicologists have had to build up suppositions concerning those responsible for his training: the great Giovanni Legrenzi, who died when Antonio was twelve, the Spada brothers, both priests and musicians? or more probably Father Partenio, *primo maestro* at St Mark's, also a resident in the parish of San Giovanni in Bragora? One thing is certain, the young man was programmed for the priesthood, a logical 'opening' at the period, especially in large families; since there was no right of primogeniture in Venice, having a son who became a priest would make it less likely that the family would have to split up property, while making certain of a good education and employment as stable as it was prestigious. The stages were therefore traversed with metronomic regularity: tonsure and minor orders at fifteen in 1693, major orders in 1699 and ordination to the priesthood on 24 March 1703, just over five months before his entry to the Pietà as a teacher of the violin.

Apart from the dates of his religious studies, few outstanding events occurred during his youth, with the exception of the Midnight Mass of 1696 which to some extent revealed the outstanding gifts of the young Antonio to the Venetian public. He had just reached the age of eighteen and had been able to join the *Arte dei Sonadori* (the Guild of Instrumentalists) to which every musician playing in public and receiving payment could belong. As it will be seen later the ceremonies at St Mark's were particularly sumptuous and music played a brilliant part in them, with exceptional splendour. The basilica had obtained a dispensation from the Pope for the midnight Mass to be said two hours before sunset, in addition to the traditional Mass on Christmas Day. For this reason it had become customary to invite singers and musicians from outside to give additional lustre to the ceremony. As far as the singers were concerned it was usually the great castrati from the opera who attended these masses, they were glad to find supplementary contracts during a period of the year when the theatres were obliged to close. The Venetian public, rich or poor, who had been applauding them in the theatre for several weeks, were very pleased to rediscover the 'stars' of the moment in the Christmas motets.

Antonio Vivaldi therefore made his first great public performance as violinist before the crowded congregation at St Mark's, during the same ceremony: history does not relate whether he played in concert with several other violinists or whether he was allowed to perform a few solos to reveal his amazing virtuosity. Since he was in minor orders he was presented as the Abbate Vivaldi. There was certainly nothing strange about the combination priest-violinist at the end of the seventeenth century, no more than the combination priest-composer; only the triple combination of priest, composer and violinist remained much rarer at this period. When the list of musicians belonging to the Guild of Instrumentalists was published in 1711, twelve priests were named out of 196 members. Being a priest and playing in an orchestra was freely permitted and since Venice was so especially tolerant in many areas it would no longer be impossible to see priests in the orchestra playing for an opera. Vivaldi was therefore known to everyone, without his priesthood being concealed in the documents and chronicles of the time. 'It is quite normal', wrote the English traveller Edward Wright in 1720, 'to see priests in the orchestra. The celebrated Vivaldi (whom they call the Red Priest), famous among us for his concertos, surpassed them all.'[13]

Today it is well known that Vivaldi never exercised his profession of priest, apart from the very early years: everything seems to show that this 'vocation', which became apparent from the time of his childhood, was his family's idea rather than his own; it was a common situation at a period when a career in the church was contemplated for endless reasons other than straightforward profound conviction. However, Vivaldi did not betray the sacrament he had received, he may have continued to say Mass in private, especially for his father. But on an official level he succeeded in convincing his superiors later that it was impossible for him to combine his fragile health (probably due to serious asthmatic attacks) with the ministry.

It was obvious that music was his life and that, without rejecting his faith or the sacraments, it occupied him totally, passionately, every day that God made.

One of the rare significant letters addressed to the Marchese Bentivoglio of Ferrara (that is to say, not limited to the strictly professional business of contracts and fees) provides us with some explanations about his health and shows why it was impossible for him to carry out his duties as a priest. It was written four years before his death, in 1737.

I have not said Mass now for twenty-five years and I shall never say it again, not because I am forbidden or commanded not to (as Your Excellency can discover), but by my own choice, and that is because of the illness which has afflicted me from birth, and it oppresses me.

Immediately after my ordination as priest I said Mass for a year or a little longer, then I gave it up, having been obliged to leave the altar three times without completing it, due to the same indisposition. For that reason I stay in the house almost all the time, and I go out only by gondola or carriage, for the pain in my chest or the narrowness of the chest prevents me from walking.

No *cavaliere* summons me to him, not even our prince, for they all know my weakness. Usually I can go out after the midday meal but never on foot. That is why I do not celebrate Mass. I went to Rome for the opera, during three consecutive carnivals and Your Excellency knows that I never asked to say Mass, but I played in the theatre and it is known that His Holiness himself wanted to hear me play and paid me many compliments. I was summoned to Vienna and I never said Mass. At Mantua I spent three years in the service of the most pious Prince of Darmstadt ... My journeys have always cost me a great deal of money, for I have always travelled with four or five people to help me.

Everything that I do well I do in my own house and at my work table.[14]

The reason that Vivaldi took so much trouble to justify himself in this defence of his lifestyle was principally because he wanted to show that his relationships with Anna Girò (also known as Giraud) and her sister, whose existence he had virtually shared for fourteen years, were entirely honourable and the fact that he no longer said Mass was not conditioned by this enduring professional and friendly relationship. There is obviously more to be said about the strange 'couple' formed by Vivaldi and Anna Girò in the context of opera in Venice. If it can be accepted that relations between these two people were always as chaste and disinterested as Vivaldi tried to confirm, another mystery hangs over this letter. It is quite plausible, at a period when there was no shortage of priests and they were totally accepted in musical activities, that Vivaldi was not able to continue his priesthood due to health reasons and had obtained the assent of the religious authorities for this. It is more surprising, on the other hand, that no one has ever remarked on the discrepancy between the so-called poor health and the hyperactivity of a man who led three lives in one, taught several instruments, conducted choirs and orchestras, composed a vast number of works, as we know, travelled everywhere as impresario and director of his own operas, all with a rare degree of physical resistance. For him music was an elixir of youth which could not be compared to the existence of a priest.

Is it possible, at the early stage of this study, to define the personality and character of the 'Red Priest'? The talent for playing both comedy and tragedy shown in the letter quoted is a challenge in itself. First, a glance at some evidence. In business dealings Vivaldi was undeniably deceitful and harsh. Did he go as far as dishonesty and immorality, as it has sometimes been stated? It should be remembered that the opera, the principal entertainment of the period, was the most important financial market place in the artistic world. Large sums of money were constantly negotiated by the impresarios over the score that was to be used in a performance, large fees had to be paid to the great singers of the moment . . . The operatic 'market-place' was subject to the inexorable laws of profit and competition; everything was permitted. What might have seemed shocking was that a priest, for Vivaldi remained a priest in the eyes of everyone, could enter into and accept all kinds of wheeling and dealing, for his letters reveal the honeyed arguments of a compulsive liar. He was no less rapacious when selling his concertos, as the Président de Brosses described:

Vivaldi arranged to become one of my close friends, so that he could sell his concertos very expensively. He partly succeeded in this, and I partly succeeded in what I wanted to do, which was to listen to him and find frequent good musical entertainment: he is a *Vecchio* (old man) with a prodigious fury for composition. I have heard him boast of composing a concerto, with all its parts, more quickly than a copyist could copy it.[15]

This was the other aspect of his uncontrollable hunger for composition. Vivaldi seduced those who approached him through his passion for music and his irrepressible enthusiasm, qualities which pour out from his innumerable concertos. A famous account by Carlo Goldoni reveals the anxious agitation and the overwhelming delight of which the Red Priest was capable within the space of a few minutes. The young Goldoni had been sent to the musician to arrange the necessary alterations to his opera *La Griselda* in order to shorten it and adapt some passages to suit the taste of the singer. The person concerned was in fact Anna Girò, who was 'protected' by Vivaldi, and was asking for an aria of 'passionate agitation', with sighs, action and movement rather than an aria full of pathos which had originally been intended. The poet asked to see the libretto for the drama: ' "Yes, yes, of course," replied the maestro: "but where on earth is *Griselda*? It was here . . . *Deus in adjutorium meum intende* [God, help me]. *Domine . . . Domine . . . Domine . . .* it was here just now. *Domine ad adjuvandum . . .* [Lord, hurry to my aid] Ah! here it is!" ' Goldoni then suggested retouching that particular scene there and then, to Vivaldi's great astonishment: he had not thought it possible. Finally the playwright ended his account as follows:

The Abbé sneered at me but gave me the libretto, paper and a writing desk, took up his breviary again and recited his psalms and hymns, walking up and down. I re-read the scene that I already knew; I went over what the musician wanted and in less than a quarter of an hour I had on paper an aria of eight lines divided into two parts; I called my Ecclesiastic over and showed him my work. He read it, he relaxed, he re-read it, he uttered cries of joy, he threw his breviary down on to the floor, he called Madame Girò. She came 'Ah!' he told her, 'here is a rare man, here is an excellent poet: read this aria, this gentleman has written it here, without turning a hair, in less than a quarter of an hour'; and, turning to me again: 'Ah, sir, forgive me', and he embraced me, protesting that he would never have any other poet but me. He handed the libretto over to me, and ordered me to make other changes; he remained satisfied with me and the opera was a wonderful success.[16]

This account shows Vivaldi as an over-excitable man, dealing with several things at the same time, becoming agitated and worried, he received Goldoni coldly then fell into his arms and praised him to the skies. All his life the Red Priest agonised, raged, exulted, exploded with anger or joy. His impatience was well known and his furious composing, as the Président de Brosses described it, drove him to do everything in a hurry. This is why some of his scores are marked 'composed in five days', just as other people might display a trophy. His phobia for revision was such that he often gave the copyists pages full of mistakes, irrelevant items or omissions. According to all the laws of the baroque world, all that mattered for him was the thrill of the creative moment, to the point that he took upon himself alone the responsibilities of composer, instrumentalist, negotiator for scores, and impresario. However, financial fortune did not always smile upon him. 'Unfortunately for me', he wrote, 'I am caught up in the opera that will be performed in May and will cost 19,000 ducats. Oh, what brutish times we live in!'[17]

Finally, what of the composer's portraits that adorn our music books? What can they tell us? There is little to be learned from the refined, presumed portrait of Vivaldi, with a pen and a violin, today in Bologna: it is too good to be true and differs too much from the most life-like portraits. It is better to look at the caricatures, for if they certainly exaggerate his features they capture more closely the physiognomy of a man who was always over-excited, certainly cheerful but very authoritarian and probably cantankerous at the end of his life, which explains the not very sympathetic term '*Vecchio*' used by de Brosses. The most interesting caricatures are those by Ghezzi and François Morellon La Cave: dating respectively from 1723 and 1725, when the maestro was about forty-five. There are many similarities: large protruding eyes, strongly arched thick eyebrows, fairly long chin and oblong face. The nose is more or less hooked, depending on the artist or the pose, while a dimple enlivens the centre of the chin. Several specialists in modern morpho-psychology have seen in him an austere, obstinate man, capable of intense excitement and excessive delight for a few moments, not always understanding towards his entourage, unyielding in his choices and his passion, always anxious to be the central figure, the key man in any situation, however complicated it might be. A long way from the ailing asthmatic!

But all the written accounts in our possession leave us with the image of a lying scoundrel, who insisted that he had composed ninety-four operas and wrote only a mere fifty; or a man always ready to 'recycle' a concerto for the highest price, offering second-hand music as 'new' or concluding a deal to his advantage, like a perfect Venetian of his time, aware of his value and of the fierce competition surrounding him. If anyone offered him a contract for 90 sequins* instead of 100, he had better look out! The German Uffenbach was astounded by his encounter with the Red Priest. One day the traveller spoke to him about certain *concerti grossi* that he wanted to take back to his own country and ordered some from him, having first taken care to send him a few bottles of good wine. Three days later Vivaldi knocked on his door again and gave him ten concertos, maintaining he had written them expressly for him, in three days! The crafty priest was not satisfied with this large order and cleverly took advantage of it to offer his German client a few violin lessons which would help him to perform his music with *buon gusto* . . .

A masterful way of handling the situation!

---

*Small gold coins used in the Venetian Republic

CHAPTER 2

Discovering Venice in Vivaldi's day

There is no place in the world where liberty and
licence reign more supremely than here.
Charles de Brosses

As already mentioned, few cities have been so much visited, admired
and described as Venice in the seventeenth and eighteenth centuries.
While many travellers gave up Spain and Portugal which they
regarded at this period as something resembling the end of the
world, as far away geographically as they were austere and uncomfortable, they now rushed off instead towards the Italian peninsula,
an essential stage in the Grand Tour, where they could satisfy their
craving for artistic and musical discoveries, enchanting entertainments and lavish festivities, pleasing landscapes and favourable
weather. Along with Florence, Rome and Naples, Venice was one of
the most prized destinations, but it scored easily over all its rivals
through the originality of its unique geographical situation, the
effervescence of its carnival and festivities, more or less unique of
their kind, and most of all through the amazing development of its
artistic and musical productions.

During the late seventeenth century and the first part of the eighteenth, the Venice that Vivaldi knew, loved, and to which he helped
in his time to make famous throughout Europe, was living through
its last carefree days, trying to forget everything through pleasure
rather than face up to its tragic economic situation. Over two centuries the inevitable decline of the most Serene Republic had set in
and by then nothing could prevent the slow but inevitable end.

Venice now withdrew into a neutrality which it could no longer afford. All foreign observers became aware of this paradox: on one side was an aristocracy in power which, with the exception of a few more realistic individuals, concealed its face but kept up an untimely self-glorification and unquestioningly believed its government to be perfect for all eternity:* on the other side was a city that lived only on its past splendour, had suffered a drastic reduction in its political influence in Europe but was trying to keep up its way of life without the benefit of the necessary commercial income. As Monsieur de Silhouette wrote in 1729:

> The Power of the Venetians is a mere shadow of what it was in the past . . . Money is very short . . . commerce is declining from day to day . . . Since the Embassies in the Republic are ruinously expensive and individuals are not as rich as they were in the past, the Republic sometimes has difficulty in finding subjects to keep up the splendid display that the Ambassadors are used to making . . .[1]

With a few families who still possessed vast fortunes, an economy in great danger, a government still trying to cut a good figure and the lower classes apparently unaware of its decline, Venice, in the time of Vivaldi, had entered into the most joyous and carefree of death agonies.

During the baroque era most States had been quite capable of soothing their inhabitants with the illusion of feasts and pleasures while at the same time supervising and watching them, but Venice had always shown a matchless refinement by granting on one hand an apparent freedom of lifestyle, with games and entertainments, and on the other hand controlling politics, social life and religion, thanks to a regime that was among the most highly policed in Europe. Venetian society constituted on its own a more or less unique example on the continent: the Venetians, cut off from the

---

*The problem was not the inactivity of the patricians who continued to modernise agriculture and farming programmes on the mainland, and developed industry, taking on major works of hygiene improvement and dykes. The difficulty came from the fact that they were no longer productive (in the past they had been merchants, ship-building magnates or navigators) and were content with their agricultural revenues, private incomes and other investments in State bonds.

world by the relative isolation imposed by the lagoon and commu-
nications with the mainland, convinced by centuries of government
by a doge that they were a kind of chosen people, born more or less
from some alliance between God and the sea, lived day by day in a
cheerful and protective autarchy: they were dominated by an
unusual taste for work, a form of piety that was highly exteriorised
and brazen, sometimes bordering on superstition, and above all by a
frenzied need to throw themselves into the delights of music, festivities, gambling and love.

In this way the whole of Europe passed through Venice in order
to see for themselves whether the talk that filled the conversation in
so many western courts was true or not. Discovering the Republic of
St Mark's became a kind of essential trip for a crowd of foreigners,
involved as much in diplomacy as in business or the arts. In view of
the part played by music in the history of the city it is worthwhile
taking a brief look at the physiognomy of Venice, its society and its
festivities as they appeared to passing foreigners.

Portrait of a city and its people

The most reliable statistics concerning the population of Venice at
the time of Vivaldi's birth mention about 138,000 inhabitants, while
the figure of 150,000 was not achieved until nearly 1760, long after
Vivaldi's death. In fact the epidemic of plague in 1630 devastated the
city, which had included nearly 170,000 souls at the end of the sixteenth century, and was one of the largest capitals in Europe. In
addition the birth rate suddenly decreased, a probable sign of the
times, fortunately made good by the regular arrival of immigrants
from the mainland. This population, average in fact, still formed the
object of endless mistaken interpretations by travellers. Did they not
often mention 200, even 300,000 inhabitants or more during the
eighteenth century? In fact, through its many civil and religious festivities, which brought a seething mass of enthusiastic people into its
alleyways and *campi*, Venice created an illusion, while visitors to the
carnival brought a considerable increase as well.

This winter period saw the arrival of at least 30,000 'foreigners',
which included visitors from Rome, Florence and Naples, equal to one
fifth of the Venetian population. The city's capacity for welcoming

visitors seems astonishing at a period when the modern idea of 'mass tourism' seemed somewhat vague. But we should not forget that La Serenissima included an astronomical number of lodging houses, hotel, cafés and other eating houses where people could stay, eat and drink: there were no fewer than 4,430 in 1661 and nearly 6,000 in 1740 or so.

The attraction for this carnival that was unequalled in Europe, but also the liberty and even the licence that reigned at the time, the vast choice of gambling opportunities and the incalculable number of courtesans all added spice to the pleasure of discovering the unique charm of a city which had already become one of the first in history to achieve the criteria of our modern 'tourist centres'. Hence the popularity of the *vedute* ('views', urban landscapes), by Canaletto or later by Guardi which throughout the entire eighteenth century contributed to exporting throughout the world the image of a city as glorious in its architecture and colour range as it was dynamic and cheerful in its social make-up.

At that time the permanent population of Venice was distributed, as it still is today, over six *sestieri* (districts), those of Cannaregio, Castello and Dorsoduro were the most highly populated; next came those of St Mark's and Santa Croce, the least populated of the six being the *sestiere* of San Polo. About 88 per cent of this Venetian population was made up of *popolani*, those humble people best known for their vivacity, their febrile activity when working and their astonishing joie de vivre. Their frankness, sincerity and civic sense also earned the admiration of visitors; a strange population, it was thought at the time, they admired and respected the Doge and his administration while at the same time fearing them at every moment of their lives, since the regime prided itself on encouraging informers and close surveillance of the slightest events and activities. In short, the humble people regarded this iron hand in its velvet glove as a necessary evil: they were constantly afraid of the Council of Ten and the State Inquisitors,* but at the same time they considered the senatorial order to be the only guarantor of the Republic and the well-being of their fellow-citizens. The richest and the best educated among them, businessmen and members of the liberal

---

*The three State Inquisitors (one of the doge's councillors and two senators) were elected annually from the Council of Ten and formed a police tribunal independent of all laws.

professions, understood also what advantages there could be for their activities in this powerful regime which gave an impression of order and stability. Cardinal de Bernis, French Ambassador in Venice from 1752 to 1754, observed quite accurately this strange heavy bureaucracy, the reverse of all excessive behaviour:

> On the Monday of Shrovetide there were more than forty thousand people assembled in the piazza of Saint Mark's; you could have heard a pin drop during the entertainments given for the people; not a single handkerchief was lost, and yet you see no bailiffs or archers to contain the population; the reason for this orderly behaviour that reigns in Venice is the certainty that the government is informed of everything and that the State Inquisitors put to death without question anyone who disturbs public order: the fear of secret executions frightens people more than the fear of torture in public.*

Above the *popolani* was an intermediate class which might represent 7 to 8 per cent of the population. They were called *cittadini originari* (for they were all citizens who had been born in Venice) or *segretari*, secretaries; they made up the current administration of the city, a kind of *grande bourgeoisie* who dealt on a daily basis with the patricians to whom they were totally devoted in inverse proportion to the scornful attitude they displayed towards the ordinary Venetians. They were in general well educated and very much at ease with the complexities of the State administration. They made a point of not mixing with ordinary people when in cafés and private gambling clubs. In fact they represented the '*nouveaux riches*' of Venice, and notably their wives, who were idle and proud of their social success, displayed an affectation far removed from the true nobility of the great patrician ladies. The 'citizens' of first rank had participated in the past in State government but were excluded from it when the Council was reduced in size. The citizens of the second rank had often obtained their title through their merits or their money.

*In fact people feared the Supreme Tribunal more than they suffered from its severity. The Venetian government had become much more relaxed in the eighteenth century. Sentences to death were rare (and never for political reasons), the prisons were half empty, the police force scanty, and torture abolished.

Lastly, completing this rapid sketch of the social pyramid, was the aristocratic class which accounted for 3–4 per cent of the population, itself divided into three distinct orders, three subtle degrees distinguishable only to those with a perfect understanding of the city: the age of the dynasty, the riches, behaviour, education or culture could explain in this way how this or that noble and his family belonged to one of these three orders. The first of the three naturally formed the absolute summit of the hierarchy, related through these qualities to the greatest princes in Europe. The older Venetian families are estimated to have been twenty-four in number, producing most of the doges and procurators: they formed the elite of the senatorial order, the only true defence for the preservation of the Republic: the twelve oldest families dated back to the election of the first doge in 709*; four others appear in the foundation deed for the abbey of San Giorgio Maggiore in 800†; finally the last eight distinguished houses were added later.‡ The nobles of the second class all appear in the catalogue of 1289 which lists sixty-five names.§ Lastly those of the third class had bought the right to nobility and were rarely employed in the high offices of the Republic.

These patricians of the two first classes, citizens *par excellence*, were those who would be eligible for the highest functions in the different Councils which governed the State, and even for the rank of doge, if the name was chosen after an electoral consultation so complex that it was unique in Europe. La Serenissima held so closely to the republican principle and was so afraid of any form of dictatorship (the doge Marino Faliero had paid for it with his life in 1355) that it continually adopted measures for limiting the real powers of the doge and for avoiding sectarianism and political scheming at the time of his election.

The procedure for the election seems astonishing to us nowadays; on the appointed day the *ballottino*, a boy aged between eight and nine, chosen with care and destined to remain at the doge's court, drew by lots in the Major Council, the names of thirty nobles over

*Among the best known names were those of Contarini, Gradenigo, Tiepolo, Faliero and Micheli.
†These were the Giustiniani, Cornaro, Bragadini and Bembi.
‡In particular the names of Querini, Delfini, Sagredo, Salomoni …
§Among these are found the names of the main doges of Vivaldi's time: Mocenigo, Toscarini, Grimani, Venier, Loredan, Gritti, Pisani …

the age of thirty (forty after 1722) who then drew the names of nine, who elected forty, who drew by lots the names of twelve, who elected twenty-five, who drew nine, who elected forty-five, who drew eleven by lots, who elected forty-one, who by a majority of twenty-five finally elected the doge. Shortly afterwards the people proclaimed him by acclamation on the steps of the Scala dei Giganti (Staircase of the Giants) in the palace courtyard. This 'assault course' shows how everything was done to prevent the leading personage of the State from having too much personal power: he was elected by majority tendency rather than through a programme, he became a kind of prisoner of his electorate. Moreover, the result of the final vote by the forty-one was not easy to obtain since the majority of twenty-five could take time to emerge. The electors were then locked in until the end of the procedure, as with the papal conclave in Rome. In 1615, for example, it took thirty days to agree on a name, while in 1623 seventy-nine ballots were necessary.

As can be seen from reading about such an election, the risks of any fraud remained more or less non-existent. Yet that all the same did not give the doge more power. In fact he was no more than a splendid window for the Republic, a golden figure, indispensable and admired, certainly, but without real authority and liable to incredible forms of humiliation: his work room could be searched at any moment and he was forbidden to leave Venice for the mainland without authorisation from the Council. At the end of the eighteenth century the French traveller Misson summed up his function perfectly in laconic fashion: 'The doge is none other than a princely figure, an animated statue and a phantom of grandeur.'[3] The entire grandeur of his role, and in that lay the spirit of this 'patrician republic', consisted of displaying the fame and riches of the State through one individual person, so that all those who truly ran the government were relieved of this duty in their day-to-day work, while profiting from the advantages that this fame procured for them. Misson ended on a highly relevant note: 'It must be admitted therefore that the gold and purple have only a deceptive lustre, if the grandeurs of this world are no more than illusions and magnificent burdens, this is especially so with the doge of Venice.'[4] For example, Antonio Vivaldi knew nine successive doges during his lifetime, a good average. Since the nobles appointed by this election were of a certain age

a doge often retained his title for only eight to ten years on average
before dying. But some could die prematurely, often carrying out
their functions for three or five years only, which explains why so
many doges could succeed one another during the course of one lifetime.

It is not very easy to assess the interaction between these different
social categories which formed so many distinct social hierarchies.
Everything was somewhat deceptive in Venice due to the famous
carnival which took up six months of the year and ensured such a
mingling of the population that all segregation seemed provisionally
out of the question. In fact inevitable tension could bring the
different social classes into conflict, but never in any head-on violent
clashes. The Venetian republic was indeed one of the few States
which experienced neither civil wars nor revolutions and unlike so
many others was not subjected to divisions between a sovereign, his
court and the rest of the population. True, as we have seen, the group
of 'city-dweller citizens', essentially civil servants, and social
climbers, looked down scornfully on the lower classes; the latter gave
as good as they got and, thanks to their sense of duty and their
devotion to La Serenissima, preferred to show their attachment to
the two first degrees of the aristocracy, the senatorial order. This did
not prevent certain modest Venetians from taking reprisals for a past
offence or sentence, from whistling at some noble in the street and
jeering at him These poor people, acting in a more systematic fashion, showed little feeling for the nobles of the third order, patricians
with very little fortune or none at all, who benefited from free education due solely to their family origin: these minor nobles who gave
themselves airs while living off the State, did no more as a rule than
exasperate the *popolani*.

As for the highly placed aristocracy, they maintained a certain dis-
tance from the lower classes and especially from their domestic staff:
their perpetual fear of plots and denunciations forced them to be
more feared than appreciated for their kind-heartedness; but their
manners and their education forbade them to show their scorn:
during the periods of carnival they showed familiarity and accepted
proximity with people of all levels which very few monied classes
tolerated during the baroque era. This mingling of the social classes,
so evident in the paintings of Guardi or Bella (but already present

in the descriptions or paintings of the sixteenth century), is explained also by the very conditions of life in Venice. There are no people in these paintings like those who, as in Paris or Madrid, are travelling in gilded carriages, wearing clothes trimmed with jewels while others walk through the mud bundled up in garments of rough cloth; there was rather a degree of uniformity, to be mentioned again later, but also due to the fact that everyone in the city walked or travelled by boat. The modest *peota* certainly had little in common with the Bucintoro, the doge's magnificent galley, but in essence navigation over the water, common to every-one, in gondolas that were uniformly black, reduced the over-aggressive difference so usual in other countries. 'In Venice', the English writer Joseph Addison noted, 'a gondola with two oarsmen is just as magnificent as a carriage and six and a large equipage is in other places.'[5]

On some Venetian lifestyles

Just as Venice was original in its manner of government and its indi-vidual stratification of social life it was equally so in its daily func-tioning, its customs and morals. It should be understood that arriving in Venice during the seventeenth and eighteenth centuries produced an effect quite different from arriving there today. Travellers usually left their carriages at Fusina on the mainland before taking some transport by water to the capital of La Serenissima. Some people even began their journey further away, on the banks of the river Brenta, in a comfortable craft, drawn by horses along the towpath. The saloon on board was luxurious and passen-gers could pass the time pleasantly, sipping Cyprus wine. Then came the entry to the lagoon; oarsmen replaced the horses; this journey covered nearly twenty-five nautical miles.

The visitor arriving today by train or car is immediately propelled, without any transition whatever, along the banks of the Grand Canal, but the traveller of the past had the good fortune to experi-ence the rites of passage, that beneficial break: he slipped gradually into this landscape of low ground and water; he immersed himself serenely into what he considered to be a different world, a city out-side normal life, reached not immediately or violently but patiently awaited, desired then contemplated in time with the slow and regular strokes of the oarsmen.

From a world of dusty roads and cultivated fields, horses and carriages, he moved into an aquatic and silent universe which caused him gradually to forget the territories he had crossed and gave him the impression of being outside time. He also found to his astonishment that Venice was a kind of open city, different from all the other cities of the time for it possessed no gates, no fortifications, no guards or garrisons of soldiers. It could not be captured by land, nor by sea, for the lagoons were too shallow and prevented any warship from approaching. The traveller would learn very quickly that this city, which received all the wrongdoers from the surrounding places also revealed itself to be the city which suffered fewer thefts and assassinations than any town in Italy.

The traveller's alienation would be further reinforced by a kind of daily life based on a foundation quite different from those existing in other European countries. It should be remembered that during the time of the Republic Venice did not follow the same calendar as its neighbours, and at the end of the eighteenth century it was even the last place to follow the Julian calendar. In 1564 France, which had previously begun the year at Easter, had adopted the custom of Germany and Switzerland, Spain and Portugal, in establishing the new year on 1 January. Russia, where the year had opened at the equinox, and England, where it had begun on 25 March, also conformed respectively in 1725 and 1752. Venice was therefore the last (with the surrender to Bonaparte in 1797) to begin the year on 1 March and not 1 January. A French or German traveller who, according to his own calendar, thought he was arriving on 6 February 1723 in fact found himself in Venice in 1722, since the months of January and February still belonged to the year that had just ended.

The calculation of the time in Venice was also affected by the fact that the city continued to believe that 00* hour was reached when the sun set. Therefore, depending on the months and seasons, the first hour of the day was moved in relation to this sunset. When in the eighteenth century mention was made of a theatrical

---

*Today only the Theocratic Republic of Mount Athos still follows this Byzantine timetable.

performance starting at three o'clock in the night, this was obviously not in the middle of the actual night as we see it but three hours after the end of the day. The Frenchman Guyot de Merville was amazed on his arrival in the city to hear the Venetians talking of 'seventeen hours' when logically, for him it was noon. The conversion tables patiently established by Gastone Vio show that what we now call midnight corresponded in Vivaldi's time to 3.45 on 8 June and slightly after 7.00 on 8 January.[6] That is also the reason why the few remaining public clocks in Venice today, or those that can be seen in the paintings by Canaletto and Guardi, are divided into twenty-four sections instead of twelve.

Once the traveller had assimilated these strange facts it remained for him to familiarise himself with the milling crowds in day-to-day Venice. Once he had recovered from his stupefaction when faced with those 145 canals crossed by 312 stone bridges and 117 wooden ones, those 140 towers and campanili, those 70 parish churches and the innumerable palazzi artistically placed at water level, he discovered the incessant coming and going of the vast flotilla of boats and gondolas, as well as the considerable throng of those who made this traffic possible. It is estimated that nearly 60,000 Venetians from near and far made a living from water transport. Among them the mass of gondoliers constituted a kind of State within a State, a homogeneous and powerful group who ruled the roost in the theatre but also played a considerable role at every moment of life. They formed the second most important corpus in the State after the nobility, and their best defence in any uprising against them. Through an oath that was jealously kept the gondoliers were obliged to keep absolute secrecy about the talk they inevitably heard while transporting their passengers. If any one of them was discovered revealing the nocturnal adventures of some lady to her husband he could have been drowned by his companions. No amorous confidence, no political intrigue must leak out from their craft which served both as a means of pleasure and a sacrosanct place of asylum. This dutiful silence was to save many a Venetian in flight, starting with Casanova who, while escaping from the Piombi, the famous prison in the doge's palace, was never denounced by the gondolier who took him to the mainland. The patience shown by this corporation when they had to wait for hours until a prince or

an ambassador chose to appear, was only equalled by the courtesy
and fraternity their members displayed towards each other during
this service. 'Compared to the savage rudeness of coachmen in Paris
or London,' wrote Grosley, 'the gondoliers could be described as
religious and holy persons'.[7]

Their witticisms, their lively repartee, their relative sobriety as far
as wine-drinking was concerned, made them into accomplices
wanted by the other social classes and by foreigners, who knew they
could rely on them for arranging an intrigue, finding the secret staircase or the rope ladder which would allow them to reach a lady's
bedroom, or for their warning, in a subdued barcarolle, of a husband's unexpected return. The sober and dignified beauty of their
craft was admired by the whole of Europe, so much so that Louis
XIV wanted to have one on the Grand Canal at Versailles. By tradition all gondolas were black, and it was firmly stated that those
owned by patricians should not be embellished by any carvings.

This was in keeping with the etiquette of the Venetian nobility
whose members could wear only black with no ornamentation to
their dress, and must not wear a mask when acting as banker in a
gambling club. Women aristocrats must also dress in black and
could only wear jewellery during the first year after their marriage:
during this period they were obliged to wear the ring given to them
by their husband and the pearl necklace given by their mother-in-
law; families with less money were obliged to hire a pearl necklace
for a year. During other years women could dress as they wished for
special occasions such as the great ball which followed the coronation of a doge or the election of a procurator: their hair was then
decked out with flowers, diadems and jewels to the point where they
were wearing fortunes in precious stones. For the entire rest of the
year patrician austerity prevailed when only ambassadors seemed to
lead extravagant lives: their gondolas were gilded and took on
extreme magnificence, perfectly in keeping with the richness and
glowing colours of their princely clothes.

From the first week of his arrival, every foreigner realised that the
relationships that he was to have with the Venetians depended very
much on the social class he was going to encounter. Contact with the
working class was fairly easy for these people showed themselves to be
generous, frank, naturally cheerful, much inclined to amusement and

all sorts of extravagant behaviour. However, it was already traditional for these people not to mingle very much with foreigners in order to avoid trouble with the government. Denunciations were frequent and took place in Venice daily: any unsuitable attitude, any dubious conversations with foreigners, any suspect relationship could be immediately reported to the doge's palace through an anonymous note or in the confidential note of a secret agent: 'The undermentioned Domenico Querini', wrote one of them:

> frequents nearly every day two ladies from Brescia at San Geremia, two sisters, who pride themelves on being musical virtuosi. One is called Meneghina and the other Domitilla. The house of these two ladies is also frequented by the Marquis de Grille, ambassador for the Emperor. Although I cannot confirm that they have been there together – and although I remain on guard every day – it is no less true that both the women go there and the Ambassador often sends a gondola for the said Meneghina and has her taken to his palace.[8]

Letters of this sort were two a penny: the least important things said and done by a foreigner, especially in the case of ambassadors, were examined, discussed and sent on to high places, but only political matters formed the object of particular espionage, although even love affairs could also be the source of denunciation. Therefore there was no point in foreigners, nor the Venetians themselves, seeking dangerous contacts.

For the same reason those in search of rapid and safe sexual adventures could be content with the group which enlivened all the gossip of the seventeenth and eighteenth centuries: the 'courtesans', the Venetian prostitutes who were reinforced during the carnival period by hundreds of 'sisters' from the continent. Although during normal times their number amounted to more or less double that of the women operating in Paris, it is difficult to estimate their total during carnival, for men were delighted by their trade but also by their charm, politeness and gentle conduct. Foreigners lost no time in searching through the crowd of these creatures, who varied from the simplest working-class girls to the upmarket courtesans described by Président de Brosses: 'Agatina is the most splendid of

all the courtesans in Venice. She lodges in a small palazzo, her furniture is superb and she is adorned with jewels like a nymph.'[9]

The abuse of this trade seems to have reached its height during
the first part of the eighteenth century, so much so that the Signoria
had to take action. 'Brokers of love' used to offer the women's services in the middle of the Piazza San Marco, they would arrange a
meeting, take an advance and the business was concluded. The problem, according to de Brosses again, was that 'they went about offering to everyone . . . this lady procuratess or that lady chevalière; as a
result a husband was sometimes offered his own wife. This deceitful
and brazen trade has been prohibited.'[10] As a result nearly 500
'brokers of love' were arrested in the spring of 1739, not that much
harm was done to a practice that continued, in a variety of ways,
until the end of the Republic.

When a foreigner arrived in Venice to conduct business, or, worse
still, to work in an embassy, he would gradually move up the social
hierarchy until he reached the nobility and then found it was almost
impossible for him to communicate with the Venetian patriarchy:
according to an age-old tradition the latter avoided all danger of
compromise with a foreigner in order to escape the anger of the
Senate. One day, Jean-Jacques Rousseau, a secretary at the French
Embassy, went to the house of a Venetian senator, during some festivities. Rousseau was wearing a mask, and when he took it off, the
senator paled in astonishment and immediately rushed off to the
State Inquisitors before the latter found out what had happened
from another source. After a severe scolding by the Inquisitors the
senator got away with it on that occasion.

So the nobles lived among themselves. When people took a walk
during the daytime along the Piazzetta, situated in front of the doge's
palace, still called the 'Broglio' by the Venetians, it was possible to
see the nobles grouped together on one side of the square, on the
sunny side in winter, on the shady side in summer. It was there,
wearing their black cloaks lined with squirrel fur in winter and
ermine in summer, their only ornament a silver buckle on their
black belts, that they exchanged news, finalised their political
or commercial affairs, and wove their intrigues. If any foreigner
dared to venture on to that side to exchange a few words he had
better look out! Even the Venetian people were duty-bound to

pass along the side where they did not want to be in order to avoid any trouble.

'It is well known,' insisted Baretti:

> that the Venetian nobles and all their servants are forbidden, by a very strict law, to speak to or correspond with foreign visitors residing in Venice on behalf of their Sovereigns. This law exerts a powerful influence over the thinking of the Venetian nobles: it is even fairly frequent in Venice for bourgeois people or merchants, or other people of that class who give balls open to the public, to employ a servant from a foreign ministry to stand at the entrance in order to keep away the nobles who would not fail to come to one of these occasions.[11]

Foreigners, and not only ambassadors, were perfectly aware of the gap which separated them from the influential society, and they could only keep to themselves and make the best of things. In 1688 the French traveller Misson regretted that he was not better able to encounter this society whose mysteries he had hoped to penetrate. 'Foreigners have so few dealings with the people who live here that it is not easy to learn the domestic customs and way of life: that is why I have so little to tell you on the subject.'[12]

In fact the job of ambassador, like those of all foreigners who made long stays in the Republic, was considerably saddened by these laborious contacts, as Charles de Brosses explained: 'They have no other resource except to live together, and they cannot possibly see any nobles, who are forbidden, on pain of death, to visit them. This is in no way a mere threat, and one noble has been put to death simply for having walked past an ambassador's house, without saying a word to anyone, on his way to visit his mistress in secret.'[13]

In these circumstances, therefore, must we believe Cardinal de Bernis, French ambassador to Venice from 1752 to 1754, when he maintained that he had succeeded in changing this state of affairs? Bernis, as everyone knows, was not famous for his modesty. His memoirs are a brilliant theatrical presentation of himself and all that he did. But it is also true that when he arrived in Venice the French were regarded 'with much horror in this city' and something had to be done. So, conscious of the traditional isolation of foreigners in

Venice he tried as hard as he could to reverse the situation, and noted in all simplicity:

> Before I came to Venice as ambassador the nobility never acknowledged the ambassadors at the theatre or when they met them and were not greeted in return: I changed this uncouth habit; I accustomed the nobles and the ladies to being greeted by me and to return my greeting; gradually they became so used to this custom that in the end they did acknowledge me. I alone enjoyed this distinction that other foreign ministers tried in vain to acquire.[14]

If the aristocrats limited their contacts with the Venetian people and foreigners as far as possible, they did not overdo encounters between themselves, with the exception of the ritual walk on the Broglio. As a rule they did not visit each other, avoiding in this way any chance of being compromised in some political situation. The patriarchy, in fact, beneath the apparent cohesion in the service of the Republic, was nothing more than a set of factions and groups whose interest lay in access to the most important posts. Isolation remained a guarantee against treason, as explained perfectly by Baretti:

> The Nobles . . . like other Venetians, appear to like each other and overwhelm each other with caresses; if they meet they greet each other, embrace and express total friendship. But no great understanding is needed to realise that all these signs of politeness are normally a mere farce. Members of an Aristocracy cannot be susceptible to these tender feelings since their rivalry for posts in the magistracy makes them impervious to anything else, including the delights of friendship.[15]

Was it for all these reasons – the fear of intrigues and denunciations, the ban on talking to foreigners, the apparent austere behaviour – that libertinage and gambling became more or less second nature, a kind of distraction from political repression? If there was one custom that foreigners observed as soon as they arrived, leading them to fill whole pages of their correspondence and memoirs on the subject, it was surely the astonishing behaviour of the Venetians concerning marriage and every form of amorous badinage.

As a general rule the Venetians were deeply preoccupied with the delights of seduction and love: men worshipped women and collected amorous adventures with imagination and humour; women regarded their husbands mainly as the head of the family, more or less freely accepted as such, and as the father of their children, but it was the last word in low-class and bourgeois behaviour to go out with him. When Goldoni was staying in Paris he was utterly amazed to see husbands and wives going to the theatre together. Venetian women, whether patricians or shopkeepers, spent their time in surrounding themselves with beaux, with whom they went out everywhere, to church, to the theatre or for a walk. 'They would rather be without bread than without a *cavaliere servente*,' said one of the characters created by Abbé Chiari.[16]

In short every woman had to have a lover, chosen if possible from the highest society in order to obtain privileges and recommendations. Giving shape to these adventures by adding a sexual element to them was not however the preoccupation of most women: all the interest was in love-play, seduction, ardent signs, mad outings by boat at night, in short what Laclos described as 'dangerous liaisons', but transported in Venice to heights of licentiousness and gaiety, and without a shadow of remorse: 'In Holy Week,' wrote the Abbé Conti, 'our ladies express their so-called universality; they go to confession accompanied by their lovers, but what is amazing is their belief that they had expiated their sins at the same time as they were committing others. The squaring of the circle holds no greater mystery for me.'[17] Husbands often seemed to show an amazing compliance and it was not unusual to see husband and lover become the best friends in the world, they would even go out together with their lady. Every outing, even the most showy, earned cheers and enthusiastic compliments from the people in the street for everything about it expressed homage to the beauty and frivolity of women: one day, when the greatest Italian woman singer of the day, Faustina Bodoni, wife of the composer Hasse, was noticed in the Piazza San Marco in the company of a famous courtesan, arm in arm with men of the aristocracy, the crowd hastened to applaud them as though they were both queens for an evening.

At the approach of the eighteenth century it was among the aristocracy that the relaxation in lifestyle was most significant. The reserve, gravity, even the austerity of the aristocratic ladies during the sixteenth and seventeenth centuries was then over. From that time on women observed a year of relative good behaviour after their marriage, then they would go out freely to the gambling clubs, theatres and cafés, protected by their masks that they were obliged to wear for six months of the year. Intrigue of course was one of the privileges of this new freedom, so much so that according to a satiric poem of the period they would talk politics 'at the casin',* in the café, in bed and even on the bidet.[14]

The kindheartedness of the patrician ladies, their goodness, their courtesy, their culture too, were noticed all the more because it was now easy to meet them in their own homes or to encounter them here or there. In this connection the German Baron Pöllnitz established in 1730 a splendidly detailed portrait, especially in the last few lines:

In the past it was a crime to see a woman on her own, and a foreigner hardly dared take the risk. It is different now; there are several houses of quality where I am tolerated, and I often find myself alone with the mistress of the house, without being watched any more than would have happened in France, where the freedom and ease of manners is so highly praised. Ladies visit each other a good deal; there are gatherings every evening, which they attend; they go out alone in their gondolas, accompanied by one valet de chambre who acts as their equerry. They go to the theatres, masked, and they also go wherever they want. This ease in seeing ladies helps not a little to make my stay in this city pleasant ... One is in the midst of honest pleasures and debauchery. God receives the same exemplary worship as in any other place in the world. Few people observe the externals of religion more than the Italians do, especially the Venetians. *It can be said of them that they spend part of their life in doing wrong and the other half in asking God to forgive them for it.*[19]

---

*The 'casin' or *casino* was in fact a little pleasure hide-out where the aristocrats, men or women, could receive their friends in private, play cards and arrange rendez-vous with their lovers. Usually the casin' consisted of a few small rooms rented in a palazzo.

As for gambling, the other rage of this population, even if in the eighteenth century money was not circulating well since the price of wheat, the principal wealth of this State, had collapsed. 'The Ridotto still remains open but money is short,' admitted the Abbé Conti in 1728. This famous Ridotto remained, through thick and thin, one of the most celebrated and invulnerable institutions of Venice. It was the most famous gambling saloon, situated in the quarter of San Moisè, and reproduced endless times over across the city by many casinos or 'bassette' academies, named after the most popular card game in Venice: they all opened at the same time as the theatres and kept their door open from October to Shrove Tuesday. A gambling club consisted of ten or twelve small rooms on the same floor with gaming tables everywhere. Apart from bassette the gamblers played Pharaoh, *biribi*, *meneghella* and backgammon, 'the game of three tables'. Even if there was quite a crowd, making it difficult to circulate between the tables, silence was the rule and masks were essential to gain entry. Noble ladies and courtesans came to play on the same footing, their masks permitting the pleasure of anonymity, even if they were often seen to be followed by spies or husbands. According to the customs of this State, which encouraged the mingling of social classes, Venetians and foreigners, aristocrats and ordinary people, mixed closely together, always wearing dominos. Only the nobles who held the bank had to do so without a mask, as established by a new law in 1704.

In addition to the salons reserved for gambling, a few rooms served as boudoirs for conversation: people could buy liqueurs there, preserves and other delicacies. Along with the theatres the Ridotto in this way was like another essential meeting-place for Venetian society away from their homes, combining the passion for gambling with the pleasure of meeting in groups in a warm comfortable place during the winter. It was here that people played for a few ducats or pledged an entire fortune; here too, as in a box at the opera, people came to prolong amorous encounters or to have a little sleep. A famous engraving by Pietro Longhi recalls, in the form of a quatrain, those multiple pleasures offered by gaming houses:

One man searching, another walking about and wanting,
One man sleeping, another warming himself without playing,

A last one thinks he is rich and doesn't even see
That in the end he hasn't a ducat left.

It is remarkable that the Republic allowed great families to squander
their fortunes this way at the Ridotto: while the State did not feel
directly involved it did not seem to worry about this phenomenon,
while it was obvious that the loss of great fortunes could only harm
the endangered economy of La Serenissima. The casino, moreover,
was one of the many systems which Venetian society discovered for
getting round the law: while overlong possibilities for meetings and
gambling sessions were forbidden in the private palazzi, the Ridotto
favoured gambling outside the law, about which nobody complained. Seeing that the private system escaped its control the State
then imported in 1715 a game that was popular all over Italy in the
sixteenth and seventeenth centuries, the *lotto genovese*, Genoan lotto,
and set it up on the Rialto, keeping it under their own control.
Lotto, originally a private game, became a public game as from
1734, with an official draw which took place in front of the *loggetta*,
at the foot of the campanile of St Mark's: five numbers were drawn
by lot out of the ninety possible, and everyone could bet on one,
two, three, four or five successive numbers, ensuring that the wins
were more enticing with each one. It became a truly permanent
Venetian institution, amusingly derided by a famous proverb – 'He
who plays lotto runs fast to his own ruin'; lotto soon crossed the
frontiers of the Republic and 'converted' other nations. It was in this
way that the most ingenious of the Venetians, Giacomo Casanova,
was to contribute to the creation in France of the Ecole Militaire
Lottery, first drawn on 18 April 1758; from 1776 it was renamed the
Royal Lottery of France and became the ancestor of the modern
French Loterie Nationale.

Feast days and rituals as guarantees of stability

Few societies have cultivated the taste for ritual as much as the
Venetians. It can even be said that Venice laid its foundations on
the endless re-enactment of the same ceremonies, feast days and
rituals, giving the world the impression of an unchanging state,
untouched by political and social upheavals. We are still amazed

today on finding, year after year, unchanging festivals as exceptional
as those of the Redentore (the Redeemer) on the third Monday in
July, a date unchanged since 1575, or the festival of the Historical
Regatta on the first Sunday in September. People will reply all the
same that Siena has its *Palio* twice a year, or Florence its *Calcio
storico*, historical football, while so many other Italian cities hold
annually at least one festival dating from the Middle Ages.

However, no Italian city has ever experienced one quarter of the
festivals celebrated in Venice and what we see there today, among
many thousands of tourists, is nothing compared to the ritual festivals during the period of the Republic and what they represented.
They had accumulated, they had been superimposed one on another
and reinforced over the centuries to the point that the eighteenth-
century traveller could see, on the same date, and with unchanged
ritual, a festival that had already taken place the previous year, and
also in the seventeenth century, in the sixteenth, in the fifteenth and
as far back as anyone could go in the search for the origin of this
commemoration, which might be religious or secular. Early in the
nineteenth century Giustina Renier Michiel, niece of the last doge,
Ludovico Manin, listed the festivals observed in the defunct
Republic.[20] There were forty of them on her list, repeated each year,
to which she added one exceptional party: the reception given in
honour of the king of Denmark in 1708.

These detailed descriptions of each feast day, including its origin,
completed the many accounts found in periodicals and memoirs of
the baroque area, that is to say, the last significant evidence before
Venice became an empty shell after 1797. The same constant attention to detail, the same desire to recall how the same processions, the
same acts by the doge, the same entertainments for the public, contributed to preserve the unity of the city for they all went back to
events or glorious deeds that took place during the history of the
Republic. It was in this way that they conferred an unassailable legit-
imacy on the government and gave the impression of associating the
lower class of people with the destinies of the State. The strictly religious festivals were also a reminder that Venice was a miracle, a
promised land, blessed by God, to which the most exaggerated
descriptions were applied. In 1697 the *Guida de' Forestieri* proudly
enumerated some fourteen terms which illustrated wonderfully well

the very substance of La Serenissima: Queen of the Sea, Sole Virgin of the Universe, Refuge of Virtue, Source of the Laws, Subject to the One God, Concept of Catholicism, Wonder of the World, *Urbs Orbis Miraculum* (Miracle City of the World). In a State where nothing must change, where the constitution and laws were totally rigid, pleasure and festivals must in that way merge with the politics of the State, contribute to its fame and longevity. This was why, unlike many other countries, Venice had no privileged class, keeper of all its pleasures, and a working class which received only the leftovers, but a truly unique society which at every level and dozens of times during the year participated on an equal footing in the collective festivities which contributed to the glorification of the State. There is no doubt that members of the managerial class could ease their consciences by inviting the people to the same entertainments as they attended themselves. Once the feast day was over, daily life for each social class reverted to what it had been before, but at least, for a few hours or a few days, each group had participated in a spectacle so magnificent that all the rest was forgotten. From this point of view it can never be repeated often enough how far away the romantic image of Venice, transmitted by the painters and poets of the nineteenth century, with its train of nostalgic impressions and morbid states of mind, could be from the 'other' Venice, that of the Republic, the true capital of celebration, pleasure, laughter and free living.

If we examine more closely the types of festival recurring towards the end of the Republic three categories can be considered. The first was that of immoveable feast days, that is to say those that were celebrated every year on a fixed date. This was true of 1 January, the date on which the doge, followed by a royal cortège, came down to hear Mass at St Mark's where the Holy Sacrament was displayed for three days. On the evening of the third day a solemn procession, in which the entire aristocracy participated, crossed the Piazza of St Mark's. More interesting for its importance in the commemoration ritual was, the feast day of 25 March, described with many details in the *Forestiere illuminato*:

His Serenity [the doge] comes down to St Mark's to hear Mass; after luncheon he listens to the sermon which is usually given by the preacher of San Lorenzo, in memory of the union of the neighbouring people who inhabited the small islands when the building of the prestigious city was begun in 1421. On that day the Procurator from On High ... clad in purple, goes to the church of La Salute to display the Image of the Blessed Virgin, brought here from Canea in 1669.[21]

As can be seen, memories of the history of Venice and its gradual construction are mingled here with a religious memory: the return from Crete of a protective Virgin Mary. Secular and religious life made one together, associating the doge and the entire population through ritual. On 16 August the same ritual obliged the doge, accompanied by the Senate and the Ambassadors to go to the church of San Rocco, then to the Church of the Frari, before returning to the Palace: such were the sumptuous and highly coloured scenes which inspired the most famous *vedute* by painters like Canaletto and Guardi.

At Christmas time Venice surpassed itself once again to make the Palazzo San Marco into the most fairytale place in the world. During Christmas night the three storeys of the Procuraties were illuminated by 2,000 wax torches which, through a highly special skill, all burst into flame at the same time. The Abbé Conti also described, not without humour, the cheerful atmosphere of a simple annual religious festival:

> We have been celebrating the Feast of Saint Martha with much gaiety here. At night everyone walks along the quay which leads to the church named after the saint, the streets are filled with huts on either side. On the Grand Canal there are a vast number of gondolas and *tartanes* where people have supper and enjoy themselves ... As for me, I was with a party of twenty-five people, in a kind of Bucintoro, but although I had the honour of supping with the most beautiful and noble ladies of this city, I will tell you in confidence that I fell asleep at table ...[22]

The second category is that of the 'moveable' feasts which were observed each year but changed their day depending on the liturgical calendar. It is in this group that the most sumptuous and impres-

sive festivals were to be found. This was the case of Carnival
Thursday (the Thursday before Lent), which will be mentioned
again in connection with the Carnival, and again that of Good
Friday which occasioned a solemn service at St Mark's: the doge,
with bare feet and formally dressed in mourning clothes, attended
the ceremony; after the meal he listened to the sermon and then
presided over the great procession along the piazza; once the statue
of Christ had been replaced in the Sepulchre the Grand Chancellor
closed it with the doge's ring. A day so sombre for Christians did not
prevent the Piazza of St Mark's from being illuminated in the
evening, and on Good Friday with double torches at each window,
gaining the admiration of visitors and the Venetians themselves. The
Feast of the Redemption, on the third Sunday in July was no different from the one we can still see today, on the same date. People still
commemorate, as they have done for four centuries, the vow made
in 1576 to build a monumental church on the Giudecca if the city
should survive a highly lethal epidemic of plague. Nowadays the
doge is no longer there to preside over this ceremony and go with a
procession to the church of the Redentore on Sunday mornings, but
the pontoon, made of boats, and linking the Zattere to the
Giudecca, so allowing the lagoon to be crossed dry-footed is still
very much there, as is has been since the first celebration in 1578. In
the same way the wait for the sunrise over the Lido continues to
attract thousands of people today, who temporarily forget their
desire to sleep. As for the fireworks display which takes place on the
Saturday evening along the banks of the canal by Saint Mark's, above
the thousands of boats which appear as though by magic each time
the sky is lit up, it remains incontestably one of the finest spectacles
to be seen in Europe today.

Of all the moveable feasts which disappeared with the former
Republic the feast of the Ascension (the *Sensa*) constitutes a kind of
pinnacle in the ritual glorification of eternal Venice. This was the day
of the 'Marriage with the Sea', recalling the victory of the Venetians
over the Emperor Frederick Barbarossa in favour of Pope Alexander
III. For La Serenissima it was more than a commemoration of a fortunate historical event, authorised by the Pope at the end of the thirteenth century, it was the means for continuing to comfort
themselves with illusions and to believe, through an exaggerated

maritime celebration, that they still wielded an influence over the seas in the seventeenth and eighteenth centuries, although it had been reduced to nothing a long time before.

On that day the doge, surrounded by the Signoria, the papal nuncio, the ambassadors and guests of note, went aboard the Bucintoro, by far the most beautiful and impressive craft ever built, with its gilded woodwork and delicate carvings, its two decks and its 168 oarsmen (all workers at the Arsenal) who sang as they rowed, four to each oar, to establish the rhythm, the Bucintoro took the doge out to sea, beyond the Lido, where he could throw a wedding ring into the Adriatic and pronounce the famous phrase *'Desponsamus te Mare, in signum veri perpetuique Dominii'* (We wed thee, Sea, as a sign of true and perpetual domination). The entire artillery of the Venetian fortresses then fired simultaneously, to the applause and cheers of the thousands of Venetians who had set out in modest *tartanes* or gondolas, following the doge's cortège. Through a somewhat ridiculous tradition the employees of the Arsenal felt responsible for the weather on that day and were prepared to die if the sea should be stormy. Casanova, not without humour, described this strange custom:

> The next day I put my mask on early before going to follow the Bucintoro which, since the weather was good, was definitely going to the Lido. This function, which is not only rare, but unique, depends on the courage of the Arsenal admiral, for he must swear, on pain of death, that the weather will be set fair. The slightest breeze could blow the vessel over and drown the doge and all the senators of La Serenissima, the ambassadors and the papal nuncio, who instigates and guarantees the worth of this unusual sacramental ceremony which the Venetians correctly hold in reverence bordering on superstition. Through additional misfortune this tragic accident would cause laughter throughout the whole of Europe where people would say that the doge of Venice had at last gone to consummate the marriage.[23]

In fact such a risk would never arise for if the weather did not favour the ceremony the doge would simply postpone his outing for a day or two.

After hearing Mass at the monastery of San Nicolò on the Lido the doge returned to his palace for a huge banquet* given for the ambassadors and all the aristocratic members of the Senate, but the public could attend during the serving of the first course. This founding feast of the Republic lasted for two weeks through the Fiera, a great fair held in wooden huts erected on the St Mark's piazza and the nearer half of the Broglio; all kinds of Venetian specialities were sold there, from glass and mirrors to tools, leatherwork and fabrics. The Sensa also allowed Venetians to wear masks again and amuse themselves by watching marionettes and mountebanks or visiting fortune-tellers; in this atmosphere of totally carefree gaiety people could spend the last two weeks of the carnival season before the long summer period.

Described in this laconic way the feast of the Ascension, and the marriage with the Adriatic may seem to be only one more celebration, with its cortège of sumptuous sailing craft and its compulsory expression of joy. In fact it represented, for those who were present, especially the passing foreigners, a miraculous moment of beauty, magnificence, vivid colours and the sincere rejoicing of ordinary people. It is difficult today to imagine these water festivals and the deep impression they made on all the contemporaries: 'The sight of all those boats on a calm sea,' admitted Monsieur de Silhouette, 'I think I can say without exaggeration, creates the finest spectacle that exists in all the world.'[24]

Finally the category of the 'exceptional festivities', which fluctuated each year because they were linked to precise political events: the finest of them all, but by definition not very frequent, was the election of a new patriarch at San Pietro di Castello or better still that of a new doge, a supreme opportunity for reviving the unity of an entire population and providing them with the illusion of playing their part in the enthroning of the Venetian leader. After all, was it not a child of the streets, a son of the people, who signalled the first stage of the alarming election procedure described earlier? For a better understanding of the complexity involved in this elaborate ritual we can be guided by the account given by a Venetian writing in 1722. At that date Vivaldi, who was surely in the crowd or in the

---

*A banquet given by the doge consisted of thirty courses. The final preparation of the bread, the gilding of oysters and candles, had to be carried out on the tables.

basilica, was forty-four years old. On 24 August that year Venice was present at the enthronement of the doge Alvise Mocenigo, who was sixty:

> A secretary sets out in a gondola along the Grand Canal, clad in crimson velvet embroidered in gold, with cushions in identical colours behind him and goes to the palazzo of the doge Elect where he receives him in this gondola . . . and accompanies him to the doge's palace, where he is received by the 41* and stays to take luncheon with them.
>
> After the meal they perform the ceremony of placing him on the throne in the Collegio, then in the Sala del Maggior Consiglio where he receives congratulations before remaining for a short time in his own apartments; then bread and money are thrown to the people, they could drink as much wine as they want and in the evening there are bonfires with a 'machine'† in the piazza while there is a great ball in the palace.
>
> The next morning the 41 lead the doge into the basilica of Saint Mark's and he goes into the musicians' Bigonzo‡; there the eldest of the 41 speaks in praise of his merits before the doge addresses the people. Then he goes to the high altar where he meets Monsignore Primicerio who sprinkles him with holy water and incense, then he goes beyond the altar and takes the oath on the New Testament, after which he receives the standard. He then takes his place in the 'well', a kind of litter in gilded wood shaped like a well, and was carried by workers from the Arsenal across the piazza, while he throws money in all directions. Arriving at the Staircase of the Giants (the ceremonial entrance to the doge's palace) he goes up it and is crowned with the cocked hat encrusted with precious stones and shows himself to the people.

*The 'Holy of Holies' of the Venetian government were known as 'the 41'. They included the Council of Ten (that is ten ordinary members elected each year by the Grand Council, from different families), the doge and his Council of 6 members, 1 lawyer from the community, the 3 section leaders of the Quaranzia and, after 1350, a commission of 20 members (the 'zonta'). These 41 members formed a special court of justice which safeguarded the security of the state, making use of secret funds and informers.
†A large construction in painted wood, a setting for magnificent fireworks displays.
‡The *bigonzo* was that octagonal platform supported by delicate columns that can still be seen today to the right, between the choir and the transept, where the cantors stood.

Immediately afterwards they go into the hall of . . . carrying out
the same ceremony and take him to his own apartments,* throwing bread and silver coins to the people at the same time, while
the same thing takes place after the meal, with a celebration in the
evening.

The following morning the doge, wearing his golden cloak,
comes into St Mark's church for High Mass with the *Te Deum
Laudamus*, then he returns to the palace while money and bread
are thrown to the people, before the evening celebrations. As soon
as he reaches the palace he goes first before the Grand Consiglio,
wearing his golden cloak, surrounded with the 41 and others still
wearing their ducal clothes. Next he devotes himself to his
prayers, and finally he goes to the Collegio. The following day the
ambassadors from different countries begin to go to the Collegio
to congratulate him, one at a time, until they have all been. Each
year a *Te Deum* will be sung to commemorate his election.[25]

As can be seen, these four days of festivities accompany a ceremonial
as complex and unchanging as the election procedure itself. It should
be noted here that the entry of the doge's wife into the palace was
also the object of a ceremony with great pomp.

The details of the description given above illustrate the attachment shown by the senators and also the people themselves towards
this immutable ritual based on multiple symbols, the more or less
permanent presence of the ordinary people who acclaimed the newly
elected doge, the inseparable nature of political and religious power,
reminders of the maritime hegemony of Venice through the power
of the Arsenal workers carrying the doge in triumph into the piazza,
the close proximity, as the 'well' was carried, of the doge (leader of
the Venetians) and the humble *ballottino*, the boy who launched the
election procedure . . .

In this way, forty or fifty times a year, according to the number of
exceptional feast days which could join the fixed calendar (others
should not be forgotten, such as the ceremonial arrivals of procurators, visits by foreign princes or sovereigns, marriages of the senior

---

*This account fails to make it clear that the new doge was taken at once to the room where
the body of the late doge was lying, so that he will realise that one day he too will be there in
his turn.

aristocracy etc.), Venice reinvented time and time again the 'state celebration' which favoured individual well-being while reinforcing the
idea of collectivity and national unity. Remote historical and religious feast days led to a legend which each inhabitant of Venice
appropriated to himself in his own way and made his own. Then
each one considered himself as the fortunate link in an everlasting
story, explaining the enthusiasm that was constantly renewed on
each one of these feast days: no lassitude, nor the blasé attitude of
some spoilt child, but truly the spontaneous reaffirmation of a pleasure which resembled a vital need and the guarantee of their own
survival.

Carnival, quintessence of the Venetian spirit

Many readers will feel they are already familiar with the famous carnival, so much a legendary phenomenon that the very word Venice
is associated with it. In 1980 it was decided that it would be a good
idea to revive it after 183 years of abandonment. Care should be
taken, however, not to associate what can be seen and experienced
today in this big international and somewhat artificial celebration
(despite the lavish and much admired costumes) with the reality of
the carnival during the former Republic, the culminating period of
the year when every Venetian broke away from his everyday life,
came out of himself, broke every rule and became part of this collective rejoicing.

During Vivaldi's lifetime the carnival lasted longer than at any
time in its history, and lasted that way until the collapse of the
Republic. As October approached every Venetian experienced a rise
in tension, like Eskimos waiting for the sun to return after months
of darkness. The festivities finally began on the first Sunday in
October and ended two weeks before Christmas, the Signoria having
banned entertainments and theatres during this period as from
1699. Then everything began again for the central episode which ran
from 26 December (sometimes only from Epiphany) until Shrove
Tuesday, with a constant rise in collective madness until the fatal
twelfth stroke of midnight on that day: then came Lent, a thousand
leagues away from the carnival celebrations. Finally, to the utter
delight of the Venetians everything began again with even more

enthusiasm for the two weeks following Ascension and the Marriage with the Sea. There remained St Mark's Day and the possible election of doges or procurators.

Altogether nearly six months of the year were given over to the most liberated and joyful festivities that could be seen in Europe at that time, and it was understandable that so many foreigners, even from other Italian states, rushed into this city that the population was increased by a quarter. Five or six months* during which everyone, from doge to soubrette, could go about masked, could risk doing and saying everything thanks to the incognito which ensured impunity. No more day or night, no time, no rules, no more social classes; 'You can see the nobility mingling with the people,' explained Casanova, 'the prince with the subject, the rare with the ordinary, the beautiful with the horrible. There are no longer any magistrates or laws in operation.'[25] Not only was there no limit to folly but it was inconceivable that any event, however serious it might be, could cast a shadow over it; for this reason, in 1781, the death of the doge was kept secret in order to avoid interrupting the whirlwind of pleasure.[†]

As always happened in Venice, the carnival was in no way an entertainment handed out to the lower classes to make them forget their poverty: it was really and truly a collective pleasure which brought together all sections of society, and during this time the doge made several appearances to re-affirm that the entire State expressed itself in this manifestation of the Venetian spirit. The government of course, in addition to the profits that it gained from all this, continued to send its spies right and left and prohibited all forms of resistance and insubordination, even while aware that so much folly and so much pleasure cheek by jowl made people turn away willingly from political intrigue and social unrest. Pleasure, yes, but pleasure that was constantly observed. As for ordinary mortals, or for the passing visitor, nothing could equal in his eyes the explosion of delight where everyone could be an actor in a fabulous

---

*The duration of the winter carnival depended in fact on the date of Shrove Tuesday, which could fall early or late depending on the year.

†The reason was also economic. In the eighteenth century the carnival was the principal source of revenue for Venice: innkeepers, gondoliers, businessmen and artisans of all kinds lived on this manna dispensed by thousands of foreigners. There could be no question of cutting it short even by two or three days.

entertainment: 'Normal libertinage is taken to the limit,' wrote Misson,

> All pleasures are enjoyed to the full; people immerse themselves totally in them. The entire city is in disguise. Vice and virtue are disguised more than ever, changing their name and performance … Foreigners and courtesans come to Venice in thousands from all the courts of Europe: there is bustle and general confusion. You might say that the world had gone suddenly mad … I am assured that the last carnival was attended by seven sovereign princes and more than thirty thousand other foreigners: think, I ask you, how much money all these people bring to Venice.[27]

Here, perhaps, in addition to its exceptional duration, lies one of the great differences between the Venetian carnival and those of other European cities: the obligation, and not the mere possibility, of wearing masks everywhere, in the street, in a gondola, at the theatre, in church, in the doge's palace, in the gambling clubs. All social barriers were down: the plebian became a prince, the noble lady became common. Everywhere, side by side, you saw nothing but satyrs, Moors, kings, devils and Turks plus the many characters from Italian comedy. The most impossible situations occurred side by side: one day Montesquieu saw a man kneel down before the papal nuncio, dutifully masked, and ask him for his blessing; the Baron de Pöllnitz was amazed to find himself approached by two rather forward ladies:

> 'Mask, from your appearance, which is more impressive than our escorts, my friend and I can tell you're a foreigner; and we can easily tell that you're not an ordinary man. We should be delighted to talk to you and would be glad if you take a walk around the piazza with us.'[28]

The baron did not say precisely how this evening adventure ended …

Everyone, patrician or rascal, could change their sex to suit the situation and allay suspicion, provided that the sound of his voice did not betray him. Even *galanterie* attained heights of refinement, as Addison found:

At this time the Venetians, who are naturally serious, like to indulge in follies and conversations when incognito, and act out the personality of someone else ... These disguises and mascarades lead to many romantic adventures; for there is more intrigue in Venetian galanteries than those of elsewhere ...[29]

Pöllnitz confirmed how easy it was to start relationships:

Mascarades are more usual here than anywhere else. People wear masks when out walking, when attending theatres or balls. This is the favourite pleasure of the nobles and the people. It gives rise to amorous adventures, and sometimes when masked one can succeed in making acquaintances which would be difficult to achieve if disguises were not in use ...[30]

The skill of the Venetian people was not only evident in amorous conquests: sporting events took place everywhere in those periods of collective enjoyment. The most famous among them was the *guerra dei pugni* (fist-fights or *pugnali*), often depicted by artists in their genre paintings and remaining popular until 1705. They consisted of a pitched battle between inhabitants of different *sestieri*. Standing closely packed together on each side of a bridge (that of Carmini and that of San Barnaba), the 'Castellani', at the given signal, hurled themselves on the 'Nicoletti'* and tried to take over this narrow footbridge (which had no handrail at the time) by throwing into the canal as many of the inhabitants of the opposing *sestieri* as possible. Windows, terraces and surrounding boats had been invaded by noble ladies, patricians and ordinary people, keen to miss nothing of this warlike spectacle; the spectators joined in the game and began to bombard the fighters with tiles, boiling water, chairs, household utensils and other projectiles. It was normal for a dozen or so men to die, they were drowned, trampled on, choked in the mud, crushed by others falling on top of them, as the Comte de Caylus described in laconic fashion:

*The 'Nicoletti' were mainly fishermen and represented the *sestieri* on the east (San Polo and Cannaregio) while the 'Castellani' tended to be sailors and represented the three western *sestieri* (Castello, San Mareo and Dorsoduro).

The *pugnali* contests, or fist-fighting, bring the common people more closely together than all the rest. They take place in summer on a bridge. The men are almost naked, each group guards one side and tries to take the other side of the bridge. This thing does not happen without several deaths. The bridge is narrow, several are drowned, others have their heads cut open.[31]

Carnival Thursday was the day when bulls were let loose in certain parts of the city: after a desperate chase the *popolani* would try to catch them with ropes at the moment the animals reached the Campo San Polo as well as a few other small piazzas in the city. Three bulls were sacrificed with a stroke of the sword on the Piazzetta, to the sound of drums and trumpets. On the same day the '*vola*' took place before the astonished eyes of a fair-sized crowd. A young man slid down a rope, as though he were flying, with a bouquet of flowers in his hand, from the top of the campanile of St Mark's to a window in the doge's palace. After offering his bouquet, or a sonnet in his honour, to His Serene Highness, he then went back up as he had come down, still attached to his rope, apparently flying through the air like some Ganymede. The record for eccentricity seems to have been reached during the carnival of 1727, described by the Abbé Conti:

> On Carnival Thursday a man from the Arsenal was bold enough to go up the spire of St Mark's in a gondola drawn by ropes; halfway up he changed his clothes and reorganised his gondola as if he had been drifting. Nothing like this has been done for more than thirty years but you would have to be mad to attempt it; I watched it with admiration but in the end I began to tremble for him and it was with pleasure that I saw him arrive at the columns of the spire.[33]

This Thursday was also the day when the Nicoletti and the Castellani began Moorish dances in the Piazza and competed in forming human pyramids called 'pillars of Hercules'; using perches placed on their shoulders they succeeded in forming four or five rows, the summit being taken by a little boy; finally he threw himself down into the arms of a man standing below and the pyramid collapsed. The next day, the last Friday of the carnival, was the only one when everyone was obliged to wear masks from morning to evening. During all that time a temporary building, the *macchina**, was put up on the Piazzetta; it served as a platform for orchestral concerts and was the starting point for a grandiose fireworks display which concluded the carnival.

The following Sunday, Carnival Sunday, brought the bull races, an essential stage in a carnival where barbarity was sometimes as refined as pleasure. Before the eyes of the doge and his suite, eight bulls, either free or held by ropes fastened to their horns, were shut into the palace courtyard and delivered to a pack of angry dogs. After fighting in vain the exhausted and bleeding bulls were beheaded by a huge two-handed sword: the whole art of this decap-itation consisted in cutting off the head with a single sword-thrust, preventing the blade from touching the ground. This was the 'enter-tainment' offered every year by the butchers of Venice to their supreme chief.

Finally came the long-awaited Monday and Shrove Tuesday, the culminating moments in a mood of excitement which had risen con-stantly day after day. All the shops were closed and there was not a single old man, nor a child of five, nor even a baby at the breast who was not wearing a mask. A coffin was carried across the piazza, accompanied by parodies of psalms belted out by students: it was the burlesque funeral of the carnival. In this way the whole of Venice seemed to be overwhelmed by a frenzy of entertainments, proces-sions, laughter, singing and dancing, in a kaleidoscope of costumes and masks. Exhaustion was inevitable, nobody would be nostalgic for those days of madness, once the twelve strokes of midnight had struck at the church of Santa Francesca della Vigna. After all, another period of carnival would soon be there! Such was the Venetian temperament, naturally accustomed to sharing a year between celebration and work, jubilation and compunction, sin and repentance over sin. 'The carnival is over', wrote the Abbé Conti,

> and in a single instant people have passed without the slightest effort from excessive madness to good behaviour, they are just as

*See p. 43, note †.

moved by the sermons of the Jesuits as they were by the tunes of d'Ambreville or the voice of La Pierri, the machine moves in the same way but the object is different, you can see in this the character of the nation, they like to be deeply moved by something, and care very little what that something is . . .[33]

Summary of the 38 immoveable religious feast days in Venice

[There were 38 immoveable feast days which the doge, the Signoria and the ambassadors were obliged to attend. The place mentioned here is that of the official ceremony, which did not prevent certain festivals from taking place at the same time in other parishes. The year chosen was a typical year during the Abbé de Pomponne's time as French ambassador (1705–10). Depending on the years, certain 'moveable feasts', such as Easter or the Ascension, might take place in different months.]

January	Circumcision (morning at St Mark's)
	Epiphany (morning at St Mark's)
	San Lorenzo (morning at San Pietro di Castello)
February	Santa Maria Formosa (vespers at the eponymous church)
	Candlemas (Purification) (morning at St Mark's)
	Carnival Thursday [the Thursday before Lent] (afternoon at St Mark's)
March	Annunciation (morning and afternoon at St Mark's)
	Ash Wednesday (afternoon at San Giovanni di Rialto)
	Palm Sunday (morning and afternoon at St Mark's, then at La Pietà)
	Good Friday (morning and afternoon at St Mark's)
	Easter Eve (morning at St Mark's)
April	Easter Sunday (morning, afternoon and evening at St Mark's)
	Low Sunday (morning at St Mark's)

Saint Isidore (morning at St Mark's)
Eve of St Mark's day (afternoon at St Mark's)
Feast of Saint Mark (morning at St Mark's then banquet at the doge's palace)

May   1 May (morning at the monastery delle Vergine at Castello)
Eve of Ascension Day (afternoon at St Mark's)
Ascension (morning at San Niccolò del Lido then banquet at the doge's palace
Whitsuntide (morning at St Mark's)
Annual commemoration of Cardinal Zen's funeral (morning at St Mark's)

June   Saint Anthony of Padua (morning at La Salute)
Saint Vitus and Saint Modestus (Vito and Modeste) (morning at San Vito then banquet at the doge's palace)
Vision of Saint Mark (morning at St Mark's)
Saint John and Saint Paul (morning at San Zanipolo then at St Mark's)

July   Redemption (third Sunday) (morning at Redentore, on La Giudecca)
Saint Marina (morning at Santa Marina then at St Mark's)

August   Assumption (morning at St Mark's)
Saint Roch (morning at San Rocco)

September Nativity of the Virgin Mary (morning at St Mark's)

October   Santa Giustina (Justina) (morning in the nuns' convent)

November   All Saints' Day (morning at St Mark's)
Presentation of the Virgin (morning at La Salute)

December   Christmas Eve (afternoon at St Mark's)
            Christmas Day (morning and evening at St Mark's)
            Saint Stephen (San Stefano) (morning at San Giorgio
            then banquet with the doge)

CHAPTER 3

The Ospedali, or musical fame for the poorest of people

At the Pietà they pray God with the violin
at the Mendicanti with the flute;
at the Ospedaletto with the bassoon
and at the Incurabili with the drum.
Anonymous, eighteenth century

The general passion for music among all classes of society, from the lowest to the most cultivated, was to produce in Venice one of the most noble educational experiences in Europe during the baroque period. It is true that charity towards the most disinherited in society (orphans, invalids, beggars . . .) was practised in many countries and had been so for a very long time. But Venice was destined to give its *ospedali* (hospices, hospitals) a musical dimension which was to be of great value to a population marginalised by their birth and the ups and downs of life.

By providing a good education for girls of the most modest origin Venice soon rose to the rank of the greatest European centre for vocal and instrumental music.

The four ospedali: orphanages and conservatoires

Ever since the sixteenth century, sometimes even earlier, many European cities, ravaged by epidemics, wars or malnutrition found themselves faced with increased numbers of abandoned children and the impossibility of providing decent conditions of life for orphans. The ecclesiastical authorities had then begun to take responsibility for these disinherited children, placing them in caring institutions which constantly became more important, in size and reputation, as the eighteenth century gradually approached. The Catholic Counter-Reformation had wanted to add a new dimension to these institutions: training the children in a Christian way, naturally, but also in a cultural and professional way, thus making them capable of earning their living and assisting in the caring work in their turn.

Music soon occupied a central place in the daily life of these *ospedali*; children and adolescents, in addition to the traditional studies in Latin, rhetoric and theology, received an unusual education which would provide them in future with training at a very high level, that would help them in a professional way when they left the institutions. In this way the four *ospedali* in Naples developed into conservatoires,* the first in Europe (they had even invented the word). It was these, especially in the eighteenth century, that produced the greatest castrati and the best stage musicians in Europe.

These four prestigious institutions were essentially reserved for boys, only one of them accepted girls. Also, far from there, in northern Germany, poor boys or orphans filled the ranks of the Mettenchor in Luneburg: the young Johann Sebastian Bach was orphaned at the age of ten and since his elder brother could no longer finance the boy's studies, which had become very expensive, he was admitted to the choir and received a very good education.

Things were no different in Venice where the four *ospedali* destined to welcoming and training the most destitute, were opened in the course of its history. The oldest, dating from the thirteenth century, was San Lazzaro dei Mendicanti, taking in beggars, lepers, people suffering from undiagnosable illnesses, together with all kinds of disabled subjects, old people and beggars. Santa Maria di Pietà had been founded in 1346 to help orphans and abandoned children. L'Ospedale degli Incurabili dated from the years 1520–22 and was originally intended to care for syphilitics. Finally, in 1527–8 there appeared Santi Giovanni e Paolo dei Derelitti, generally known later

*More details about the organisation and musical life of the Neapolitan conservatoires in *The World of the Castrati*, Patrick Barbier, Souvenir Press, 1996.

as the Ospedaletto, originally dedicated to helping the population in times of serious famine.

The buildings where Vivaldi and the girls of the Pietà worked together no longer exist today. All that remains is the church situated on the Riva near St Mark's which is the third so named: it was rebuilt in 1745, that is, after Vivaldi's death. Only two columns from the second church, the one known to the composer, can be seen today in the entrance hall of the Hotel Metropole. The visitor must be content with imagining its position without being able to see the slightest section of wall. However, there is much more satisfaction to be had in the case of the three others. The Incurabili building, entirely restored and rehabilitated, is situated on the Zattere, facing the island of La Giudecca. Its plain but elegant façade, its well designed interior patio, surrounded on four sides by buildings occupied today by various administrative organisations, give some idea of what the former *ospedale* was like, even if the church where so many masterpieces were created no longer exists.

But the most interesting finds for the traveller fascinated by the musical history of Venice in the seventeenth and eighteenth centuries are certainly to be discovered in the two other *ospedali* which are more or less intact, real mines of information about the social and musical life which existed at the time. Few buildings have been painted over three centuries as often as the Mendicanti: its proximity to the adjacent church of Santi Giovanni e Paolo (San 'Zanipolo' to the Venetians), with its immense façade along the rio of the same name as well as the various bridges which cross this stretch of water between the piazza and the distant lagoon have inspired, perhaps more than any other part of Venice, the painting of the eighteenth-century *vedute* artists of the Romantic period, as well as modern photographers. It has to be said that this high spot of musical Venice in the baroque period has moved on from the status of hospice for the most needy to that of municipal hospital; nothing important has changed: neither the buildings, nor the church that serves as its grandiose epicentre, nor even its previous medical vocation. In walking in the district round the church of Santi Giovanni e Paolo and the hospital of the Mendicanti you will encounter several centuries of history in a décor that is virtually untouched. Going into the church, open nowadays only for Masses on Sundays and the funerals of patients, means that you can already understand the musical organisation of the institution in the eighteenth century: two *cantorie* or platforms face each other, the one on the left for the girls and the one on the right for the boys, who were also allowed to sing in this *ospedale*. The public could not see them during services; at the most only the tops of their heads were visible.

Equally satisfying is the Ospedaletto, situated less than 200 metres away, at the start of the street called Barbarie delle Tole. Today it is a rest home for elderly people, which has preserved many elements from its rich past: the superb baroque façade of 1674 by Baldassare Longhena, the church built in 1575, based on a project by Palladio, with many paintings by Palma the Younger, Longhi or Tiepolo, the oval staircase completed by Longhena in 1670 and lastly the superb music room, completed in 1777 and very recently restored: with its trompe-l'oeil effects by Guarama and Mengozzi Colonna, it recreates perfectly for us one of those elegant salons where the girls from the *ospedale* came to perform, concealed by grilles, before guests of note, admitted in a small group into the Holy of Holies of Venetian music.

This church remains today an inexhaustible source of interest for any devotee of baroque Venice, not so much for its intrinsic beauty (many churches surpass it in refinement and grandeur), but for its unchanged arrangement: facing the congregation, much higher in relation to the high altar, is the famous platform where the girls, the '*putte*' (as they were known in the Venetian dialect) would sing like angels, partially concealed by the long grilles running from left to right and yet visible enough to arouse the passions (not solely musical) of Venetians and foreign visitors. Below the *cantorie*, on both sides of the tabernacle, two alcoves, also with grilles, and still visible today, sheltered the girl musicians, trumpeters or others, who, according to the ceremonies and types of instruments required, accompanied the choristers. The voices, mysterious and celestial, reached the ears of the visitors, seated below yet fairly near, and transported them into an unreal world, as ethereal as it was sensuous: 'The girl musicians of the Ospedaletto', wrote a Venetian newspaper in 1707, 'sang the pastorals like angels, the voices echoed so well around the crèche that the listeners felt they were in Bethlehem.'[1]

In Naples boys were the principal beneficiaries of the four conservatoires but in Venice the girls were the only ones to profit from

the teaching of music. The *ospedali* certainly welcomed disinherited children of both sexes, but the boys figured only temporarily
in the registers, for as soon as they were old enough they were
apprenticed with different corporations in the city: in this way
they were no longer the responsibility of the institution. It was
quite different for the girls, for there could be no question of let-
ting them go out into the world before they were adult and they
could only leave if they were getting married or taking the veil in
some convent. In either case they received a good dowry, given by
the *ospedale* itself which replaced in this way the parents they had
never had. At the end of the eighteenth century this dowry
amounted to about 2,000 ducats, a sum corresponding to about
20,000 euros in 2002. But it is clear that in exceptional cases some
girls received much larger sums, in proportion to their fame and
the income they had brought into the *ospedale* through concerts
with entance fees. All the girls could also take away with them the
linen and sheets they had embroidered.

The length of their stay in the institutions was therefore extended
and long-lasting activities had to be found for them, suitable for
occupying them for an average of ten years. The more modest among
them, who showed the least capacity for artistic or intellectual pur-
suits, were called 'community girls', their education was of a general
nature and their activities were concentrated round various domestic
tasks, nursing care, but also craft work of a high standard, particularly
lace-making or embroidery, in which they excelled. It was obviously
a hardworking life (they were allowed only one day's outing each
year), but it was preferable to the wretched existence they would
otherwise have had in the city or the countryside. The most gifted
among the girls whose disposition was for things of the mind were
called 'choir girls' and received a specifically musical education. As the
following pages will show, each *ospedale* had its own organisation, its
rules of life, its own special recruiting system, music teachers, its days
for ceremonies or concerts and of course its musical specialities.

Organisation and social life in the ospedali

Originally, as already mentioned, the *ospedali* had been created for
medical and caring purposes. This objective remained the same

during the baroque period and the children were all admitted for the same sad reasons: great poverty, illness, death of both parents or the incapacity of the remaining parent. The statutes of the Ospedaletto, revised in 1667, provided clearly for access to be limited to girls who were the most poverty-stricken and abandoned, often without father or mother, without relatives capable of providing them with help or lodging; the girls had to be no older than ten and no younger than six.[2] The registers of these institutions remain moving catalogues of social problems, desperate pleas, insufficient places when the numbers of applicants were clearly too great. In 1733, for instance, the Ospedaletto register mentions a special dispensation made for 'the poor Laura Anzola . . . whose mother is dead and her father, who is mad, has been in prison for a year.' Two years later came the plea from several girls asking for permission to leave the institution for one day, which was allowed on condition that they told the prioress exactly to whose house they were going. Another page mentions that seventeen little girls were asking for admission to the *ospedale*, but owing to the shortage of places only six could be accepted, including twins whom the authorities did not want to separate.[3] Any page in the register of the Mendicanti tells the same story: each one of the administrators could propose ten names of the poorest people they had found in the city and who wanted to be admitted. Time after time one can read: 'Poor children selected by Signore X from the [. . .] sestiere.' Sixty young people entered the *ospedale* in this way on the single day of 9 January 1720.

In fact, at the end of the seventeenth century, and even more so in the eighteenth, the purely medical reasons which prevailed for the admission of children or adults were largely ignored. The Ospedaletto, which was first and foremost an orphanage for 125 girls and 40 boys, continued also to treat skin ailments, especially ringworm, and undiagnosed illnesses. Its numbers did not exceed 200 boarders. The Incurabili, destined at first to treat syphilis, the incurable illness *par excellence*, came to accept all kinds of patients, as well as male orphans and even seventy girls from noble families, which brought its numbers up to 500. The Mendicanti included even more people, and had now become a vast caring institution capable of receiving orphans, beggars or cripples as well as widows or elderly nobles. Although its entry conditions were strict, its population nevertheless inevitably varied between 600 and 900. Finally, at the top of the pyramid, as far as inmates were concerned, was La Pietà, which developed rapidly from a population of 400–500 inmates in 1663 to more than 1,000 in 1738. Like its sister organisations the Pietà added to its vocation of orphanage the care of those suffering from ringworm, help for beggars coming from the country and vaccination against smallpox. It seems astonishing that while dealing with so many scourges La Pietà could also be the bastion of musical excellence; due to the presence of Antonio Vivaldi within its walls it will be described separately.

The European fame of these four Venetian institutions therefore was not due solely to their healing talents, which were common to many other cities, but to the unprecedented musical education they gave to their young boarders. This education which at first had been no more than a means of entertaining and educating girls who, unlike boys, could not decently go to work with a craftsman or a worker-manager, soon became the *raison d'être* of these institutions and the leading cause of competition between them. The four *ospedali* were run by private secular bodies, while the clergy only took responsibility for the teaching side. Nobles, Venetian citizens and rich merchants financed and administered them with the same unanimity and benevolence as the council of admisnistration of an association or a company would do today. They shared out the tasks between different commissions (finance, clothing, nursing care, church, communal business etc.) and they all belonged to the leading families of the Venetian Signoria: throughout the registries there appear the names of Loredan, Mocenigo, Tron, Dona or Contarini. These protectors, appointed by the senatorial magistrates, soon understood, towards the end of the seventeenth century and especially during the first part of the eighteenth, that the musical talent of these young ladies, which had then reached its zenith, was a worthwhile source of revenue, as much through the new donations that it brought in, as through the considerable charitable gifts left by the rich visitors who had hurried from all over Europe to hear them.

'In Venice,' wrote a Russian in 1698,

there are convents for girls where they play the organ, different instruments, and sing so admirably that nowhere else in the world could one find such sweet and harmonious singing. So people come to Venice from everywhere with the desire to feed on these angelic songs, especially at the Incurabili.[4]

The 'choir girls' therefore were the pride of these honourable institutions. Having entered music as people enter religion from the time of their arrival, that is to say for most of them between the ages of six and ten, sometimes later, they 'owed' the institution by statute a minimum of ten or fifteen years of good and loyal musical service, after which they had three options: they could stay, marry or take the veil. This makes it clear what degree of perfection could be reached by these young musicians, selected at the age of about ten by the *maestro di coro* for singing or for this or that instrument, then instructed each day in their respective discipline over so many years by the best teachers that Venice could produce. A few girls who paid for their teaching, sometimes Germans or Austrians, could be admitted in order to acquire perfection in the art of music, even if they were not orphans. The teaching was not carried out only by the great teachers but also by the older choir girls, generally those who had decided to spend all their lives in the *ospedale*, or who were not able to do anything else. This teaching that was handed down, also usual among the boys in the Naples conservatoires, guaranteed the quality of these studies, since the best students were admirably capable of transmitting what they themselves had received. After their time as beginners they could become *sotto-maestre* (sub-mistresses) at the age of twenty-four, then *maestre* (mistresses) after thirty. When they were forty they could retire, but many of them remained to an advanced age, the record belonging to a woman of seventy-six at the Pietà who had totalled sixty-five years of service.

If discipline was strict and daily life somewhat austere, especially on the religious level, the girl musicians still benefited from a certain number of favours and relief from discipline which were not unlike the relaxed lifestyle reserved for the young castrati in the Neapolitan conservatoires. Distinguished in this way from the 'community girls' they had the advantage of better food and warmer clothes to preserve their valuable throats and banish attacks of bronchitis or numb fingers in winter. They were also partially or totally excused from '*la tasca*', the daily tasks assigned to the other girls. In the same way,

although the poor laundry workers or lace-makers could go out only
once during each year, the choir girls were given a more relaxed
régime which permitted short holidays in the countryside and some
outings to the islands in the lagoon or to the drawing-rooms of the
aristocracy for musical performances, by invitation, obviously. Their
rare escapes into the outside world formed a kind of attraction for
their admirers who were delighted to see them by daylight, and not
behind a grille. In 1704, *Pallade Veneta* described how 'the girls who
sing in the Mendicanti choir were taken by their gentlemen governors to an aristocratic recreation and were followed by a crowd who
venerated them and considered them the most celebrated musicians
to be heard these days.'[5] Some comments in the press were not without humour, such as the article of 1702 which described the unusual
outing by the '*putte*' to the island of Torcello, 'where they made
nature stand still through the staccato notes in their singing.'[6] If a
few outings were authorised it was not usual on the other hand to
receive visitors in the *ospedali*, the rules there being similar to those
in a closed convent. In the eighteenth century some income was
given to the girls who deserved it. In 1717 the Pietà awarded some
payments to these girls on condition that they taught a girl from the
aristocracy; in 1739 an annual payment was granted to the twelve
girls who most deserved it. In 1731 the Mendicanti, followed by the
Ospedaletto in 1743, decided to encourage the 'choir girls' by granting them a sum corresponding to half the price of the tickets to
public concerts, but the girls still had to render some services in
return by copying scores. The small sum of money, patiently collected, could be invested in the school funds at a privileged rate of
interest. In this way the eighteenth century marked the beginning of
a certain rise in social status for the choir girls, even if it was the last
time in their history.

An international musical reputation

The transcendent music here is that of the hospitals. There are
four of them, all made up of illegitimate girls or orphans, and
some whose parents are not able to bring them up. They are educated at the expense of the State, and trained only to excel in
music. Therefore they sing like angels and play the violin, the

flute, the organ, the oboe, the 'cello, the bassoon; in short no instruments are big enough to frighten them. They are cloistered like nuns. They alone perform, and each choir is composed of forty girls or so. I assure you there is nothing so delightful as to see a young girl, a pretty nun, in a white dress, with a bunch of pomegranate flowers at her ear, conducting the orchestra and beating out the time with all the grace and precision imaginable. Their voices are adorable for their phrasing and lightness; for here the rounded and extended sounds in the French style are unknown. Zabetta at the Incurabili is particularly astonishing through the range of her voice and the violin-like sounds she carries in her throat. I myself have no doubt that she has swallowed Somis's violin. It is she who wins all the votes and you would be attacked by the people if you compared anyone else to her. But listen, my friends, I believe that nobody can hear us and I will whisper to you that Margarita at the Mendicanti is just as good as she is and I find her more pleasing.[7]

Charles de Brosses, Président of the Dijon *Parlement*, wrote this letter in 1739. Vivaldi had only two more years to live, but Venice exercised all its powers of seduction in the musical field and the *ospedale* girls were at the height of their popularity both in the Italian peninsula and the surrounding countries. The capital of the four institutions was certainly that described by the French traveller. Forty or so girls performed in each 'hospital': half were singers and half instrumentalists, the latter slightly outnumbering the former. The mysterious beauty of their appearance* in addition to the delicacy of their voices or their perfect mastery of the instruments were the cause of veneration on the part of the travellers: 'I cannot imagine anything so voluptuous, so touching as this music,' stated Rousseau apropos the Mendicanti, while Goethe, visiting the same place later, maintained that he had 'never imagined such voices'. 'I do not know what delighted me most about the performance or the

---

*The girls obviously excited the spectators' imagination. But reality could be cruel. Rousseau, admitted one day beyond the enclosing barrier, was heartbroken to see so many ill-favoured girls. Then he pulled himself together and concluded in elegant fashion: 'I continued to find their singing delicious, and their voices lent such a fictitious charm to their faces that, as long as they were singing, I persisted in thinking them beautiful, in spite of my eyes (*Confessions*, Book VII).

composition', wrote the English musicologist Burney after going to
the Incurabili. Anyone could draw up a list of the most outstanding
girls, as shown clearly by the Président de Brosses, fascinated by
Zabetta of the Incurabili or Margarita of the Mendicanti and each
man could boast of having found the most beautiful, most spiritual
and most accomplished voice, the surest stroke of the bow ... 'On
feast days,' wrote Casotti in 1713, 'we never fail to go to the
Incurabili to hear Vespers with music and listen to Greghetta, and
Anzoletta, along with others, who do not sing but delight us.'[8]
Charles de Brosses, once more, in the same letter, was proud of
having found the two best girl instrumentalists in Venice: 'Chiarretta
(at the Pietà) could certainly be the leading violinist of Italy if Anna
Maria of the Hospitalettes [the Ospedaletto] did not surpass her. I
was rather pleased to hear the latter, who is so capricious that she
plays barely once a year.' In fact visitors were guided in their search
for deep emotional reactions by the Venetian newspapers themselves
which never failed, at various periods, to indicate the musical stars
of the moment. In this way the Guide for Foreigners for 1697 told
passing visitors:

> The girls from the four *ospedali* are greatly applauded and much
> attention is given to Appolonia, Caccina and Oseletta at the
> Incurabili, Antonina at the Mendicanti, Vicentina at the
> Ospedaletto and for the playing of the archlute, to Jamosa at the
> Pietà.[9]

It only remained now to go and enjoy the delights of this music in
the feminine gender. There was no lack of choice and visitors had to
check with the calendar and the customs of the four institutions.
First came the regular services, the easiest to attend. As a general rule
complines and litanies on Saturday, vespers on Sunday and the
masses held on important feast days were the principal times for
going into one of the churches and hearing the *putte*. With the growing popularity of these services during the period which concerns us
and the growth of what might be called the 'tourist demand', the
ospedali arranged for the services in each one to avoid any clash, with
the exception of vespers which took place in each church every afternoon and at more or less the same time; it was arranged that the

solemn services and exceptional feast days should not take place on the same day nor at the same time. For example the solemn Mass at the Mendicanti took place on the second Sunday of the month and on the fourth Sunday at the Ospedaletto, and so on.

But it was certainly the oratorios, motets and concerts of instrumental music that constituted the *nec plus ultra* of the *ospedale* productions and therefore became the most sought-after entertainments for the Venetian public and for visiting foreigners. The greatest teachers had trained these students: the great woman violinist Giacomina Stromba, at the Incurabili, had learnt everything from the famous Tartini. Moreover this *ospedale* possessed an exceptional collection of instruments: spinets made by the craftsman Donato Undeo, harpsichords by Bortolotti, harps, psalteries and all kinds of violins and 'cellos. For the young girls in this institution Porpora, the undisputed master of the Neapolitan school and teacher of the great Farinelli had written a *Salve Regina* and the oratorio to Latin words *San Petrus Urseolus*; Lotti had also composed for them the oratorio to Italian words *Joas re de Giuda* and the Saxon Hasse a *Miserere*. Between 1683 and 1716 the Incurabili and the Pietà competed fiercely over oratorios. Seventeen of these were created at the Incurabili thanks to the maestro Pollarolo, rather fewer at the Pietà with Gasparini. But it was especially at the Ospedaletto that Porpora became *maestro di capella* in 1743. His contract was approved that year with a salary of 400 lire per year and his work began at the start of 1744.[10] An archive document entitled 'list of the musical works composed during the current year by Maestro Nicolo Porpora' mentions no fewer than forty works written specially for the students in one year, with notably fifteen pieces for the Feast of the Assumption and twelve for Christmas.[11] At the end of the seventeenth century the great composer Giovanni Legrenzi was engaged by the Mendicanti in order to extend the school repertoire. His oratorio with Italian words *L'Erodiade o vero la morte di S. Giov. Battista* was the event of the year in 1687; the people of Venice, in addition to an audience of princes and princesses were present at its first performance in January, and the following month it was the work performed for the Elector of Bavaria, who was making an official visit to Venice.

He was taken to the pious institution of the Mendicanti where for his entertainment they sang again the oratorio [*L'Erodiade*]

... which was received with the greatest satisfaction, before a great gathering of people; and His Highness warmly praised the young lady virtuosi and rewarded them well, proving at the same time both his generosity of spirit and his noble birth.[12]

After 1700 the maestro Biffi took the place of Legrenzi and remained attached to the Mendicanti for thirty years. Examples like this, in addition to those we shall see later concerning the Pietà, provide only a brief glimpse of the many great teachers and the instrumental or sacred works made available to the girls at the *ospedali*, since the aim here is not to provide exhaustive lists but to demonstrate the vitality and musical influence of these institutions.

As we have seen, all visitors of note, any royal or princely presence in Venice implied as an obligation one or more attendances at this or that *ospedale*. The appearance of the girls, dressed in white but discreetly concealed from all eyes by grilles, sometimes draped with black gauze, their position, always higher than the audience, the relative quiet behaviour of the latter, who listened in silence and were not allowed to applaud, the perfection of the vocal parts and instrumental accompaniments, which was unanimously acknowledged: all this combined to transform these evenings into times of delight and intense emotion. At a period, and especially in a country where opera ruled the scene, it was altogether remarkable that the girls of the *ospedali* could often be compared to the greatest voices of the eighteenth century, although they lived in an enclosed world, without even being able to hear the greatest names in the musical theatre or participate in that permanent musical and commercial extravaganza, the opera. 'Last night,' wrote Lady Mary Wortley Montagu to her husband,

> there was a concert of voices and instruments at the Hospital of the Incurabili, where there were two girls that, in the opinion of all people, excel either Faustina or Cuzzoni [the two greatest Italian women singers of the moment, well known to her husband and all Londoners], but you know they are never permitted to sing on [sic] any theatre.[13]

Jean-Jacques Rousseau, a fervent admirer of vespers at the Mendicanti, went so far in fact as to affirm that 'even operatic singers came to form their taste after these excellent models'.[14]

Venice could also pride itself on having taken to the heights of perfection a musical art performed by the most humble people and earning international fame, far removed from the élitist practices that were current in other places. These impoverished orphan girls who, without the *ospedali*, would have known deprivation and prostitution, enjoyed a highly honourable quality of life and even attained some fame while remaining anonymous, for their Christian names (and sometimes their surnames), were more or less all that was known of them. The institution certainly took its share. What the girls did not earn (at the most they were granted a few payments now and then, as we have seen) went entirely to the profits of the *ospedale*. In this way, and with sound logic, they moved from charity pure and simple, to a kind of tit-for-tat situation. The girls, through the fame of their performances, brought considerable revenues to the institution in exchange for the education they had received: the oratorios and concertos led to a sale of tickets for seat reservations and 'programmes' (the texts of the motets or oratorios that were to be heard). But through the near-voluptuous pleasure they gave to the listeners, the success of the girls encouraged legacies or donations along with all types of generosity, most of which went into the school funds. This system therefore formed an original compromise between non-commercial production (unlike the opera) and a reliable source of profit.

Lastly, these girls, who formed a far from negligible element in the social scene, established a musical and spiritual link between the interior and exterior of the *ospedali*. It should not be forgotten that these young musicians formed only a small part of the population living within those walls. There were also the 'community girls', who were far more numerous, orphan boys, before they left to take up apprenticeships, as well as patients, paralytics, and old people who could all hear their 'sisters' during the services. Music of this kind possibly had the power to ease in part the wretched state of such people and prevent the hospices from appearing to be mere old people's homes, while most of all it constituted a kind of link between the internal world and the crowd outside which represented at one and the same time Venice, Italy and Europe. Nobody, and this can be seen clearly in the many commentaries and descriptions of the time, could forget that behind those sublime performances there were the charitable institutions, full of disinherited people who still were not forgotten rejects of the ruling class. Thanks to music, the Venetian hospices were in fact the most famous and the most fashionable of their century.

Were things equally simple for the young musicians? And can we speak in their name when not one of them left an account of their life and their musical experience? They were certainly aware of having escaped from a much harsher fate, especially the choir girls, freed of many menial tasks and raised to an enviable intellectual and artistic status which united them in one entity, beyond social, linguistic or cultural differences. They formed an élite among people of their class and could only have been aware of it, despite their modesty. The first frustration could surely arise from the anonymity to which they were constrained. Aware of their musical gifts and the effect they produced in public, they also had to accept that they must remain in the shade, deriving no personal satisfaction from their art and working in fact more for the institution than for themselves. But the greatest frustration no doubt awaited those who left the *ospedale* to be married. It was true that a promise of marriage could constitute a form of liberation for these young women who had been cloistered from an early age, but it was certainly not easy to find a husband when there was so little opportunity to go out and meet men. The problem was not marriage, then, but on the contrary the total prohibition for the former *fanciulle* from practising their art once they had left the institution. This was one more injustice in the treatment of the sexes. Whereas the young men who left the Neapolitan conservatoires, singers or instrumentalists, castrati or not, only emerged to fly with their own wings and turn their years of musical studies to profit, the young Venetian girls could only resign: their career ended with their marriage. The rules were very strict: once they were back in the outside world it was out of the question to practise music or singing, and certainly not in public. The husband had to sign a document to this effect, under oath. Any infringement of the rule could entail the loss of the famous dowry granted by the administrators, and it was substantial, as we have seen. This measure reinforced the spirit of free educational care and benevolence in which the musical studies of the young boarders took place. But it is difficult to refrain from thinking of their sadness at not being able to practise an art which had been taken to an extreme degree of refinement over at least six years of study and even less at having received inadequate payment for it. A woman, even if she has married well, acquires a status known everywhere in other situations: that of the woman at home, the mother dependent on her husband and excluded from the professional, even the artistic world. It will be argued that the great women singers of the eighteenth century succeeded in continuing their careers along with married life, starting with the greatest of them all, Faustina Bordoni, wife of the composer Hasse. But we should not forget that they practised their art against the background of opera, a commercial activity *par excellence*, which could not have survived without them and rewarded the best of them with considerable salaries. The young women who left the *ospedali* had hardly been trained for that type of repertoire, even if they had sometimes come close to it for this or that festivity. In any case such a destiny was not possible, due to the rules in force, both in the theatres of the Venetian republic and on foreign stages. There remained the consolation, not unimportant, of having found a place in society, sometimes even with great families, who were often cultivated and passionately fond of music; these families approved greatly of a marriage between a young man and a young girl who was not only a musician, but had received an education, the concept of piety and a lifestyle instilled by the *ospedale*, all quite worthy of the best society. There perhaps lay the best recompense for these young girls who had been disinherited by their birth but in the end were promised to the best husbands.

One of the best romantic stories known is that of Cecilia Guardi whose request for entry to the Ospedaletto was dated June 1717, as described in the registers:

Request heard by this Congregation from the poor widow, mother of Cecilia Guardi, who described her extreme poverty, her many children, the danger to her daughter's honour ... Her voice is stable and would be useful to the choir, as proved by our administrator responsible for music, assisted by our choir master Don

Antonio Pollaroli, stating that her soprano voice is beautiful and provides hope that it can lead to another distinguished success. For all these reasons, to the glory of our Lord God, may the young Cecilia Guardi, daughter of Domenico Guardi, be accepted, although she is past the age set out by our rules and her mother is living . . . [15]

In fact Cecilia was already fifteen when she was admitted, late in relation to current practice. She owed this entry entirely to the recommendation by Count Giovanelli, who was then administrator of the Ospedaletto. Thanks to her beautiful soprano voice she was placed among the choir 'angels' but apparently she was not content with ethereal pleasures and soon noticed the young painter who was carrying out some work in the church: his name was Gian Battista Tiepolo and he was to become the greatest name in eighteenth-century Venice, the pride of the palaces and churches in the declining years of the Republic. History does not relate the looks exchanged and the furtive meetings between the young genius of painting and the frail singer. The fact remains that two years after her admission Gian Battista 'abducted' Cecilia and secretly married her. The registers of the Giovanelli family, who had protected the girl, mention again the marriage gift offered to her in 1719. This episode quickly forced the *ospedale* to take some new measures, for it was clear that making a gift to a boarder who had supplied only two years of good and loyal service was hardly justified. From 1720 onwards therefore the Ospedaletto decided that a dowry could only be given if the young musician had trained at least two students to a stage suitable for service in the choir. Then it was decided to demand ten years of good service in the choir before the famous dowry of 300 ducats could be claimed. The source of the severe rule in the institution was to be found thus in the delightful idyll of the angel and the artist.

Vivaldi and La Pietà

La Pietà differed from the three other *ospedali* not only because it was the 'home' of Vivaldi but also because it enjoyed a special prestige, possessed the greatest number of students and was the only one that practised single-sex admission. Women and girls only, from young orphans to elderly ladies belonged to the community of 1,000 people situated on the Riva about 200 metres from the doge's palace. Little girls abandoned by their parents were left in a niche set in the outer wall, some succeeded in being adopted by peasants on the mainland, but most of them remained in the *ospedale* where they were divided, as in the three others, into 'community girls' and 'choir girls'.

During the seventeenth century and the early part of the eighteenth liturgical music, which had been content to remain limited to choral polyphonic work with organ accompaniment, began from 1650 to make much more use of instruments. It is true that this new conception of sacred music, this *stile moderno*, responding to the great progress of the Counter-Reformation, did not concern only the Pietà. But this institution very quickly earned itself a particularly special reputation in the instrumental field, with strings at first, then woodwind and plucked strings such as lutes and mandolins. Benefiting gradually from the contributions by different *maestri* as well as from the enthusiasm of the students, the Pietà specialised more and more in instrumental concerts, and even tried to outstrip its competitors by developing rarer instruments such as the French bagpipe or the psaltery, very popular during the Vivaldi period. As from 1716 the Pietà introduced the clarinet, in 1728 the transverse flute, in 1747 the horn and in 1750 the kettledrum. The girls, particularly impressed by the innovations introduced by Vivaldi, as we shall see, began, during the first half of the eighteenth century to acquire an unrivalled skill in the playing of instruments, while not excluding the excellent performance of the young singers. From 1712 to 1722 many travellers mention the famous 'Anna Maria of the Pietà' who played with equal talent the harpsichord, the violin, the 'cello, the *viola d'amore*,* the luth, the theorbo (a large bass lute) and the mandolin.

In this radically feminist universe, male teachers were appointed as rarely as possible, while the maximum use was made of the *maestre*, former choir girls who had become adult and reached an

---

*Viola d'amore: stringed instrument producing a sweet tenor sound, due to the resonant 'sympathetic' strings beneath the keyboard.

excellent musical level for training the young students. They were forty years old, sometimes younger, and usually performed the solo parts, vocal or instrumental, during public performances. If the *maestro* was absent they could even take over what we call the 'conducting' of the ensemble, corresponding at that time to mere time-keeping. The number of men was reduced as far as possible, although they could not be dispensed with altogether, due to their own personal skills. Between 1703 and 1740 the Pietà engaged a (male) teacher for the violin and the *viola inglese*,* a teacher for the 'cello, a teacher for the oboe, and another for the transverse flute, a teacher of singing and one for musical theory, in addition to a man for the maintenance of the organ and a further man to maintain the harpsichord.

At the top of the hierarchy was the *maestro di coro*, who created the works necessary for the different services and oratorios (Easter and the Visitation constituted the principal celebrations at the Pietà), while ensuring good progress in the various teaching areas and the careful recruitment of young singers or instrumentalists, which took place after a vote. Vivaldi knew only four choir-masters during his professional life: Francesco Gasparini (1701–14), Carlo Grua (1719–26), Giovanni Porta (1726–37) and the Neapolitan Alessandro Gennaro (1739–41); after the departure and death of Vivaldi the celebrated Neapolitan Porpora arrived, first at the Pietà from 1742 to 1744, then at the Ospedaletto until 1747.

It should be made clear in the first place that the word *coro* should not be taken at this period in its literal sense (a choir of voices only), but in the wider sense of an ensemble of voices and instruments. However, it is not easy today to determine the exact number of participants, for it varied according to the seasons and the descriptions that we possess. An archive document of 1707 mentions fourteen singers and fourteen instrumentalists,[16] but Charles de Brosses mentions forty performers in 1739 and a more detailed text from the mid-century lists eighteen singers and ten instrumentalists, plus two soloists and two copyists, in addition to eight singers and six instrumentalists, who were beginners.[17] The number of 'active' performers only amounted to thirty or so, an average number which varied,

---

**Viola inglese (or *all'inglese*): similar to the *viola d'amore*, with six strings.

depending on the importance and magnificence of the ceremonies. But the number of singers remains more of a mystery; the scores indicate a range of four voices (soprano, contralto, tenor and bass) whereas there were only female singers. Every hypothesis has been put forward, Robbins Landon has suggested that on occasions some bass voices could be recruited from among the male staff at the *ospedale*, which is very unlikely: their musical level would not have equalled that of the well produced girl singers. Michael Talbot emphasises that the parts for female voices were usually repeated an octave lower by the bass instruments. Various documents also mention that some young women sang the lower parts themselves, thanks to their exceptionally deep voices, like those one can still hear today in traditional music all over the world. It should be noted also that Vivaldi wrote more for the baritone voice than for the bass and in fact always supported voices by low chords. Whatever the truth, several cases are known to us. In 1687 the monthly news sheet *Pallade Veneta* especially mentioned Maria Anna Ziani 'who, although a woman, sings naturally with a man's voice, but a voice so tender and full, and with a tone so sweet, that she sings baritone with sufficient grace to transport and bewitch the listeners.'[18] The lists of young singers at the Pietà preserved in the State Archives of Venice also mention fairly frequently the following names: Anastasia, soprano, Cecilia, contralto, but also Annetta, bass, Antonia, tenor, Vittoria, tenor, etc. However, it is clear that low voices of this kind, by definition fairly rare, would hardly be very powerful nor would they supply the necessary balance to the ensemble. That is why the most plausible hypothesis remains the transposing of the male parts an octave higher: the sopranos would sing their part, the second sopranos would read the tenor part an octave higher, the mezzo-sopranos would take the contralto part and the contraltos sang the bass part an octave higher. This redistribution therefore produced an all-over colour of a very unusual kind, as shown by a recent recording of *Juditha triumphans*,[19] surely very close to the original performance.

It was for these girls therefore that Vivaldi wrote, among other works, his oratorios *Moyses Deus Pharaonis* (now lost) and *Juditha triumphans*, in 1714 and 1716 respectively, as well as many motets (*Magnificat, Gloria, Beatus vir, Lauda Jerusalem* . . .), amounting to about fifty pieces of sacred music. Some of his manuscripts give the actual names of the singers, even if they were only Christian names, since the Pietà performers had to remain anonymous. In the case of *Juditha triumphans* the names of Caterina, Polonia, Giulia, Silvia and Barbara can be read.

The fact that Antonio Vivaldi never attained the supreme rank of *maestro di coro* often remains a paradox for the music lovers of today who are accustomed to classify him among the important leading composers of his century. In fact his speciality was the orchestra, in particular the strings, and he probably never wanted to take responsibility in the choral field. He came to the Pietà on 1 September 1703 in the capacity of violin teacher: he was twenty-five and had been ordained six months earlier; after which, on 17 August 1704 he was given the additional task of teaching the *viola inglese*. His appointment was in response to a genuine wish by the *maestro di coro* Francesco Gasparini, who had occupied the post for two years, to consolidate and strengthen the string sections. Since this post was essentially that of teacher, Vivaldi at first was under no obligation to compose, which justified the annual salary of sixty ducats for one teaching session and 100 ducats for two: the 'choir-master', obliged to teach three days a week, morning and afternoon, and always responsible for new compositions and for the liturgy, received 200. The latter was assisted in his work by the instrument teachers and by various *maestre* who guaranteed a kind of moral authority and added their own skills to the musical education of the youngest girls. Over the three days when the 'choir-master' was there, and lessons were given by all the other teachers, the work took place every day and had to be conducted in several rooms at the same time.

The socio-professional situation of these male teachers could not really have been simple, for their employment was called into question every year by the vote of the administrators. If teachers were not suitable they were dismissed; and if they fulfilled their function well they could spend years dispensing the best teaching in the world to young girls who would never become professionals: a thankless task which had to reconcile the great art of music with a certain kind of renunciation. The contracts were renewable annually and the vote by the governors was final. Until 1708 there had to be an absolute majority, after that it had to reach two thirds. Vivaldi was one of the

first to suffer from this. Since no man is a prophet in his own country the composer who during his lifetime and after his death was to
confer a major reputation on the concert performers of the Pietà was
obliged to suffer the disappointment of finding votes against him.
On 24 February 1709, after always having been confirmed until that
day, Antonio did not obtain the required majority and had to leave
the congregation until 26 November 1711, the date on which he was
again appointed violin teacher. The same setback happened once
more on 29 March 1716 and forced him to leave, but only for two
months until he was recalled, after a vote, the following 24 May. The
reasons for these dismissals are not known precisely, but they seem
to have been caused by economic difficulties and not from any form
of disapproval. They are surprising, however, especially in the case of
the second one, since we know how much work Vivaldi himself took
on in 1715, during the absence of the 'choir-master' Gasparini, in
order to carry out extra functions and compose the liturgical pieces
that were necessary, and for which he was in fact paid.

Vivaldi's important role in developing the Pietà repertoire can,
however, never be adequately acknowledged. Even if we know very
little about his personality, his teaching or his relationship with his
students, it is quite evident that his presence and his teaching stimulated the development of instrumental concerts in the *ospedale*
church, where the concerts had been mostly devoted to vocal music.
The first reports from outside confirm this very rapid evolution and
show how far Vivaldi must have imposed his style, both through the
quality of performance and through the new effects achieved
through the rearrangement of space. In May 1704 the *Pallade Veneta*
wrote:

> On Sunday, at vespers, the girls of the Pietà performed a sym-
> phony of instruments that were placed at each corner of the
> church, producing such harmony and such novelty of ideas that
> the music became a marvel of ecstasy and gave the impression that
> such a composition came from heaven rather than from
> mankind.[21]

This is an early document demonstrating the 'imprint' of Vivaldi on
a concerto that was probably of his composition, with a surprising

increase in the string section and an arrangement in the church that
strengthened this effect of surprise. There was much praise of this
kind for the unprecedented orchestra at the Pietà without Vivaldi's
name appearing, all the same. Two articles of April–May 1711 ran:

> His Serene Highness granted plenary indulgence in the Pietà
> church where he was greeted by the wonderful symphonies of this
> choir . . . On Sunday, for the third time the virginal singers of the
> Pietà performed an oratorio that is already known [*Maria
> Magdalena* by Gasparini] and the audience was larger than ever,
> left in ecstasy by the spiritual harmony of such a variety of
> instruments.[22]

All the enthusiasm for this repertoire led the administrators in May
1716 to create for Vivaldi a totally new kind of post: that of *maestro
dei concerti*, 'master of concerts' or of 'concertos'. He occupied this
post in 1716, then in 1723, 1727, 1728 and 1729, no longer permanently but in sporadic fashion, his remuneration corresponding
only to the compositions he supplied; he returned to the post finally
in 1735 until his departure for Vienna in 1739, again with a fixed
salary. If we add to this the first (intermittent) period between 1703
and 1716, then it can be seen that Vivaldi dedicated more than
twenty years of his life, totally or partially, to the Ospedale della
Pietà.

It was during that same year, 1716, that Vivaldi was to produce
Juditha triumphans, an oratorio in Latin that remains a symbolic
choral work among those he reserved for his students and certainly
the most impressive of all his religious compositions. The performance of this 'sacred melodrama', with a libretto by Giacomo Cassetti
dates from the month of November. It is a work for women *par
excellence*, composed for the best students at the Pietà who sang the
principal roles of Judith, Holofernes and Lieutenant Bagoas. Lasting
nearly three hours, half way between oratorio and opera, this is an
original work in Vivaldi's religious production through the theatrical
effect it creates, the quantity of arias and the compact nature of its
few choruses which were treated in syllabic fashion in order to rein-
force their warlike effect.

The instrumental arsenal anticipated for this *Sacrum militare ora-*

torium was highly significant in the instrumental development at the Pietà after Vivaldi had been teaching there. With two recorders, two oboes, a soprano pipe, two clarinets, two trumpets with kettledrums, a mandolin, four theorbos, organ obligato, five *viole inglese*, one *viola d'amore* to which must be added the string ensemble and the continuo, the orchestral score is infinitely richer than that of many operas of the period. Only a few girls could achieve the principal roles for the singers, but many of the ospedale musicians took part in this performance. Although it formed a powerful moment for the public who paid for their right of entry, an oratorio like this remains also a magnificent example of the high-level collective event which gave meaning to the years of work by the young boarders. On the vocal level an infallible technique was needed to perform the many and varied arias which sometimes outstrip the most highly dramatic scenes in opera. The crucial moment when Judith takes action may be disappointing through the lack of dramatic expression, but nothing can replace Bagoas' aria of revenge (*Armatae face*) when he discovers the decapitated body of his master Holofernes: it is a minor masterpiece.

Apart from the great beauties revealed in this oratorio, *Juditha triumphans* is also an interesting transposition of a biblical text into the politico-military context of the eighteenth century. As from 1714 Venice had reopened warfare against its eternal enemy, the Ottoman Empire; despite various defeats due to Austria, it still maintained a certain military presence in the Mediterranean, at least until 1748. During the year of this oratorio the Republic even enjoyed, during August, two sound victories, one by Prince Eugene leading the Christian allies and the deliverance of the Venetian fortress of Corfu. In the Apocrypha Judith is to sacrifice herself in order to save the city of Bethulia by agreeing to go with her servant into the camp of her Assyrian enemy Holofernes: during the night, torn between her faith and her desire to liberate her people from tyranny she decides to cut off the head of the hated general with his own sword. The Judeans then counter-attack and put the demoralised army of Holofernes to flight. For Vivaldi two things were clear: Bethulia, besieged, represented the Church, Holofernes was the Turk, Judith incarnated Venice and her servant the Christian faith. Hence the magnificence and the ardour, but also the tenderness and emotion expressed in the vocal and instrumental parts of the oratorio, truly a hymn to the glory of Venice and encouraging the Venetians, who were constantly at war, to hold their heads high.

Many travellers saw this Pietà 'conservatoire', comparable to those of Naples, as the quintessence of instrumental music in Venice. The governors' objectives were all directed to one end: the tireless per-fecting of the young musicians' technique, particularly through the purchase of new instruments which Vivaldi was responsible for selecting from among the best. 'It will be a duty', ran one order, 'to instruct them as well as possible in the understanding and knowl-edge of these instruments that they play . . .'[23] From 1709, shortly after Vivaldi's early work, but two years before his first concertos were published, it was to the Pietà that King Frederick of Denmark was taken to hear an oratorio. During the years to come there was no lack of visits by celebrities, who attended private concerts: Cardinal Ottoboni in 1726, the Contessa Grimaldi from Genoa the following year, the Elector Prince of Saxony in 1740. The visit of the Président de Brosses also dates from this period:

> The hospital where I go most often and enjoy myself the most is the hospital of the Pietà; it leads in the perfection of symphonic music. What rigour of performance! It is only there that you can hear that first stroke of the bow, so much praised at the Paris Opera. They have a kind of music here that we do not know at all in France, and it seems to me more suitable than any other for *le jardin de Bourbonne*. These are large-scale concertos in which there is no first violin.[24]

So it was essentially for the students at the Pietà, but also for private commissions and various publications that Vivaldi was to compose his 500 concertos and sinfonias for strings and continuo, to which ninety sonatas should be added. This colossal body of work, excep-tional in its unity, was to represent a commercial value that was not negligible for him, while ensuring him a posthumous fame which does not decline. Was it the over-regular form of these concertos (usually in three movements, lasting more or less the same length of time, almost always quick-slow-quick contrasting with each other) that led Stravinsky to regret intensely that Vivaldi was 'a tedious man, capable of composing the same concerto six hundred times over.'[25] According to the composer of *The Rite of Spring* for whom every new work had to be unique, exceptional, a perfect renewal of art, the regularity of Vivaldi's concertos represents monotony and a lack of ideas. This shows inadequate knowledge of the baroque period during which music formed part of a daily ritual, on the stage, in church, and needed an impressive quantity of compositions without anyone feeling the need to change their form each time and without taking the risk of displeasing the public. This led sometimes to an amazing output by many composers of the baroque era: Alessandro Scarlatti's 125 operas, Johann Sebastian Bach's 300 cantatas or Vivaldi's 500 concertos!

The contribution by the Red Priest to instrumental music was, however, considerable. After two or three decades dedicated to the *concerto grosso*, in which a mixed group of instruments are opposed to the *tutti*, he imposed and ennobled the concerto for a single soloist, or possibly two, well contrasted. The violin, the Red Priest's personal instrument, is logically the most frequent of those for which he composed: 253 of the 500 concertos are consecrated to it, and introduce a 'colour' and virtuosity which were entirely fresh and sometimes reminiscent of the great operatic arias of the time. But the concertos are also fascinating through the variety of the other solo instruments which add a special atmosphere and renew the listener's pleasure on each occasion: 'cello, *viola d'amore*, mandolin, flute, bassoon, horn, trumpet ... Vivaldi composed for the classes he gave and for the best students available to him at the time: it was for them, probably, that he wrote thirty-nine concertos for bassoon, when that instrument was fairly unusual in Venice during the early part of the century. But he also had to take into account the other instrument teachers who worked with him: hence the oboe concertos, written for the first teachers recruited (the oboe players Erdman in 1707 and Siber in 1713) or the concertos for 'cello composed after 1720 for the newly recruited teachers Vandini and Aliprandi.

In most of the concertos the form in three movements (allegro–adagio–allegro), inspired by the so-called 'Italian style' overture already used by Torelli, was from then on firmly adopted by Vivaldi and was to remain a model virtually unchanged until the twentieth century. The Venetian's originality therefore resides not in the somewhat systematic arrangement but in what he did with it. The allegro sections which begin and end the concerto break out into jubilation and melodic invention unsurpassed in the eighteenth century: the instrumental combinations are infinitely varied and express an imagination dreamy or capricious in turn. These allegro movements also show how far the Red Priest knew how to take advantage of the technical perfection achieved by the lute-makers of his period. As for the slow middle movement, which is somewhat reminiscent of the arioso style in opera, it attains poetical heights, as much through the sweetness and melancholy that emanate from the solo 'song' as through the suspensive and mysterious nature of the pizzicati or the long-held chords that accompany it. In this is the true genius of the composer who knew how to transcribe into his instrumental music the transparency and sparkles of light along the canals in spring as well as the thick fog that envelops the city in winter like cottonwool.

Even if Vivaldi did not need titles or detailed descriptions to introduce images into his music, his 'programme' concertos, although there are not many of them, were perhaps the first to reach posterity. What could be more seductive in fact than the orchestral breaking waves in La *Tempesta di mare* (The Storm at Sea), the haunted dreams of *La Notte* (Night), or the cheerful singing in *Il Cardellino* (The Goldfinch), all three for solo flute? Several other 'programme' concertos still hold our attention, although they cannot reach the total perfection of *The Four Seasons*, the work most universally attached to the name of Vivaldi. It is indeed programme music *par excellence*; the composer not only takes us with him, like a true landscape painter, to hear murmuring streams, to see village dances or feel flakes of snow, but he succeeds in creating a thematic link between the three movements of a single concerto: in this way, in 'Summer' we suffer during the first two the unbearable heaviness of a heat wave, and in the third movement we are relieved by the sudden violent onset of helpful rain. For a long time *The Four Seasons* were performed in the Mozartian manner with over-classical elegance but thanks to recent recordings they have at last revealed the breathtaking contrasts, the turbulent rhythms, the sharpness and power of the descriptive effects of which Vivaldi was capable. It is no surprise that later composers, Haydn, Beethoven and Berlioz followed in his footsteps.

Thanks to the publication in his lifetime of nearly a hundred concertos, that is a few less than one out of five, the Red Priest quickly became a European figure. The word 'concerto' which occurs in de Brosses's writing, had already entered the French vocabulary and began to occupy an important place in the Concert Spirituel* given at the Tuileries, the first example of concerts open to the public in France from 1725 onwards.

Vivaldi was very soon a celebrity in Paris, and 'Spring', performed there for the first time in 1728 along with the three other 'Seasons', won the votes of the French public. Auber, Leclair and other Parisian violinists were already beginning to imitate its exuberance and infectious joie de vivre in their first French concertos, while Louis XV demanded that 'Spring' from 'The Four Seasons' should be played to him at Versailles. In London *The Post Man* of 16 October 1711 announced the sale of the twelve concertos of *L'Estro Armonico* as an event. In Germany, when Johann Sebastian Bach was staying in Weimar, he discovered the totally southern energy of Vivaldi's work and was already beginning to transcribe it for the organ or the harpsichord. As for the flautist Quantz, when he was a young man and discovered the many innovations of the Vivaldi concertos, he suffered a shock.

> At that moment I saw for the first time at Pirna [near Dresden] Vivaldi's violin concertos. The pieces made a great impression on me for at that time they were completely new. I did not fail to acquire a stock of copies. Vivaldi's splendid *ritornelli* served me later as models.[26]

Vivaldi, becoming aware of the growing demand for his works and the high reputation they acquired in various countries through foreign visitors, quickly had recourse to the modern publishers in Amsterdam. He knew that the two big Italian publishers, Sala and Bortoli, were very out-of-date on the technical level and could not

---

*See the chapter on the Concert Spirituel in *La Maison des Italiens, les castrats à Versailles*, Patrick Barbier, Grasset, 1998.

meet the competition from northern Europe. Like many other composers therefore he began to send scores directly to Amsterdam, going over the heads of the local publishers. This was notably the case of the cycle *Il Cimento dell'Armonia e dell'Invenzione*, which included *The Four Seasons*, published in the Dutch city in 1725. This procedure was to facilitate the distribution of the concertos and make them into that European model as previously mentioned.

Just as La Serenissima was to disappear in the midst of celebrations, remaining unaware of its fate until the very end, the four *ospedali* were to experience a fabulous musical conclusion against a background of financial disaster. The greatest masters of the classical period were to contribute to the success of the concerts and ceremonies: Galuppi at the Mendicanti then at the Incurabili, Sarti at the Pietà, Traetta, Sacchini and Cimarosa at the Ospedaletto . . .

During this time the four institutions were financially without resources. Major collapse overwhelmed the Incurabili in 1777 and took the others with it in its wake. Since the income from shares had fallen sharply creditors became alarmed and demanded checks at every level which would only reveal the insolvency of the *ospedali*. Severe cuts, dismissals and drastic measures were hardly able to save the institutions even if the latter were able to survive thanks to the musical dynamism which characterised them: they were kept going even to the very end by composers such as Traetta, which meant that the *ospedali* could even, somehow or other, continue until the 1780s, even until the collapse of the Republic, which was the case of the Ospedaletto and the Mendicanti. The administrators took things in hand and 'saved the furniture'. Like La Serenissima the secular congregations faded away without a ducat to their name, but with heads high, with panache.

1. The Ospedaletto church, showing the grilles behind which the girls sang

2. Girls' Concert (given at the Philharmonic Society, 1782),
painting by Gabriele Bella (courtesy, Museo Civico Correr, Venice)

3. The Mendicanti, Venice, as it is today (photo, Patrick Barbier)

4. The Nuns' Parlour, painting by Francesco Guardi, based on the nuns' parlour at the convent of San Zaccaria (courtesy, Ca' Rezzonico, Venice)

5. Interior of the Teatro San Benedetto, engraving by Antonio Baratti
(courtesy, Museo Civico Correr, Venice)

6. The Ridotto, or Gambling Room, painting by Francesco Guardi
(courtesy, Ca' Rezzonico, Venice)

7. Carnival Scene, painting by Domenico Tiepolo (courtesy, Musée du Louvre, Paris)

8. Masked Conversation, painting by Pietro Longhi (courtesy Ca' Rezzonico, Venice)

CHAPTER 4

Sacred music and religious festivals

We are Venetians first, Christians next.
Seventeenth-century saying

For the girls in the *ospedali* life closely resembled that of enclosed
nuns: few outings, if any, no visits from outside, services and concerts performed behind grilles and daily existence based on intensive
religious practice. But there the resemblance ends, since the institutions were run by lay administrators and, after all, the girls
had the choice of marrying, taking the veil or remaining in their
orphanage.

The *ospedali* were just one small aspect of Venetian piety, half-
way between a spiritual life similar to that of a convent and a
form of commercialisation of music through their public
concerts with paid admission. At the same time Venice had highly
intense religious concerns in which music held pride of place. That
life was omnipresent through seventy-two parish churches, twenty-
two convents for regular priests (monks), thirty-one convents for
enclosed nuns and twenty oratories, which was no small number in
a city of medium size after all and out of a population of about
40,000 inhabitants at the end of the seventeenth century and the
beginning of the eighteenth. In Venice one in every twenty adults
was a priest or nun. There lay the other original feature of this oligarchic Republic, apparently far removed from the monarchies by
divine right, and yet established in people's minds, over several centuries, through a kind of miracle, a mysterious alliance between God
and the city.

The religious organisation of the city

Due to its prestigious eastern and western past, Venice had been elevated to a patriarchy from 8 October 1457, rising in this way to the
level of the metropolises on which Christianity was founded. The
bishop of Venice received at the time the title of patriarch which had
been borne by the bishop of Aquileia, later installed at Grado. If
Venice inherited this at the time, it was obviously thanks to the role
it played in the eastern Mediterranean and the symbol it incarnated
in the Christian world, four years after the fall of Constantinople.*

Until the end of the Republic, therefore, Venice could count on
the double presence of a patriarch observing the Roman rite, and of
a *primicerio*, a kind of leader for the chapter of canons at St Mark's,
who was always chosen from among the leading patrician families of
the city; his role as 'chaplain to the doge' also conferred on him a
sizeable amount of political power. While the patriarch officiated at
San Pietro di Castello, the *primicerio* resided at St Mark's and was
responsible for celebrating the local Venetian rite, which is still called
the 'marcian' rite. As far as protocol was concerned, the *primicerio*
ranked above the bishops of the region, in Chioggia and Torcello for
instance, and was responsible for the lay clergy of the city, that is
nine congregations with an archpriest and seventy-two parishes,
each with a curate and a chapter of twelve priests. Six of them
enjoyed a prebend – that is, a sort of salary – but the other six would
only receive it after the death of the other six: so they had no remuneration beyond the offertory at Mass and the fees produced by bap-
tisms and burials.

Contrary to what one might expect, the basilica of St Mark in the
eighteenth century was under the jurisdiction of the doge and did
not become the cathedral of Venice until 1807; that function was
fulfilled by San Pietro di Castello, the church situated on the island
of the same name, to the extreme east of Venice, beyond the Public
Gardens of today. It was there, beside the cathedral, that the patriarch's residence stood, and this was the scene of his ceremonial
arrival, shortly after his nomination: he would arrive with great

*In the early twenty-first century there remain eleven Catholic patriarchies: one, for Latin
countries, is the patriarchy of the West, situated in Rome (which is confused with the Holy
See), six are oriental and four remain purely honorary: Latin Jerusalem, Goa (East Indies),
Lisbon (West Indies) and Venice.

pomp, escorted by a cortège of gondolas, dressed overall, to celebrate Mass at San Pietro; after the ceremony the Signoria and the doge, walking under a golden parasol, accompanied him to the door of his palace before parting from him. This ceremony was symbolic in two ways: through the lavish ritual accorded to a personage apparently as important as the patriarch, but also because he was greeted and accompanied to his residence by the doge, the only true master of the place and the incarnation of the State: it was the outward sign of a Venetian Church perpetually in the pay of power, always carefully 'protected' by the doge and the superior figures of the Republic. Such an unusual situation did not fail to strike visiting clerics. 'The Church in Venice is like the State,' observed the Bishop of Salisbury,

> for the man who is its leader has a great title, receives many honours and is called the Patriarch in the same way as the Duke [doge] is treated as Prince and 'Serenity' and the coinage carries his name: but all that is no more than a set of honours for both of them, as I have just said, without authority. As for the Patriarch, not only is the Church of St Mark's not within his jurisdiction and is directly dependent on the Duke: but his authority in everything is so closely subject to that of the Senate that you might say he only has what the Senate passes on to him; the result being that the Senate is truly the supreme head of the State, without any distinction of things and people.[1]

In addition to the regular clergy, those who followed the monastic rule, there was the very large group of monks and enclosed nuns, highly respected by the Venetians, if not venerated. These religious people occupied an infinite number of convents situated in the city itself and on the islands in the lagoon. For this reason the figures might vary, depending on whether account is taken of the city alone or of the entire area under the authority of the doge: for men there were twenty-two convents in the city but a total of forty or so over the whole lagoon area, with a population of about 1,500 monks in the eighteenth century; as for the nuns, there were about 1,600 divided between thirty-five convents.

The orders represented were very numerous at this period and it would be tedious to establish a complete list of them. It should be noted that certain more intellectual orders, such as the Benedictines or the Dominicans, usually lived in luxurious monasteries and, as will be seen later, lived like princes without in any way failing in their total respect for the offices, chanting of psalms, prayers and other contemplations imposed by the rule. At the summit of the hierarchy were the Benedictines, the richest of all the orders, who benefited in Venice from an exceptional place: the convent of San Giorgio, on the island of the same name, which also enjoyed huge buildings, a superb garden and an ideally isolated situation, a few minutes by gondola from the esplanade of Saint Mark's opposite. No less imposing was the Dominican convent where the church of San Zanipolo (San Giovanni e San Paolo), steeped in an atmosphere of austerity through its totally plain Gothic vaulting, still earns the admiration of visitors today for its vast nave, the largest after the one in the Frari. Then came the secondary orders, known as '*Berretti*' which represented all the tendencies of Venetian monastic life, from the most liberal, such as the Somaschi, who said Mass and chanted psalms when they felt like it, slept in their convent sometimes and cheerfully frequented 'society', to the most rigid who, like the Philippines, passed their lives in the confessional, restored ageing courtesans to an honest way of life and practised a religion fairly close to that of the French Jansenists.

As in several other countries nuns were more numerous than men in the Venetian convents because it was the rule in well-off families to arrange for one son only to marry. As a result there was no patrician family which, at some moment in their history, did not force a young girl to enter a convent. In the context of the eighteenth century, when people lived in a monastery as in a drawing-room, it was preferable to settle a girl comfortably in a convent rather than fear the pain of divided inheritances. As will be repeated later, the cloister no longer had much in common with the austerity and the more than Spartan lifestyle of the preceding centuries: there was little difference between a nun's parlour and the anteroom of a palace.

Ordinary people in the great Venetian ceremonies

The Venetians in general are ignorant in religious matters, to a scandalous extent, that is to say that the mysteries of religion

hardly touch them; this means that they do not take much trouble to study them: therefore all the pomp of their ceremonies and
all the riches of their churches can only be attributed to their magnificence or rivalry between families. However, superstition reigns
among the people as it does all over Italy; quite a few of them as
well have a hint of atheism, but of the coarsest and most stupid
variety. Young gentlemen in Venice are usually so corrupt in their
morals and live in such ignorance of everything that it's difficult
to conceive how vice-ridden and ignorant they are.[2]

This laconic but very realistic account in 1690 by the Bishop of
Salisbury, Gilbert Burnet, recalls some basic facts about the
Venetians and about the inhabitants of many other regions of Italy
in general: there is a mixture of highly exteriorised faith, very close
to superstition, along with an exaggerated taste for the pomp of ceremonies against a background of a somewhat dissolute lifestyle.

Grosley was amused one day by a scene which took place very
close to him: during a service in Venice an Englishman did not kneel
down during the Elevation, although everyone else had already done
so. A senator, who was most displeased, told him to kneel; the
Englishman replied proudly: 'I do not believe in transubstantiation'.
'Neither do I,' replied the senator, 'but you will either kneel down or
leave the church.'[3] Many foreigners noticed this strange superimpo-
sition on very regular and orthodox religious practice, of rules, rituals, gestures and attitudes which bordered on superstition – avoid
black cats or two nuns walking together, touch your sex to ward off
danger, wear amulets more or less all over the body. In the eighteenth
century, Venice, like Naples, did not escape this ritual of which many
aspects dated from the older pagan cults. This led to the permanent
confusion between a very free life, relaxed morals along with a super-
ficial faith on one side and on the other a total, or almost total con-
stancy in their assiduous attachment to the great ritual Christian
celebrations, which guaranteed the stability and spiritual power of
the Republic. There was an official State Church, where every religious event existed to remind people of the unity between the tem-
poral and the spiritual, the divine inspiration of the laws and
institutions, the protection received from on high by the privileged
population 'descending from the Hebrews'.

Travellers' tales, like the articles in the Venetian newspapers of the time, never stopped describing the considerable crowds which flocked into St Mark's and the large churches in the city, so much so that they made Venice look like the beacon of religious practice in Europe. Music certainly remained the essential element in these ceremonies: the smallest parish church would set aside large sums of money in order to provide for the duration of a patronal festival a maestro worthy of it, as well as violinists and a high quality organist.[4] But what Venice offered, outstripping all other cities, was the unrivalled beauty of the processions along the water, fleets of gondolas with passengers clad in richly coloured clothes, backing up the least important religious festival, as Président de Brosses described:

> I have also seen what they call a 'function', that is to say a cere-
> mony in which all the leading magistrates go in a body to a
> church festival . . . the ambassadors' procession being the princi-
> pal attraction. They go there alongside the doge, with their
> household; but the best thing, in my opinion is the progress. A
> procession in gondolas is for me a divine moment, all the more so
> because on this occasion they are not ordinary gondolas, but those
> owned by the Republic, superbly carved and gilded, accompanied
> by those of the ambassadors, even more luxurious and attractive,
> especially ours. They are the only ones in the State which are
> allowed to be other than black. The State gondoliers all wear red
> velvet capes with gold embroidery, and large Albanian-style caps.
> They are too proud of their uniforms to concern themselves with
> rowing, so they have themselves towed along by small boats full
> of musical instruments.[5]

As for the number of religious festivals, La Serenissima knew hardly any rivals. There was no parish, convent or oratory, in addition to the basilica and the cathedral, that did not organise lavish celebra-tions, which led to rejoicings over the whole area for several days before ending with impressive processions and, equally lavish fire-work displays. For those fortunate enough today to go to Malta between June and September, that is the only place which can still give us a glimpse of what this life in the Venetian parishes was like, just as effervescent and festive, with the churches decorated and illuminated throughout, inside as well as outside, with treasures displayed to the admiring faithful:

> On Saturday 6 [September 1687], the day when the glorious body of San Zaccaria, the prophet, is transferred, you can see in the rich and beautiful church belonging to those illustrious and most reverend nuns, decorations so nobly magnificent that I doubt if anything more splendid could be achieved. Bright red damask was wrapped round those tall columns, while smooth velvet ornamented the base and the capitals; a similar décor extended to the space higher up: it was so well arranged and so carefully integrated with the smallest architectural details of this vast and noble temple of stone that one could not tell if it had been achieved by the needle or the brush.[6]

All the magic spells of baroque pomp can already be found in this description: luxurious materials, the triumph of illusion. The Counter-Reformation tried to make the church into a perpetual feast for the eyes; its duty was to attract the crowds through a magnificence which brought them into direct contact with the wonders of the world beyond: the columns danced, the reredos sang, the saints trembled, the cherubs capered, through trompe-l'oeil effects the ceilings opened on to celestial immensities. The faithful churchgoer was overcome with dizziness, his eyes and ears opened to sensual delights: it only remained for him to desire with impatience eternal life . . . while awaiting the next feast day, surely more lavish than the previous one.

Everything therefore was a pretext for large crowds to gather: the major festivals in the liturgical calendar and the usual saints' days, certainly, but also secular events in the Republican calendar, heroic anniversaries commemorating great victories, receptions for foreign monarchs, *Te Deums* in honour of a new doge or a patriarch. It is worth reading again the description of the procession on 7 June 1716, celebrating the recent victory of the Christian allies against the Turks:

> After the midday meal there was a solemn procession round the Piazza [St Mark's] . . . The six leading Scuole were obliged to

come, carrying twenty torches, each one strengthened with fabric. First came forty torch-bearers and two congregations chanting the litanies and following them the miraculous image of the Virgin. Then came forty more torch-bearers with two congregations, then the relic of the Madonna's veil carried by Monsignore the bishop of Chioggia. Next forty more torch-bearers with the relic of the Madonna's hair, carried by Monsignore Sansogi, bishop of Caorle. Then forty torch-bearers again with the three congregations and the relic of the Madonna's milk carried by the Monsignore the patriarch Barbarigo, accompanied by the canons of St Mark's and Castello. There followed the commander, secretaries, and His Serene Highness [the doge] D. Giovanni Cornaro with Monsignore Aldobrandini, the apostolic nuncio to the Senate and all the nobility. Once the Holy Relics and the Senate were back in the church it began to rain.[7]

Despite their pious intentions, these 'republican' festivals were pretexts for overwhelming pleasures in the palaces, especially the ambassadors who supported the ruling party: fountains of wine flowed for the Venetian people while bread and money were scattered to them. In the evening serenades brought a special atmosphere to the palaces, where hundreds of masked revellers devoured the food and drink set out on the buffets.

As for *Te Deums* or funerals: there were the same solemn observances and, it could be said, the same rejoicing. The funeral pomp of the baroque period was no meaningless phrase and in Paris and Madrid, as in Venice, nothing was spared in order to make a funeral ceremony the most lavish of spectacles. At a period when the art of the theatre prevailed in the palaces, the parks, the convents and the street celebrations (in addition to the operas) the church was forced to rise to the occasion and contribute to removing the tragedy from death through its lavish presentation. The paintings or prints of the seventeenth and eighteenth centuries are eloquent: roofs and walls draped with black and grey, the bier atop a pyramid surrounded with angels, skeletons and thousands of candles, draperies arranged like a dais high up in the church, a motley crowd all round, sometimes even seated as at the theatre, chatting as though in their drawing-room, accompanying the deceased.

The burial of a doge was an event of special brilliance and always took place at San Zanipolo, the second 'official' church of the city after St Mark's. For the Venetians of the baroque age the tomb had to be as sublime as the throne: tears and candles proved that the Republic knew how to remain seigneurial in its sorrow as in its principles. When the doge's death was announced, church bells rang the death knell nine times. The doge's knight, dressed in deep mourning, went to inform the Collegio. In accordance with an unchangeable ritual he announced: 'Most Serene Signoria, the doge is dead!', to which the vice-doge replied in the same invariable way: 'If he is dead, we shall create a new one!' The ceremonies would last three days and only the Signoria would wear mourning. On the third day the doge's corpse left the palace to be carried in procession: thirty gentlemen clad in red preceded the body and thirty more followed it. After being taken round the piazza of St Mark's it was lifted up nine times in front of the basilica and then carried through the streets for three hours. When it finally reached San Zanipolo it was placed in the top of a large octagonal mausoleum 80 feet high and 165 wide at the base. Corinthian-style architecture supported the edifice which was obscured behind thousands of torches and candles. Venetians could climb up it by taking a series of eleven steps to a first level, then by following another series of five steps which led into the mausoleum. Inside was a true funeral chamber hung with black and silver, surmounted by a cupola where everyone could go to pray. In this way a continuous coming and going by the noisy crowd invaded the church for hours.[8]

Perhaps this was the most astonishing, even seductive aspect of these people who were both mystical and resourceful, turning the church into the anteroom of an apartment. And then, what a difference between Misson's account, written about 1690, and the later descriptions of the mid-eighteenth century.

> Their churches are divided into four parts [wrote Misson]. The altars are in the place they call holy, at one end of the church: normally only the officiating priest and his servers go there. The second place is reserved for the other parts of the service. The men of the congregation are in the third part which is separated from the second only by a balustrade. And the women are behind a

trellis, at the other end of the church, or in the galleries. The entire service is conducted in vulgar Greek, which is their own language and the people understand it: they condemn loudly the unknown language used by the church. They stand up when they are worshipping and bow their heads only, while placing their hands on their chests. Those who are married can acquire ecclesiastical posts without leaving their wives, but if they have been received into the church before being married, they are not allowed to marry afterwards . . .[9]

This was a more or less fair description which reveals a population quietly disciplined in religious observance and occupying different parts of the church in orderly fashion. Did Misson not notice any excessive behaviour or was his period still favourable to a more austere form of piety?

Nothing resembles this monologue less than the many eighteenth-century accounts which were full of juicy details about Venetian behaviour in church. It was a cool place during heat waves, people felt comfortable, they greeted each other and played with their fans. Lovers met there, so did the adventurers in galanterie, intriguers and idle people, all of which led the Abbé Caccia to say: 'While a priest is celebrating Mass they play with a dog, they act like fools, read some Gothic inscriptions beneath the statue of a famous warrior, make agreements, busy themselves with flirtations, make a noise, wink at each other . . .'[10] In the second half of the century the moral decadence became more and more obvious and in certain cases the church was to become a place of near-debauchery, causing a growing number of denunciations:

I humbly inform you [wrote a secret agent in 1711], that for a long time recently the church of San Salvatore has become the object of profanation, on feast days, by a great number of women of all types, who, instead of going there to hear Holy Mass, come to be admired and courted. I have heard many devout people say that the church of San Salvatore has become a brothel. The one cause of this is none other than the late hour at which Mass is celebrated there.[11]

A strange conclusion to a phenomenon which, from one parish to another, seemed to affect Venice during its twilight. Carnal and spiritual: two constants incessantly recalled in a famous Venetian saying:

La mattina una messetta	In the morning a little mass
L'apodisnar una bassetta	In the afternoon a little game of bassette
E la sera une donnetta.	And in the evening a little woman.

Music at St Mark's and its performers

So all parishes experienced an intense musical life during the great ritual festivities in the calendar. None of them, however, exceeded in grandeur and prestige the mother church of St Mark's. Regarded as the Palace chapel and placed directly under the jurisdiction of the doge, it allowed the nobles to acquire the highest responsibilities, those of procurators. Their leader, named the *primicerio*, took the oath before the doge that he would preserve the dignity of this church, he wore the mitre and the other episcopal accoutrements. The three oldest procurators also swore on oath that they would watch over the treasure of the basilica. They were people of a totally exceptional culture in both private and public life, exercised power and upheld the special nature of the city. Venice, constantly proud of its past and its originality, did everything possible to stand apart from Rome; it intended to preserve its traditions and a ducal ceremonial which was quite distinct from the progress to uniformity undertaken by the Catholic Counter-Reformation throughout Italy. St Mark's, as the symbol of the hegemony of the Republic over the Church, was therefore under the perpetual control of the Senate: any preacher who tried to upset this fragile equilibrium between civil society and religious society had better be on his guard! Thus in 1727 the Abbé Conti was present for a few days at the rise and fall of an over-bold cleric:

> The Jesuit who used to preach at San Lorenzo, and was followed with such a crowd that people climbed the altar columns to listen to him has just been dismissed; on the Virgin's day he preached at St Mark's in the presence of the doge and the Senate and a vast number of people. He took it into his head to teach the govern-

ment a political lesson, to correct the old Plan and suggest a new one. People complained, the State inquisitors had the Jesuit removed from Venice and were applauded by everyone. The Jesuits are highly mortified, they condemned their brother but there is no doubt that in a short time they will attempt to justify him by having the sermon printed, with corrections it must be said; the talk here is of nothing else; the Jesuits have their protectors, and especially the French people, whose confessions they hear.[12]

On the musical level, the most responsible post at St Mark's was that of master of the chapel; when it was vacant the procurator appointed a new composer and awarded him an excellent salary, more or less unchanged during the seventeenth and eighteenth centuries of 300 to 400 ducats a year. In general the procurators preferred to find recruits among the top-level musicians known in Venice rather than open the post to artists in the whole of Italy, even if they were famous. After the departure or death of a maestro it was logical that a 'vice maestro' took his place. Cavalli and Legrenzi 'reigned' at St Mark's at the end of the seventeenth century (respectively from 1668 to 1676 and from 1685 to 1690). The early eighteenth century, until the death of Vivaldi, experienced the direction of the mediocre Biffi (1702–32) and the excellent Lotti (1736–40). The composer of *The Four Seasons* would therefore never occupy this much coveted post. Yet would he have been the ideal (and likely) candidate if Biffi had not monopolised this post for thirty years? Would he have even wanted it? These questions will remain forever mere conjectures.

However, the prestige of being able to work and sing at St Mark's was extremely high, as much for the *maestri* as for the singers and musicians. To describe someone as 'a singer at St Mark's' corresponded to the most splendid visiting card, even if the real level of the performance depended very much on the master of the chapel and the choir-master at the time. These performers were carefully selected, and they were hardly ever granted permission to leave and go to the operatic theatres: they would be away too long and there were risks that they would not return because of the great temptations for earning more money.

In 1686 the number of singers at St Mark's was fixed at thirty-six, nine for each of the four parts, but as from the following year consideration was given to unequal divisions between the voices, although the same total number was preserved (6–7–13–10 or 12–6–10–8). In this way the records for 1708 mention thirteen sopranos, including four priests, four contraltos including two priests, eleven tenors including five priests and eight basses including one priest and one friar. The total therefore was still thirty-six, divided between twenty-three lay singers and twelve ecclesiastics. During the baroque period the soprano parts were all taken by castrati, while a few falsetto voices could join the castrati who sang contralto: several great names among the eighteenth-century male sopranos appeared at one point or another in the registers of St Mark's in addition to exceptional guests such as Farinelli and Senesino who sang together during Christmas night in 1728. As for the musicians, the same register of 1708 indicates the presence of twenty-three instrumentalists engaged for life and divided as follows: ten violins (including the father of Antonio Vivaldi), three small violas, one *viola da braccio* (a sort of alto), one *violone* (close to a double bass), three theorbos, one cornet, one oboe, two trumpets and one trombone. It goes without saying that cornets, trombones and theorbos were hardly used any more in the eighteenth century, but by tradition they remained in the stock. The documents even show a certain increase in the total number of instruments, rising to as many as thirty-four during the century. By adding together all these musicians and singers, the twenty administrators, the ninety-four members of the clergy, and the ten or so security staff, a total of about 200 people were assuring the smooth conduct of the basilica.

And there was no shortage of hard work! Few posts in the musical world were as exhausting as those in St Mark's, for the prestige of the basilica and the vast number of masses, vespers and solemn feasts celebrated there demanded from the participants a kind of perpetual marathon of prayer. A manuscript of 1677[13] lists 492 obligatory attendances in one year, including 239 masses, 210 vespers, 11 processions, etc. While opera had its seasons (divided into three distinct periods), there was no interval in religious life and it was continually reactivated by the great solemn celebrations in the calendar (see the summary table of these festivals at the end of Chapter 2), especially those which took place in the presence of the doge or when the Pala d'Oro, the famous reredos, incrusted with precious stones, the real glory of the basilica, was placed on show.

During the day-to-day services which required few performers, the singers took their places on the *bigonzo*, the octagonal platform supported by seven marble columns, which can still be admired today, on the right looking towards the choir, opposite the pulpit. During the baroque period it was also known as 'the singers' pergola'. It was from there that the day-to-day Masses, motets, psalms and vespers were sung. A pen and ink drawing by Canaletto shows us a dozen singers, somewhat crowded together in this slightly elevated and restricted area. Although they were very close to the congregation they had their backs towards them and sang from a large score attached to a board that stood against the wall. During solemn ceremonies when the choristers performed in the *bigonzo*, all the additional singers were placed on the large platforms situated high up, to the right and left of the iconostasis, where two organs faced each other, and also in the corner balconies, one facing the side above the iconostasis and one facing the nave and the congregation. In this way choir members and soloists were divided between four separate spaces, two on each side, well above floor level. Below them smaller boxes and balconies facing each other provided space for a few soloists and instrumentalists.

It should be remembered that all these spaces remain unchanged today and that it is extremely easy, when visiting St Mark's, to understand the musical organisation which was carried out before the great ceremonies of La Serenissima. Nothing has changed, and when attending a Sunday service you can hear the current Cappella Marciana singing near the organ from one of the famous raised platforms situated on the side of the choir. You can understand then what the legendary spacing out of voices and instruments was like; it was introduced at the end of the sixteenth century by the Gabriele family, then taken to heights of fairytale splendour during the whole of the baroque era. From left and right, from in front and from behind the disembodied, almost supernatural voices of the singers reached the ears of the faithful, and through their distant and lofty origin added a mysterious dimension which often moved Venetians and passing visitors alike. In this way Lotti's *Credo* for eight voices and instruments mentions two choirs of four voices, five parts for strings and organ. The congregation can really find itself in the presence of a great *concertato* destined to bring out the value alternately of the soloists, the small choir or the large one, while singling out when necessary some of the instrumental parts. The whole performance was orchestrated by the chapel master who stood on one of the two platforms or in one corner niche visible to everyone. A grouping just as complex can be seen in an anonymous painting of 1690. It shows eight singers on the platform, four musicians on the balcony situated beneath the corner niche with three more singers and a stringed instrument on the small balcony below. Since we can see one side only, it is easy to imagine the same number of performers on the opposite side, according to the laws of stereophony (or quadrophony) beloved by the period. The isolated singers in the lower box were surely soloists, while the choir, split in two, was on the two higher platforms. In any case, and it is enough to attend a service today to realise this, the music was intended to mean much more to the members of the Signoria (doge, procurators, senators, members of the council . . .) seated in the choir, behind the iconostasis, than to the ordinary people who were kneeling or standing (but never sitting) in the nave, separated from the Holy of Holies and its music. This led to complaints from some foreigners during the seventeenth and eighteenth centuries about the poor acoustics in St Mark's and the unfortunate impression that you had to strain your ears to appreciate the celestial harmonies of Monteverdi, Cavalli or Lotti. In 1714 the Comte de Caylus became a valuable chronicler of the pomp and the practices reserved for the nobility, precisely in that privileged place, the choir of St Mark's:

The day before Christmas, by permission of Pope Alexander III, Mass was said at two o'clock in the morning, which corresponds to six o'clock in France. The churches in Venice possess this privilege, the church of La Pietà, the church of the Frari or the Franciscans, and that of St Mark. I went to this last, which is the doge's chapel; he attends with ceremony, followed by a certain number of nobles wearing habits of fiery red and with a kind of sleeve over the left shoulder in velvet of the same colour, striped. This garment is trimmed with red fur and is somewhat showy. The doge was wearing velvet of the same colour, quite plain,

trimmed with gold braid. He was seated in a special chair but in
the same row as those where the priests usually sit. On his right
are the ambassadors of foreign powers seated according to their
rank. That day only the papal nuncio was present: he was the only
envoy who was in the Republic at that time. In this place the
nobles sit on wide benches, on the right and left. The Mass was
celebrated by the leading canon of the church, named the *primicerio*. This post is always occupied by a noble. At that time it was
a young man of twenty-three, a member of the Cornaro family.
The doge also had the same name. The post of *primicerio* is fairly
pleasant for as a rule those who occupy it are created cardinals by
the Pope. Apart from that he officiates with crozier and mitre but
in his church and chapter he does not have the authority of a
bishop. In my opinion the Mass which is celebrated has no beauty
other than its unusual time, the illumination of the church and
music with four choirs which this year was very fine.[14]

There remained the procession in front of St Mark's, certainly the
most beautiful demonstration of the Venetian spirit in religious display. Ever since the paintings of Gentile Bellini in the fifteenth century down to those of Canaletto and Bella in the eighteenth, no
painter ever failed to commemorate this innate art of decorum,
splendour and perfect order but also that sense of the sacred raised
to its most noble expression. More than ever Venice reaffirmed in
its grandiose processions the perennial nature of its institutions and
the unity of its people. Participants and spectators were all there, in
that highly symbolic piazza, to commemorate the unique character
of Venice and its divine protection. Whether they took place by day
or night (with hundreds of flares and white wax candles), the processions were intended to demonstrate a consensus round the doge
and the highest dignitaries of the Church and the Republic. The
host was then carried round under a dais, in a monstrance of crys-
tal, gold and silver, gleaming brilliantly during the torchlight procession. Following an order fixed by centuries of tradition, with
each great celebration the doge, the Signoria, the clergy, the consti-
tuant bodies, reinvented a vast sacred ballet which dazzled the population as much as it impressed foreigners. Once the procession had
re-entered the basilica, hundreds of candles, placed all round the

huge nave, lit up one by one, all within the space of barely more than one minute.

Apart from the Feast of St Mark, Holy Week took on an unparalleled solemnity, in sorrow and in joy. On Palm Sunday there was an imposing procession, going from the doge's palace to the basilica. The sisters at Sant'Andrea de Zirada had prepared and arranged luxuriant branches of palm which were blessed and then distributed. Then, after the Mass, the doge and the patricians came out on to the square and were present at a strange release of pigeons. This was not in fact the gracious flight that anyone would willingly imagine. On the contrary, and very much so, the pigeons were weighted down with heavy papers which forced them to fly very low instead of soaring skywards. The least nimble were then caught by the crowd on the square who would later cook them for their Easter repast. However, a few of them managed to fly away and reach the terraces on the basilica, to the applause of some fringe members of the public, ecologists before their time. Gradually the pigeons were to become a Venetian institution: people acquired the habit of building huge pigeon lofts on the roofs and feeding the birds every day until the end of the Republic in 1797. This custom of caring for the pigeons of Saint Mark's, which was abandoned when the last doge fell, was revived seventy years later, thanks to the Contessa Caterina Querini, and has never disappeared since.

On the Wednesday, Thursday and Friday of Holy Week, the doge, the ambassadors, the nobles, the magistrates and the senators went to St Mark's dressed in mourning, and on Good Friday with bare feet. On that occasion, once night had fallen, the processions that took place in every parish reached the acme of seriousness and solemnity. At St Mark's in particular the cortège went along the side of the piazza, along the Procuratie, which were illuminated by large candles, while the crowd kept to the middle. The funeral bier moved forward, surrounded by clergy dressed in mourning robes, and by nobles, still wearing black, carrying lowered candles. All through the city the nobles had covered the façades of their palazzi with torches, candles or flares, thousands of them reflected in the canals and conferring a suggestive atmosphere on this day of mourning.

At last Easter Sunday arrived, the great ceremonial occasion of the year, when the doge went in procession to join the sisters

of San Zaccaria, and was conducted to the altar by the abbess
and all the lay sisters, before hearing Mass said by the patriarch. It
was the day when the doge wore the most sumptuous 'corno', the
special headgear that was higher at the back than at the front, a
symbol of his dignity. The Easter *corno* was entirely of gold, decorated with twenty-four pear-shaped oriental pearls; on the top-
most part there sparkled an eight-faceted diamond, as large as the
ruby beside it, surmounting a cross made up of twenty-three emer-
alds. As usual when the doge moved in procession he walked in front
of the parasol, the folding chair and the sword which were his usual
attributes. For the Venetians the rest of the day was a pretext for all
kinds of rejoicing of a popular nature which lasted until nightfall;
the piazzi would be decorated with carpets, and standards, the
women would dance the forlane, the gondoliers would sing more
than ever along the canals, and everyone would say that it was nearly
time now for the third carnival period of the year, the Ascension
carnival.

Musical and social life in the convents

The licentious lifestyle that took over Venice in the eighteenth century certainly affected the world of convents and monasteries.
Among the thirty-five or so monasteries assumed to exist at the time
very few practised strict observance: lack of discipline, frivolity and
artistic pleasures existed there as elsewhere, restricted only by the
grille and the parlour. It seemed obvious to all observers that the
Republic served as a defence for the priests and those in religion
against possible threats from the Roman Curia: 'It is due to political
principle', stated Monsieur de Silhouette,

> but one that should be condemned, that the Venetians tolerate
> the licentiousness of the clergy and the monks who, according to
> a witty remark by a nuncio, 'truly need to have their cowls short-
> ened'; through this means the Republic escapes any fear of cen-
> sures and excommunications by the Popes, as happen elsewhere,
> for these monks do not worry very much about disobeying the
> Pope and their General, and they counter their threats through
> the good graces and protection of the Republic.[15]

Many young girls, on their side, who had been placed in a convent by their family, in order to avoid the sharing of property, were there without any deep conviction beyond the simple faith practised by these people.

> Nobility [Addison remarked] extends also to all brothers and they generally send the female element in the family to the convent in order to safeguard their property better. As a result the Venetian nuns are known for the liberties they take. They perform operas within their walls and, if it is true, they often leave their institutions to meet their admirers.[16]

Their daily life therefore was organised with a benevolent laxity which, without any neglect for the obligations towards the principal services, allowed a nun to receive a gallant at the grille on a regular basis: more than once it was admitted that the mere fact of being able to pass hands through the grille ruined the reputation of the Venetian nuns. On rare occasions flight could put an end to a vocation imposed by over-authoritarian parents. Without much difficulty the nun concerned could then take advantage of the delightful encounters she had experienced in the parlour to arrange her own abduction with a *cavaliere servente*. One day the desperate flight of a nun with an Englishman provoked a remark by the Abbé Conti: 'These gentlemen are not content with carrying off our coins and our statues, with corrupting our musicians and our painters: they want our nuns too!'[17]

Without going as far as flight, a discreet exit from the convent after dark, with the complicity of some older nun, could lead to strange adventures, and one of the most astonishing of them happened to Casanova in 1752, occupying ten or more chapters in his memoirs. One day a young nun in a Murano convent had a note taken to him and asked to see him. Her mysterious name, M.M., was to cause many hypotheses among those specialising in the handsome Giacomo. When he was introduced to her in the parlour, in the presence of a chaperone, to preserve appearances, the seductive adventurer fell desperately in love with this veiled twenty-two-year-old nymph. There then began an amorous intrigue worthy of the greatest novels and recounted by Casanova with sensuality, mystery and wonderment at every moment: exchanges of notes, furtive meet-ings outside the convent, patient seduction and finally exhausting nights of love in the nun's '*casin*", a small luxuriously furnished apartment where she went some evenings after her day in the clois-ter. Despite the relaxed morals inherent in eighteenth-century Venice the erotic liaison between the nun and the seducer caused a scandal and was to be the cause, among other reasons, of his incar-ceration in the Piombi, the prison in the doge's palace. However, it was to remain for us one of Casanova's most colourful accounts and certainly one of the most piquant examples of the moral liberty which reigned along the lagoons at that time.

The Venetian parlours were the scene of a thousand and one minor daily events among which galanterie, but also music, conver-sation and the pleasures of the table were constantly popular. It must be said that the young nuns knew how to let themselves be seen in the best light: 'In fact,' de Brosses would say:

> if I had to make a long stay here I would look first of all at the nuns. All those I have seen through the grilles, talking and laugh-ing throughout Mass, seemed to me extremely pretty and dressed in a way that truly emphasises their beauty. They wear a delight-ful little cap, a plain habit, almost always white, of course, which bares their shoulders and breast neither more nor less than the Roman-style garments worn by our actresses.[18]

In the sacrosanct Venetian tradition masked people could also enter the convents during the periods of carnival. It is worth taking another look at the genre paintings by Guardi or Longhi and redis-cover that easy-going atmosphere where lace and tricorne hats seem to mince about in front of the pretty young girls who were barely concealed by the grilles. Guardi's famous painting *The Nun's Parlour* takes us to the monastery of San Zaccaria on a visiting day for friends and family. Sitting or standing, masked or not, the visitors converse calmly with the nuns, honourably, it appears, while nearby the children are being entertained by a little puppet show. The one restriction imposed was that at midnight (that is to say sunset), guests must absolutely leave the parlour, but one only has to read the multiple denunciations and reports by secret agents to understand how easily the law was evaded. Only one problem remains from the many recollections known to us. Did the libertinage so often mentioned concern in particular the enclosed nuns – and it can safely be assumed that some of them, secure in their faith, did not take part in these little games – or did it concern rather the '*fie e spese*', those young ladies of good family whose stay in the convent was paid for, as with girl boarders at a school?

As described earlier, the *ospedali* sometimes took in girls of this category who paid, and it is clear that they enjoyed a special type of treatment. It is likely that in the convents they were the first to know that freedom for establishing contacts with the outside world. Confirmation of this is provided by the reports of secret agents which describe the serenades organised at night by several Venetian nobles or foreign ambassadors under the convent windows. Singers and musicians, recruited for the occasion, took their places in a flat-bottomed boat (the '*peota*'), while the organisers of this hopeful amorous party followed in a gondola. A wider craft, such as the '*burchiello*', allowed everyone to be together. The reports show that it was essentially the girls who paid for their stay, not the nuns themselves, who formed the object of so much nocturnal attention. Some of them had already been courted long before they entered the convent, others had recently been noticed in the parlour. Prosecution documents even mention adverse judgements against this 'licentious singing', those 'obscene songs' which rose below the walls of the sacred cloisters, in the Venetian night.

In any case, and more understandably, the convent sisters took part very fully in the social life which surrounded them Occasionally some of them became godmothers at the confirmation of a local child. In return the neighbouring population participated widely in the life of the convent and took to itself the principal moments of its celebrations, such as the patronal feast or the nomination of a new abbess. The most celebrated manifestation of this kind, not reserved for one district only, but famous in the whole of Venice and beyond, was the Solennità of San Lorenzo, celebrated on 10 August every year in the convent of the same name. No convent celebration in the religious calendar surpassed this event in splendour and musical quality. The San Lorenzo nuns came essentially from large aristocratic families, for the convent was the place where the girls were

forced to take the veil in order to prevent the sharing of inheritance
and the reduction of the family estate. These nuns were certainly
intent on astonishing the other monasteries through recruiting the
best musicians of the time, instructed especially not to accept
engagements by other congregations. This near-monopoly of aural
enjoyment and the post-conciliar luxury made the convent church
look like a palace where a concert worthy of the most brilliant courts
was to take place. On the appointed day people crowded round the
convent doors, opened wide for the occasion, and were welcomed by
these high society nuns who conversed with everyone as freely as if
they were in a drawing-room. They were dressed in white and added
a black veil, as thin as possible, which did not prevent a few pretty
locks of hair from escaping; transparent gauze hinted at a delicate
neck and curving breasts: it was more like the 'dress for a nymph'
than the 'dress for a nun', they said in the seventeenth century. The
interior of the church was in keeping: damascene embroidered with
gold letters, festoons, garlands, ribbons, vases of flowers, paintings
and silverware, from floor to roof without counting the hundreds of
torches and candles. The great nave of San Lorenzo was transformed
from a church into a theatre of wonders, worthy, it was thought, of
its illustrious patron saint.

Once the public was in place, the sisters hoped to temper the
effects of the summer dog-days and served cooling drinks in quantity while the vaults of the church resounded with the notes of a concerto or a cantata, performed by the best singers and instrumentalists. In 1758 Grosley heard there as many as 400 performers
placed on a raised stage near the church doors, so that the spectators,
who were seated on chairs, had their backs to the altar. More than
one foreigner would be shocked by such a practice. Between the religious ceremony proper and the concert, the crowd could stay there
five hours at a stretch, during the great August heat. Usually a chapel
master or a master of instruments from one of the *ospedali* or the
doge's chapel was needed to direct what the *Pallade Veneta* called 'a
supreme re-creation of the spirit and the senses'. Legrenzi, chapel
master at St Mark's, spent good days here during the 1680s, then
Biffi, maestro at the Mendicanti for the first thirty years of the eighteenth century, while the famous Hasse conducted the orchestra
when Grosley was there. It should be noted all the same that one of

the richest concertos by Antonio Vivaldi from the orchestral point of view, written precisely for the Solemnità di San Lorenzo (in C major RV556), was no doubt first conceived for Rome (and not for Venice), intended for Cardinal Ottoboni, titular bishop of the church of San Lorenzo in Damaso.

The feast of San Lorenzo therefore had a particular character but it was far from being the exception since music had remained present, and for a very long time, in the various Venetian monasteries, thanks to the permission granted by the doge or the abbess for a musician to be allowed to come and give lessons to various nuns, generally of aristocratic lineage. In this way, sometime about 1645, the great Francesco Cavalli, successor to Monteverdi, was authorised to teach the organ for a year to a nun at San Lorenzo, the daughter of the Cavaliero Grimani. Rovetta, in his turn, gave lessons for four months to a noble Pisani lady at the monastery delle Vergine, situated at Castello. All composers and musicians admitted to an enclosed institution had to wear a cassock and surplice and leave before sunset.

Another musical practice: that of the concerts and ceremonial services which required, as at San Lorenzo, the presence of many musicians and singers. Far from being limited to the service of Mass, cantatas and oratorios, which formed the basis of the sacred repertoire, a good place was allotted to instrumental music, and in particular to concertos for soloists, the true expression of Venetian genius as from the time of Vivaldi. These were the moments awaited by the faithful and the habitués, following the example of the concerts given in the four *ospedali*. The distinction then between the liturgical part of a ceremony and the part assigned to the pleasures of the ear remained very slight. In many cases the congregation attended a low Mass during which the finest pages of the contemporary repertoire were performed: Catholic ceremonies of the baroque period consisted essentially of 'concerts' performed against the sound of prayers whispered by the priest, even if people believed that music should enhance the Word but not replace it. Which led to the pertinent remark by Lorenzo Bianconi: 'In church the Catholic listens without singing; the Calvinist sings without listening; the Protestant sings and listens simultaneously.'[19] Many witnesses have shown us that the music received more attention than the service, and Venice was certainly not alone in this attitude during the eighteenth century in Italy: the French composer Grétry was to notice later, in Rome, how Pope Benedict XIV celebrated Mass in a side chapel in order to attract more attention from the faithful whose eyes seemed drawn to the musicians who were placed in the choir.

Of all the deviations of which Venice was capable, the double practice of balls and operas in the convents established a kind of record. In the eighteenth century balls were usually admitted during the carnival period. The nuns certainly remained behind the enclosure but could enjoy the sight of the most elegant aristocracy of Venice dancing in front of them. Invitations were issued by the sisters themselves and it was considered normal at the time to celebrate the carnival as well as Easter. Casanova was not the last to defend this practice:

> In Venice, at carnival time, nuns in the convents were permitted to enjoy this innocent pleasure. There was dancing in the parlour and the nuns remained behind their wide grilles, watching the fine celebrations. At the end of the day, the festivities are over, everyone leaves, and the nuns retire feeling very pleased at having been present at this pleasure enjoyed by secular people.

In this extreme hunger for music which affected all social spheres in the city, opera too could not fail to fascinate the friars, monks and nuns, as in the case of their fellow citizens. In fact its practice was forbidden and from time to time it earned prosecutions. But the Venetians of the baroque period had realised that any law could easily be avoided. It was not uncommon to see friars or priests playing in the orchestra at an operatic theatre. Some of them even took small roles, which Saint-Didier found when one evening he heard a spectator call out: 'Look, there's Father Pierro playing the vielle!' Half a century later Nemeiz noticed that monks were playing in a theatre which he attended. On the other hand an opera was performed in the parlour of the San Daniele convent for the sixty or so nuns, enclosed or lay members, who resided there, in the presence of a few noble gentlemen who had been specially invited for the occasion. These extravagant experiments flourished more or less everywhere despite the protests of the Catholic hierarchy: monks sang in opera, nuns formed a string ensemble, sessions for 'masked people and monks' with special timetables and reduced prices, were organised at certain theatres in Florence. One day a pitched battle even broke out between enclosed nuns who demanded opera and those who refused to hear it mentioned: several were hurt in the crush and one of them finished at the bottom of a well.

CHAPTER 5

Venetian opera and its public

> The only talk here is about the operas that are to
> be performed.
> *Abbé Conti*

Nothing was more true than this brief remark by the Abbé Conti. Venice had been the city of opera *par excellence* and the Venetians the most avid, the most insatiable opera-goers ever encountered during the seventeenth and eighteenth centuries. Yet opera, as a musical form, was not a pure product of La Serenissima. 'Drama set to music' appeared in Florence during the last years of the sixteenth century and established itself in 1600 with Peri's *Euridice*, given there to celebrate the marriage of Henri IV of France and Marie de' Medici. Several years of research by a group of Florentine intellectuals would burgeon into this total spectacle, dominated by the idea of 'speaking in song', of 'representing in music' the human passions, the *affetti*, with an emotional power stronger in a different way from that of the polyphonic madrigals of the Renaissance.

Strangely, this flash of genius by the Tuscan capital was at the same time to be its swansong. Florence was exhausted by nearly three centuries of flamboyant artistic renewal and would never regain the leading position it had occupied so proudly before then. Not in the artistic field and even less in the world of opera would the city maintain the level to which it could have aspired for a long time to come. It was worn out and would not preserve even what had been acquired in the musical and theatrical genre it had nurtured, something entirely new in the history of music. Florence, the cradle of opera, would remain for this type of entertainment a city like many others, offering no comparison with Venice, Naples, or later, Milan.

As early as 1607, thanks to the genius of Claudio Monteverdi, it was Mantua that took up the torch again by offering the first masterpiece in operatic history, *Orfeo*, an unsurpassed model of that divine alchemy between poetry and music, between the art of performance and the inflections of the voice. With *Orfeo* all was said. With Venice first welcoming Monteverdi to St Mark's in 1612, she would make this new genre her own, and it would become the most significant and fashionable phenomenon of the baroque period.

Venice, opera capital of the seventeenth century

When Vivaldi was born, Venice had held the privilege of reigning as absolute master of drama in music for nearly half a century. Florence had fallen asleep for ever; Mantua, Parma, Ferrara and other cities possessed courts that were too small to offer any rivalry. La Serenissima, on the other hand, possessed many advantages. It was a true city in the spirit of the time; the vitality of its festivals and its people, its innate feeling for entertainment, all this favoured a genre which encouraged the passions and the senses; as for its declining fortunes, it was still able to find helpful support among the big aristocratic families who were ready to invest in this new kind of spectacle which set the spirit alight.

Venice was to create an entertainment, for every type of audience, from a musical genre that had previously been reserved for the great families of Florence, Parma or Mantua, that is for a cultural elite. It was a master-stroke. This small revolution took place in 1637, led by the brothers Francesco and Ettore Tron: for the first time the Teatro San Cassiano was open to everyone, from a procurator of St Mark's to the most modest gondolier. There lay the two-fold genius of Venice: that of having transformed a luxury product, elitist *par excellence*, into a commercial product accessible to the general public; but also for having dared to imagine that social classes as far apart as princes and ordinary people could be together in the same place and could experience the same emotions while watching one single spectacle. Only a city orientated towards trade and business for so many centuries, but also a city which in its celebrations and its carnival constantly mingled all the social classes together, could have projected itself into the future like this. Everything of this kind that happened later, in Naples or in other European cities, would be imitated from Venice.

After the San Cassiano theatre, in 1637, the Santi Giovanni e Paolo and the San Moisè opened their doors in 1639, then the San Angelo and the San Giovanni Grisostomo in 1677 and 1678 respectively, to quote only the principal theatres, those that were to last into the eighteenth century.* Virtually all of them bore the name of the parish in which they were situated. In fact, the number of theatres was greater than those listed above, for some closed while others opened, there was building on one side and demolition on the other: whereas the Teatro Santi Apostoli survived for three years only, the San Cassiano would continue for 169 years, until the end of the Republic. In a city as enterprising as Venice the aristocrats soon understood that the total entertainment of opera could become a worthwhile commercial product: the exponential opening of the theatres did not signify ideal prosperity, as one might have imagined, but rather that of an alarming economic situation which the city was trying to check by all the aesthetico-commercial methods possible. The patricians invested their riches in the theatre and tried to unite the spirit of enterprise with respect for music. Their enterprise had to be entrusted, therefore, to skilful administrators. That is where the impresarios came in, the valuable intermediaries between a family having a theatre built for money-making purposes and a public who were supposed to fill it and make it pay. The problem for the impresario was obviously knowing how to succeed in his enterprise: the prince put in the capital, the impresario rented the theatre and risked his own money in the adventure. He ran the risk, therefore, of earning a great deal or of being ruined: more than one would never recover what he had spent, and suffered bankruptcy.

This was the type of system, which will certainly be mentioned

---

*The most famous theatre today, La Fenice, was not inaugurated until 1792, only five years before the fall of the Republic.

again during descriptions of the internal life of the theatres, through which a considerable repertoire was to develop, comparable only during the seventeenth century with that occurring in Naples during the eighteenth. Sixteen theatres opened in Venice between 1637 and 1699 and, through the diversity of their public they were to have a direct influence on the operatic repertoire. They began with opulent spectacles, reserved for princes and based, during the first thirty years of the century, on the great mythological tragedies, such as Monteverdi's *Arianna*, first performed in Mantua in 1608 and revived in Venice in 1639 for the opening of the Teatro San Moisè; opera then moved gradually towards a mixed kind of genre, with more appeal to ordinary people, in which the comic and the tragic, the vulgar and the sublime appeared side by side or superimposed on each other. *L'Incoronazione di Poppea*, Monteverdi's last work and the first on a historical subject, dates from 1642 at the Teatro Santi Giovanni e Paolo; this opera, the masterpiece of the century, equal to *Orfeo* but in a quite different style, offers the synthesis of an entire life at the same time as the archetype of the Venetian model: the outpourings of Poppaea, the tragic recitatives of Octavia, daring harmony, moments of high tragedy, such as the death of Seneca, alongside the amusing vulgarities of the nurse or the servants.

The Monteverdian torch was immediately handed on during the years 1640–60 through the thirty-two operas of Francesco Cavalli which maintained the dramatic art of Venice on heights which knew no equal. In *Egisto, Serse, Didone* and the incomparable *Calisto*, the composer brought more flexibility to the Monteverdi style by making it even freer and more natural, gave pride of place to the most entertaining of the 'canzonette' while introducing moments of high tragedy. When the listener of today hears the perfect fluidity of these works, full of brilliance and emotion, it is difficult to understand the reticence, even hostility of the Parisian audiences of 1660–2 when they had the possibility of hearing *Serse* (Xerxes) or *Ercole amante* (Hercules in Love). It is true that the language problem and the resentment against the Mazarin era which was just ending can explain this coldness. There was admiration for all the scenic devices which the Italians had introduced twenty years earlier. But the finesse, the natural quality, humour and dynamic imagination of the Venetian composer were never understood on the banks of the Seine.*

Cavalli, who was never surpassed during the second part of the seventeenth century, preceded however a new generation of composers: they were all to enrich an entertainment that Europe liked to describe from then on as 'Venetian opera'. In Sartorio's *Massensio* (1673) famous for its seventy-eight arias, in Pallavicino's *Vespasiano*, which inaugurated the illustrious Teatro San Giovanni Grisostomo in 1678, in the eighty-five works by Pollarolo or the spicy comic-heroic productions of Legrenzi, opera continued to fascinate all categories of spectators present in the auditorium through its highly spectacular scenes and its astonishing mixture of contrasts. As in the street, during the carnival, the prince in the opera was disguised as a slave, the humble nymph was transformed into a goddess, Jupiter appeared in women's clothes and Mercury adopted the suggestive poses of a clown from the *commedia dell'arte*. Acts of treason, battles, plots or abductions followed one another with frantic speed, while leaving more time for noble sentiments or the most daring tomfooleries.

The Venetians were delighted by all this artifice, they reacted as one to this totally baroque illusion, and were entertained by observing the reactions of foreigners who knew nothing whatever about this type of entertainment. The best account is the delightful piece offered by the *Pallade Veneta* in 1687 on the occasion when the Turkish Pasha of Romania was taken to a Venetian theatre:

> I must not fail to tell you of the surprise reserved for us by the Turkish Pasha of Romania who was taken to a musical opera [probably Pallavicino's *Elmiro*] by one of our very noble gentlemen. He was in a box, accompanied by various nobles; when he saw the chandelier which lit the auditorium descend from on high and then come to a stop he said, *good, good*, and asked if the opera was over. When the curtain went up he was full of admiration at the sight of a very grandiose stage, and by the intrigue of a sumptuous ballet. When asked if he enjoyed it he replied that people

---

*For all these conflicts between French and Italian music in Paris, see *La Maison des Italiens, les castrats à Versailles* by Patrick Barbier (Grasset, Paris, 1998) or *Louis XIV artiste* by Philippe Beaussant (Perrin, Paris, 1998).

also danced before the great [Turkish] lord but not so well. He seemed delighted at hearing the voices of the singers and he asked his hosts to bring the singers to him every evening, or to take him to the theatre. Towards the end of the opera he saw a very well produced massacre, and cried out 'brave soldiers'. He was told that they were only pretending to be brave, but that the Republic had real ones. At the end, after he had expressed his amazement at the crowd in the theatre, it was explained to him that there was not just one theatre, but that there were five for opera, two for comedy, always full, and in addition there were people who went to private entertainments and to the Ridotto to gamble. He was absolutely amazed and exclaimed with astonishment: 'Oh, in Constantinople, war, plague and famine, always starving, always weeping, never enjoying things; God doesn't see us then, since He gives all his love to the Christians.'[1]

After which the Venetian newspaper hastened to conclude that no infidel could have spoken more sincerely.

The theatre audience

More important than the repertoire and its performers, the productions and their stage machinery, the Venetian opera was first of all the encounter, the fusion, between a kind of auditorium, totally innovative in Europe and, from 1637 onwards, an amazingly diversified audience. This alchemy, this amalgamation between auditorium and spectators, was to produce the most surprising, the most talked about and the most imitated theatrical behaviour that could be found during the baroque era.

Everything began with that real stroke of genius inspired by the opening of many public theatres in the seventeenth century: the successful installation in one place and in front of the same stage of social classes that had nothing in common, had no wish to communicate with each other and obviously did not want to sit at the same level. Until then these problems had not arisen in these terms because court society, benefiting from generosity (and invitations) from the prince, shared the same tiers in the theatre. This can be seen today on visiting Palladio's famous Teatro Olimpico at Vicenza as

well as the enchanting little ducal theatre at Sabbioneta, even if they
both date from before the birth of opera and were therefore devoted
to tragedy and comedy. More interesting still is the grandiose Teatro
Farnese in Parma, proud of its 4,500 seats and inaugurated in 1628
with Monteverdi's *Mercurio e Marte*: this astounding musical entertainment even included a naval battle. In this theatre, as in the two
previously mentioned, the model remained that of the ancient tiered
theatre, shaped more or less like an opened out horseshoe: the
courtiers and other invited guests filled the tiered seats while the
reigning family (except in the case of Vicenza which formed part of
the Republic) occupied on their own the loggia situated higher up,
at the back. Apart from this one separation, all subjects were
regarded as equal in the eyes of the sovereign.

Venice therefore had to make innovations in more than one way.
On one hand it wanted to have a Republic that did not practise the
cult of personality: the doge was elected and, in the theatre, did not
occupy the same representative role as a prince or monarch. On the
other hand the city wanted to separate the different social classes in
accordance with a system that would allow proximity, not promiscuity. In 1680 Saint-Didier was pleased on behalf of the ordinary
people of Venice by the idea that there were no pleasures 'that were
not shared with the nobility'. That was certainly fair, but this sharing was not obtained at just any price. Hence the famous
Italian-style auditorium which was based on the old open-air theatres of princely tournaments: while retaining the horseshoe shape it
clearly divided the public according to a principle of verticality, and
no longer according to the horizontality of tiers. During the course
of the century Venice imposed a type of auditorium where the theatre boxes were arranged over each other on five or six levels, called
rows, each one exactly over the first level as far up as the
'pigeon-loft'. The Teatro San Cassiano, the first one open to the
public, included five rows of thirty-one boxes, called '*palchi*', a figure
identical with that of San Giovanni Grisostomo, the most luxurious
of all the Venetian theatres inaugurated in 1678. About 150 boxes
remained the average number for the Venetian theatres. The first row
of boxes, a kind of raised ground floor called '*Pepian*', remained a
somewhat ill-famed place, reserved for the 'suspect girls' who were
not shy about making conversation with the men in the nearby pit

who climbed up to the platform. Apart from this promiscuity with the '*popolani*', who were very near, the first row of boxes was also hindered by the necks of the orchestra theorbos which prevented a good view of the stage. This first row was as cheap as the top row, full of people and uncomfortable, by definition a long way from the stage. These two rows were never sold by subscription but only from evening to evening at the free disposal of the proprietor who tried to make the maximum profit from them. As for the pit, the '*platea*', where people sat on folding stools or chairs, close to the audience, or else stood at the back, this was definitely the place reserved for the gondoliers and people of the humblest origin, or even passing visitors who had not been able to find places elsewhere.

Finally there remained the 'noble' levels, in particular the two rows above the *Pepian*, which were to isolate and protect Venetian high society, not only by separating its members from spectators whose behaviour was more 'common' but also by installing them more comfortably in boxes, all separated from each other and therefore likely to produce a certain intimacy. The women, who did not occupy the front of the box as in Paris, were able to hold a salon there, maintain conversations and receive visits from good-class people. This system would not avoid the less orthodox mingling of people, as recalled by an anonymous eighteenth-century poet: 'A mere partition wall separates a respectable woman from a tart.'[2]

But how much has been written about the theatre box, that Italian institution that was to be imitated all over the rest of Europe, the starting point of all social success in many countries through four centuries! The Venetians were without doubt the first people to turn their boxes into a kind of sanctuary for all public and private life. Public because the box, according to the accepted expression, was the means of seeing and being seen. In a city where collective pleasure was central to life, where the theatre remained the most perfect expression of that pleasure of being together in order to share a moment of life, the box offered a sight of the stage as well as a sight of the boxes opposite, to right or left. Private because citizens of high rank, subscribers for a year or for life, became owners of their boxes and could probably transfer their own to their heirs from generation to generation. It became therefore a part of themselves, a second home which they could furnish and decorate with paintings and tapestries of their choice, a place where they could pass an average of six hours a day, that is to say a quarter of their life during the entertainment season.

The reason for this sale of boxes to subscribers was another discovery of these enterprising people. When a great family was about to build a new theatre they launched a kind of subscription to bring in funds. The subscribers could benefit from the priority they received in the acquisition of one or several boxes, through paying a fixed annual rent. Their loan thus became an advance on a kind of 'multiproperty' which contributed largely to the spread and growth of so many theatres within a perimeter as restricted as that of Venice. As a general rule the great families conducted a merciless struggle in order to obtain in each theatre the boxes that occupied the best position, those most deserving of their family coat of arms: it was the famous 'theatre box war', which was so often noticed by contemporary observers. Any boxes that were not occupied on a yearly basis by the families who owned them could also be rented for one evening or for one season to less well-heeled citizens, great lovers of opera but unable to purchase such a property for a long period. If the tradition of owning or handing on a box still remained alive until the end of the century who could have imagined that today, at the start of the twenty-first century, two boxes at the Teatro Comunale in Bologna, are still owned by the two leading aristocratic families in the city, a situation that has lasted from the second half of the eighteenth century?

In addition to the obvious conviviality of the boxes there were of course other advantages: warmth in the first place, for it was true that this concentration of human beings could keep people warm more easily than in the vast palaces, that were cold and damp on winter evenings; then there was gastronomy, since everything was done to make it possible to serve dainty snacks and refreshments during the performance: in this way the corridors leading to the boxes were full of servants continually stocking the buffets and waiting in readiness to serve the people who did not want to leave their box; there was plenty of mischievous behaviour too within the intimacy of these boxes: a curtain or a wooden partition could be used at any time on the auditorium side of the box to hide the cosy nest and the lovers within it from the gaze of inquisitive spectators; lastly gambling and all sorts of pastimes offered an ideal way of passing the time during the recitatives or arias by secondary characters; mirrors placed on the partition walls allowed the spectators to keep one eye on the stage while finishing a game of bassetta. 'I could not believe what I saw,' wrote Uffenbach, 'when I found that in the boxes people ate, gambled and smoked'.[3] His astonishment was shared by Président de Brosses. 'Chess was a marvellous invention to fill the void of those long recitatives, and music to interrupt over-assiduous attention to chess.'[4]

The opera, a place of multiple delights, also formed an ideal area for political life. In a city where contacts between nobles and foreigners were forbidden, the theatre, through the apparent freedom of movement that existed within it and the masks worn there throughout the entire carnival period, offered many possibilities for sybilline exchanges and intrigues. As Cardinal de Bernis showed:

> Although the Venetian nobility cannot have any commerce with the ambassadors . . . one must not think that the foreign ministers do not have a kind of relationship with the magistrates; people speak to each other through third parties: they tell each other a great deal by making signs when at the Opera, a situation which makes it necessary for foreign ministers to frequent entertainments and to use masks; between them and the Venetians close and lasting friendships are formed.[5]

What the cardinal-ambassador fails to say is that throughout this time the Venetian secret police were also at work and took advantage of masks to listen to conversations, sift through information and take the pulse of current feeling. Since opera had become available to the public it had remained a splendid example of the State hold over the free time of its citizens: the presence together of so many people in one place at the same time made it possible to supervise the population and foreigners during their nocturnal pleasures.

As a general rule the performances began at about six o'clock in the evening. A motley crowd, usually masked, arrived on foot through the maze of surrounding streets or by gondola along the nearby canals. The nobles proceeded immediately to their boxes.

They had a key to them which showed the row or level and the number on the door. Since this box was rented to them for the year or even for life, they could invite their friends there, entertain relatives or professional contacts. Whenever a new ambassador arrived in Venice the Senate informed the theatre director that he must find a box for this privileged guest. The director then suggested to various box-owners that they should let him have one of their boxes and give back the key so that the ambassador could be installed. After many discussions, sometimes even leading to arbitration by the doge, a box was finally assigned to the illustrious visitor, who would be responsible for paying the corresponding rent. When he left, the box would return legitimately to its owner.

As for the ordinary people, they had to acquire a '*bollettino di passaporto*', that is to say a ticket of admission at a price fixed at one third of a ducat, a price which did not change between 1617 and 1679. Later it was reduced to a quarter of a ducat which naturally delighted these people and angered the nobility by this continuing cheap access reserved for the 'vulgar' crowd. Only the Teatro San Giovanni Grisostomo would keep its prices high, on the pretext that the high level of its presentations would prevent what had happened in all the other theatres, namely the significant increase in the number of modest citizens. From that time, and through the entire eighteenth century, this theatre was to become a kind of sanctuary for the nobility, and, thanks to its large income, the most prestigious in the musical history of Venice.

The audience in the pit, as already mentioned, sat on folding chairs or remained standing, and therefore could move about a great deal during the show. The coming and going was non-stop, jokes flew about and confrontations between gondoliers were not rare. 'When everything was ready for the show,' wrote Misson,

> at the Comedy or the Opera, the doors were usually opened to those gentlemen the Gondoliers who form a considerable body in Venice and are used for several important purposes. On this occasion they are there to clap their hands and shout like desperate men in praise of the performers. I can neither tell you nor suggest the terms they use, in particular when they offer congratulations to the women. The latter also receive other applause in printed

sonnets that are produced for them, which you can sometimes see flying about all over the stage.[6]

The noise and chaos among the spectators 'down below' were also made much worse by the behaviour of those 'up there'. Many travellers must have discovered that it was quite usual to see the audience in the boxes, even the most noble among them, spitting or dropping all sorts of rubbish down on to the people in the pit. Far from taking offence the latter reacted with witty remarks, sometimes with rather crude jokes, called out across the auditorium in the middle of the performance. As a result, at the end of the show Uffenbach found his programme all wet and Wright found that the candles used for following the libretto were often put out by these 'favours from above'. This custom which has often been described, was once the subject of an amusing story sent to a Venetian gazette by one of its readers. He told how he wanted to show a friend from abroad, who was passing through, the various pleasures of the city, especially by taking him, wearing a mask, to an evening out at the opera. The boxes were definitely not available and the two men accepted seats in the pit, maintaining that the acoustics would be better there. The friend was amazed by the singers, applauded as loudly as he could, and was ready to swear that he had never known such delight when all at once the first gob of spit landed on his hat, then another on top of his head, after he had removed his hat to examine the damage caused by the first one. And the whole evening passed like this. When he saw his Venetian friend become horribly embarrassed the guest risked an explanation that was as courteous as it was ironic:

> I've often been afraid that the air in this place, which is limited by the alleyways that are so narrow, causes serious harm to people's chests, so much so that it's not impossible for them all to be suffering from colds! This continual rain falling from the boxes makes it even clearer to me. The lungs of all these people are so fiercely stimulated that they can't prevent themselves from spitting out what I felt just now on my hat and my forehead, and also on one shoulder or the other. What the devil, if it's only due to an illness, could it be that the infinite civility I've admired in so many other places in this polite and beautiful city, might flourish here as well?

The friend from abroad then decided to laugh at this and every time more spit reached him he called out to the audience in the boxes: 'May God restore your health! May Heaven relieve your bronchial tubes of this catarrh!' After which the poor Venetian, who was forced to join in his companion's game, decided mischievously that at the end of the opera they would both leave 'covered with the signs of this universal cold'![7]

In spite of this apparent lapse into bad behaviour, usually during the less important episodes of an opera, needing less attention, the Venetian public knew how to appear highly receptive when they listened to the outstanding moments, so much so that they would swoon in delight at an overwhelming love duet or the heady vocal acrobatics of their favourite castrato. 'Scarlatti', wrote Lalande, 'wrote a duet for his opera *La Clemenza di Tito* which moved the audience so completely that they uttered cries of transport and emotion which sounded like howling.' It was also for this reason that the Venetian public, like the Neapolitans in the eighteenth century in fact, who were always avid for new sensations, categorically refused to have revivals. An opera which had already been heard during a preceding season would no longer have any support and according to the words of Charles de Brosses it would be treated like 'last year's calendar'. Exceptions were rare, although Ristori's *Orlando furioso* would be performed on nearly fifty successive evenings at the Teatro San Angelo in the autumn of 1713, before being revived the following autumn. It must be said that opera production was so rich – Strohm estimated that in the eighteenth century 1,200 different shows were performed, that is an average of twelve operas per year during a five-month season – that spectators became insatiable and did not understand why old works had to be revived. From October to the end of the carnival the seven theatres were never empty and stimulated each other by the furious competition that led them to recruit the finest voices, seek out the best scores or offer the most grandiose productions.

The mechanics of opera production
Family owners and impresarios

The system for managing Venetian entertainments remained complex. As already described, the powerful theatres belonged to the great patrician families of the city and two of them have been discussed. The Tron family had founded the San Cassiano theatre in 1580 and then, after the fire of 1629, had rebuilt it and finally opened it to the general public in 1637: during its first years it benefited from the rich repertoire of Francesco Cavalli. The Grimani family had opened the Teatro Santi Giovanni e Paolo, built first in wood, in 1655, then in stone in 1669. In this way the family was expressing its intention to dominate and compete with the Tron family theatres which had been operational for two seasons. The same Grimani family later built the San Samuele in 1655 in order to produce comedies and compete with the Tron and Vendramin family theatres which put on comedies and operas alternately. Lastly it was the Grimani who were to build – in just four months – *the* most prestigious and luxurious theatre, the San Giovanni Grisostomo, all in gold and polychrome marbles, inaugurated during the carnival of 1678 with Pallavicino's *Vespasiano*.*

Without attempting to draw up a complete list of those owning the sixteen or so theatres open in the seventeenth century, one must add to these two famous names those of the Vendramins of the Teatro San Luca, the Capellos and Marcellos of the Teatro San Angelo, and the Giustinians of the Teatro San Moisè. It goes without saying that each theatre would experience periods of prosperity alternately with periods of recession, depending on economic ups and downs, the competition from the other theatres and the quality of the productions offered. In the same way the purpose to which all these buildings were put would evolve greatly with time. Some of them, including the San Samuele, moved over to the spoken theatre in the seventeenth century. It was there that Casanova made his début, as a musician in the orchestra, and his mother, Zanetta, first appeared as an actress, both of them protected by the Grimani family. Other theatres concentrated at this period on a type of highly specialised repertoire, *opera seria* for the San Cassiano and San Giovanni Grisostomo, *opera buffa* for the San Moisè and the San Samuele.

Once the theatres were open, with the permission of the Council of Ten, there were two possibilities for these families: they could

---

*For a good understanding of the Grimani theatre, its management, repertoire and singers, see *Les Grands Castrats napolitains à Venise au XVIIIe siècle* by Sylvie Mamy, Mardaga, 1994.

either manage them on their own, or entrust them to an entrepreneur, a manager, the impresario. The first alternative remained fairly rare (with the exception of the Tron and Grimani families), for the patricians, who had opened their theatres, attracted by profit as much as by the publicity given to their family, hardly wanted to bother with the complex practical contingencies connected with the efficient working of their enterprise. These patrician-proprietors were to limit themselves at most to a public relations role, establishing links with the other princes in the Peninsula for searching out famous singers, helping with the transfer of an artist from one State to another and the signing of contracts . . . This is what conferred another princely character on this theatrical management, which in fact was entirely 'entrepreneurial'.

The recruitment of an impresario was usually essential. It was his responsibility to prepare the new season, recruit the singers, instrumentalists, choreographers and costume-designers, negotiate with the composer and the librettist, supervise the production and the lighting and most of all ensure that the whole enterprise would be viable, since in general he took responsibility himself. It was here that the shoe pinched, for in Venice as in Paris, in the eighteenth century as today, the production of an opera is rarely profitable and the hope of making a profit is always a risky venture. During the baroque period Venice became part of a system that was openly 'capitalist' due to the unceasing competition between the theatres. The impresarios relied on the renting of boxes by the year, casual sales of tickets for the pit or secondary boxes, and the sale of refreshments . . .

Unfortunately the economic difficulties arising from the various wars against the Turks, the competition from Naples in the eighteenth century, which became more and more severe, the exponential cost of the great singers and the unfortunate choice of some operatic works were all obstacles to financial success. In addition there was the insatiable appetite of the public who wanted stage machinery to be more and more inventive and spectacular to satisfy their desire for major thrills during the performance. 'At first,' wrote Ivanovich in 1681, 'two exquisite voices and a few arias sufficed to give pleasure; a few scene changes satisfied their curiosity. Nowadays people are not satisfied with a voice that is one of the best in Europe and they would like the décor to change with every scene.'[8]

Expenses therefore could easily be guaranteed but receipts were chancy, meaning that the impresario was frequently obliged, as some observers described, to resort to subterfuge to compensate for his losses:

> The impresarios often failed to recover from their losses. They are essentially rich people of rank who band together and draw some fame from the fact that they tolerate sacrifices for the entertainment of the citizens. If they recover from the expenditure this is because games of chance, in which they hold the bank, something permitted today, compensate for the losses due to their activity as impresario.[9]

It was therefore the responsibility of the patrician families to know where to find a man who could be relied upon. This was especially the case of Marco Faustino who provided brilliant management for the Teatro Santi Giovanni e Paolo on behalf of the Grimani family from 1658 to 1668, arranging multiple contracts with the best performers. When the singers jeopardised his administration with their capricious behaviour over money, the Grimani family were obliged to take things in hand again: like real entrepreneurs in advance of their time they were always careful to pay attention to their business affairs. In 1674 the Zane family chose the impresario Francesco Santurini to take over the reins at the San Moisè, a small theatre which until then had not been a serious rival to the larger ones. The entrepreneur's chief merit was to reduce the price of admission from a third of a ducat to a quarter of a ducat. This brought a considerable increase in the audience for this small theatre which had been somewhat lacking in class, and turned it into one that was economically viable. Three years later, having separated from the Grimani, Faustino inaugurated a new theatre, the San Angelo, the future theatre of Vivaldi, on land rented from the Capello and Marcello families. Since the price of admission remained the same, the San Cassiano and the Santi Giovanni e Paolo were also forced to follow suit. This brought about a minor revolution in Venetian theatrical life, sweeping away a commercial system which had been put in place by the Tron and Grimani families: it led the two nephews of Giovanni Grimani to manage their own two theatres (the San Samuele and the Santi Giovanni e Paolo) themselves, before deciding to build the majestic San Giovanni Grisostomo. This theatre, as already mentioned, would be not only the greatest and most handsome but also the one that in the time of Vivaldi would welcome the greatest singers and the greatest operas to the repertoire. It should be noted that it was the Grimani, followed later by all the other families, who were to have the courtesy to place a box at the disposal of the composer every evening, allowing him to go there freely and invite some friends.

After Faustini or Santurini many other impresarios were to struggle, in public or in private, to bring about the triumph of a theatre. Their success would always depend on many parameters. First, intuition, which would help them to evaluate what type of repertoire would be most suitable at a given moment in a given theatre; in short they would have to decide to what demand from the public they should respond and then, depending on that, they would have to select a repertoire that was heroic or romantic, mythological or pastoral, as well as any one of the multiple variations of the comic style which became essential from 1730 onwards (comic-heroic, comic-pastoral, tragi-comic, satirical, etc.). Later the way relations were conducted with the other Italian theatres came to be important: especially from the moment in the eighteenth century when the poet Metastasio was writing librettos which were guarantees of success for an opera production, and which came to be *de rigueur* more or less everywhere – in Venice as well as all the countries of the Peninsula, and far beyond it – this 'globalisation' of opera repertoire meant that the Venetians could no longer remain locked into their own productions. Finally came the 'political' skill which consisted of knowing how to manoeuvre among the twists and turns of relations between great families or between States, how not to make a false move and how to ensure a 'cultural policy' as sound as the management of the theatre itself.

The impresario therefore was a key player on the theatrical and intellectual chessboard of his time, and his responsibility was even strengthened in Venice by the decisive aspect of the economic factor, while in Naples or Turin opera remained a court genre, generously subsidised by the king. The impresario's role could be made even more significant through his own cultural qualifications. This was the case of Maffei in Verona, who was both dramatist and impresario, or even more so of Vivaldi who fulfilled the triple function of composer, director of instrumental music and impresario.

The Red Priest, who was a hard man when selling his concertos, was equally intransigent when he had to further his own affairs during the production of a show. His correspondence with the Marchese Bentivolgio d'Aragona in Ferrara, despite the few letters we possess, shows the permanent cunning, the even suspect morality that he used in order to bring his projects to a successful conclusion. It is true that, unlike other impresarios who were acting as intermediaries between composers and theatres, Vivaldi was acting on behalf of his own operas and as a result found himself involved, twice over, in the success of his affairs. In addition this Ferrara period (1736–9) was a nightmare for him: his operas were not well received and the local organisers produced only worries for him. Hence this correspondence with the Marchese Bentivoglio, an aristocrat of Venetian origin, from whom he hoped for arbitration and support. Vivaldi claimed that he had rejected the 90 sequins offered to him by the Teatro San Cassiano in Venice since, according to him, the 'rate' demanded for a new opera was 100 sequins. In fact he had never received this proposition but it served him as a pretext for fixing his price and showing what a remarkable favour he was granting to Ferrara by asking for much less. If the new price was so low (six 'wretched' sequins for each work) it was because one of the four operas that he wanted to palm off on Ferrara was the adaptation of a work by another composer: Vivaldi merely limited himself to rewriting the recitatives and adding a few arias of his own. The Ferrara impresario, the Abbé Bollani, was not more understanding: every time Vivaldi sent him an opera the abbé changed his mind and wanted another one. In the end Vivaldi demanded the prescribed sum for each opera, while his sleeping partners wanted to pay only copyist expenses for works that he had not written out entirely in his own hand. From one letter to another there was nothing but endless haggling, criticisms, admonitions and appeals to reason. One of his worst displays of anger took place in 1739 when the producer Antonio Mauro refused to accept responsibility for the debts incurred by the opera season in Ferrara. Vivaldi, exhausted by these three years and discouraged by the failure of his opera *Siroe*, hit back with a lawsuit and did not hesitate to introduce God into his threats:

> [Remember] that it is your duty to reflect on your responsibilities and that your calumnies and sinister deceptions will not suffice to release you from paying the singers, dancers and myself. Remember that ingratitude is one of the most horrible sins. Subterfuges are only diabolical insinuations which conceal the truth. And finally remember that God sees, God knows and God judges, and that beyond the very sound justice of this Serenissima Dominante, you must always render to God strict accounts in everything.[10]

Décor and production

After Giacomo Torelli, born at Fano in 1608, had put into practice his fabulous procedure for scene changing, Italy had once more taken the lead over all the countries of Europe for inventive skill in stage production. Torelli had settled in Venice as a naval engineer and worked at the Arsenal before exercising his talents in the Teatro Novissimo. His initial idea was to link all the panels at the side and back of the stage, plus those above it, using a complex system of winches, ropes and pulleys, to a single drum placed under the stage: by revolving it, a single machine operator could, in a few seconds, transform a huge stage and change it from the interior of a palace to a park, a cloudy sky could become a harbour full of boats. From the first stage settings by the man whom the French were to call 'the great magician', the Arsenal sailors had been requisitioned to activate all these 'changes of scene' under the supervision of the admiral of the Venetian fleet: these sailors alone had the knowledge and skill to make everything work, these kilometres of rope, canvas and masts, not to mention the winches, pulleys, drums and capstans. The handling of all these materials, which came very close to sailing, meant that all over Italy theatres would have to be adapted, that is to say, they had to have huge flies and space beneath the stage to allow the '*gloria*'* to go up and the 'infernal' characters to go down into the abyss.

Venice, unlike other cities, required a prodigious effort to bring off such an operation successfully, for the muddy and unstable soil, as well as the thousands of wooden piles† that supported a theatre, hardly allowed the building of deep basements. As usual, Venice adapted to its geographical situation and succeeded none the less in achieving miracles of illusion and fantasy during performances.

It is known that opera of the baroque period certainly depended on the quality of a libretto or a score, but also and especially on the brilliance of the singers, who were regarded as gods, and on the dazzling efflect produced by the décor, the costumes, the choreography and especially on the art of the 'machines'. Dazzling was indeed the word suitable for a city where the opera season and the carnival season united the population as one, in the same atmosphere of delight: it was considered obligatory to go to the opera wearing masks, even the clerics did so, and everyone did their best to take there any foreign personality passing through the city, leading them into a dream world as they watched one of the most beautiful expressions of the Venetian genius.

For a better understanding of what a Venetian theatrical production was like in the seventeenth and eighteenth centuries it is useful to read the evidence left by spectators, Venetian or foreign, who all felt the need to describe in their memoirs or letters to English, German or French correspondents the prodigious achievements they had just watched. Thus Ivanovich, in 1681:

> today we see clever machines suggested by the story, they are very pleasing amidst the pomp of the scenery and costumes which are totally satisfying to universal curiosity. We have also seen real elephants, live camels, highly majestic chariots drawn by wild animals or horses; also flying horses up in the air, dancing horses,

---

*The '*gloria*' was a machine that moved upwards, usually decorated with clouds, which allowed the divinities and their suite to return to heaven. Sixty singers, sometimes more, could be lifted up at the same time.

†As an example, the Rialto bridge needed 10,000 piles; the church of La Salute rested on 1,156 stakes arranged in concentric circles; in the twentieth century 100,000 trees were needed to rebuild the campanile of St Mark's. According to some studies the old buildings of Venice are said to rest on a submerged forest of 12 million tree-trunks.

superb machines which move up in the air, on the ground, in the sea with amazing artifice and praiseworthy invention, going as far as to bring down from the upper air royal salons with all the characters and the instrumentalists, lit up in the darkness and with them go back up again in the most admirable manner ...[11]

At the same period Monsieur de Vaumorière emphasised the magnificence of the décor and the impressive number of extras:

All the changes take place high up over the stage and on the other sides, so that you never see a room without a ceiling. Galleries and large rooms are vaulted, the smallest rooms appear to be panelled. When an emperor or a king comes on to the stage he is usually accompanied by forty or fifty guards, some of them surrounding him while the others protect the doors and the avenues leading to his palace. The same is true of the queens and princesses: depending on their rank, their suite includes a quantity of ladies, officers and pages.[12]

It is also worth noting this interesting description by Edward Wright of a show sometime between the years 1720–22:

In one [of these operas] Nero presents Tiridate, king of Armenia, by means of a great spectacle in which he participates himself. The emperor and empress appear in a triumphal chariot drawn by an elephant. The head, trunk and eyes of the great beast move as though it were alive, and Tiridate thinks so too. Then suddenly, as soon as the emperor and empress have taken their seats, the triumphal chariot changes into an amphitheatre filled with spectators. The elephant falls to pieces and out of his body emerge a great number of gladiators armed with shields which had previously formed the innumerable pieces of the elephant's flanks, so that it seemed to be transformed at one stroke into a company of armed men who engage in a skirmish in time to the music. We saw another machine. A huge room contained representations of the four elements painted as emblems; as they opened they formed two palaces, of Love and Hymen, entirely surrounded with weapons of war. This scene was conceived with so much subtlety and the lighting so well arranged that in my opinion it was the most entertaining vision I have ever seen on a theatre stage.[13]

Castrati and women singers

The recruitment and paying of singers was certainly the crucial factor in the management of a theatre by the family owner or by the impresario. This task took all his energy, especially in a city where fierce commercial rivalry had replaced the generous prodigality of the court theatres. In addition Venice had assumed a situation as strange as it was uncomfortable by concentrating all its energy on training of young girls in the *ospedali* who would never have any right of access to the stage, ruling out at the same time all musical training for boys and castrati. As a result the city, concentrating so much on the commercial success of its theatres, had to have recourse constantly to voices imported from outside the Republic, especially for the title roles reserved for outstanding singers. This led to the essential skill of the impresario, assisted in this by the owner-proprietor of the theatre, in recruiting intelligently, securing alliances, obtaining the assent of princes and monarchs on whom some singers depended.

However, the situation was different in the seventeenth and eighteenth centuries. During the rise of the theatre economy in its links with the opera, Venice, as already described, occupied first place on the Italian chessboard. The Venetian opera, undisputed model for Europe, had the advantage of dynamic theatre, singers whose emoluments were still reasonable, and, above all original productions, by names as prestigious as Monteverdi, Pallavicino or Legrenzi, not forgetting the man whom Prunières described as 'the Tintoretto of music', Francesco Cavalli. It was this Venetian repertoire that was exported and earned the admiration of the other States. Cesti, after the triumph of his *Dori* all over Italy in 1661, took all his works to Vienna, five years later. In fact he took advantage of this to make people forget his licentious behaviour which had recently shocked the Venetians, remarkable in a city that cultivated freedom of morals to such an extent. This was how Austria came to give an ovation to his *Pomo d'oro*, a grandiose allegory of the marriage of Leopold I, in which Burnacini, the brilliant theatrical architect, presented a series of no fewer than sixty-seven scenes. On its side Mazarin's France discovered *La Finta Pazza* by Sacrati in 1645, and then the finest of Cavalli's works, *Le Nozze di Peleo e di Teto* in 1654, *Serse* in 1660 and *Ercole amante*, given two years later after the marriage of Louis XIV, in 1662. The length of the works, the failure to understand the Italian language, the long recitatives, and the voices of the castrati were all likely to put off the French; but from then on they developed a taste for the opera, and they were fascinated by the refinement of Italian singers and the art of the machines.

As the fame of the Venetian opera rose, that is to say until the last years of the seventeenth century, the recruitment of the singers was carried out in different ways. At first use was made of touring companies who happened to appear in Rome, or at various Italian courts, as well as at other theatres in the Republic such as Padua or Vicenza. Lorenzo Bianconi maintains that one of these troupes was probably the catalyst that allowed the Teatro San Cassiano to present the first opera performance in public (1637). Later, and in a more systematic fashion, the excellent chapel of St Mark's was searched for singers. Venice in fact trained its own singers on their way to the Holy of Holies, the basilica that was the pride of the Republic. Very soon the chapel was to experience the same difficulties as the Vatican, in that the singers would leave, and go to the opera theatres and the great European courts, infinitely better payers than the Church. This chapel (and the Seminario, the school of song that led there), was to produce some of the very great voices of the century, from the soprano castrati to the basses. While some would remain faithful to sacred music and the basilica others would allow themselves to be tempted by the theatres, during the carnival, and would go abroad during the other months of the year.

The last form of recruitment would consist of engaging the most varied types of singers, coming from all regions of the Peninsula, on an *ad hoc* basis. This system would cost the impresario much more, because of the payments demanded by the artists in addition to their expenses for travel and their stay in Venice. The increase in the salaries allotted to the singers accelerated during Vivaldi's youth, that is to say, the years from 1680 onwards which were devoted to the inauguration of the Teatro San Giovanni Grisostomo: as a result the impresario had to be very astute in order to offer the public voices of quality while keeping an eye on his budget. In addition to their fees the singers, be they castrati or prima donnas were tempted to play at being stars and got themselves treated like royalty, sometimes coming with part of their family, not counting dogs, cats and parrots. One singer would reject a score that did not suit him or cancel a contract that did not offer enough money, another would ask for one part to be transposed because it was too high or ask for a bravura aria to be added for his entry on stage.

The names of these stage gods in the seventeenth century are much less well known than those of the eighteenth for the scores do not give them, neither do the posters. But various accounts reveal the public's irrepressible passion for these adored performers; people would call out to them in the middle of a performance, offering compliments, and accompany them back to their palazzi after the performance with serenades.

In the first half of the eighteenth century this madness became hysteria. Curiously, this golden half-century was to correspond to the decline of the Venetian school, replaced in future by the Neapolitan school. From 1696 and the first years of the next century Venice saw the arrival of the first wave of Neapolitan singers, but did not show any mistrust. These latter were fairly isolated and did not yet represent a 'school' with marked characteristics. In this way, in 1697, then from 1706 to 1708, the Grimani theatre presented the great castrato, Matteo Sassano, known as Matteucio, who was soon to leave for the Spanish court, then Nicolò Grimaldi, known as Nicolino: he was to be one of the glories of this theatre between 1703 and 1731, which did not prevent him from going to England's capital in 1711, where he took part in the creation of Handel's first London opera, *Rinaldo*.

After 1725 or thereabouts the Neapolitan hegemony was to become total in all areas. Venice, as though exhausted by the leadership it had retained for nearly a century, no longer offered any resistance to this tidal wave of operas and singers from Naples, the new masters of musical Europe. As for the repertoire, Sylvie Mamy has shown how, in a symbolic theatre like the San Giovanni Grisostomo, the evolution became significant from 1725, the date when a Neapolitan opera by Vinci, entitled *Rosmira fedele*, arrived. From that day, and during the next ten years, fifteen operas out of thirty-one came from Neapolitan composers while only four were by Venetians.

This reversal was accompanied by the large-scale arrival of castrati and women singers, mainly Neapolitan, who now were made up of a clearly identified group, trained, in the case of the male singers, by the Naples conservatoires, which were extremely famous all over Europe. There was a moment of grace, corresponding to the rise of the Grimani theatre to the summit of success, in about 1730 or so, with the presence in Venice of the castrati Farinelli, Caffarelli and Appianino, the tenor Francesco Tolve and the Saxon composer Johann-Adolf Hasse who married Faustina Bordoni, the greatest singer of her time, in the lagoon-city. Such a plethora of famous names sufficed to demonstrate the prestige of the Republic and its theatres, even if the repertoire, as we have seen, was tending to become less Venetian and more international. Supreme praise was addressed to the art of the male soprani:* praise that came from a French subject who in the future was to make a violent attack on it in his *Dictionnaire de musique*. It was actually in Venice that Jean-Jacques Rousseau experienced his deepest musical emotion, one evening when he fell asleep in the Teatro San Giovanni Grisostomo: 'But who could express the delightful sensation I experienced from the sweet harmony and the angelic singing that woke me? What an awakening, what joy, what ecstasy when my ears and eyes opened at the same time! I thought at first that I was in paradise.'

Farinelli in Venice

The case of Carlo Broschi, known as Farinelli, is certainly significant in this context and highly representative of a Venetian sojourn by a great virtuoso. I shall not write in detail about this male soprano, unique star in the firmament of singers of his century, about whom I have already written an entire work.[14] I shall simply describe his various stays in the capital of the Republic and their impact on contemporary society. In 1729 Farinelli arrived at a time

---

*In this case the castrato Carestini who sang in Venice in 1743–4.

of severe competition beween the two great *opera seria* theatres: the San Giovanni Grisostomo had engaged him to lend his brilliant support to them against the San Cassiano, temporarily administered by Faustina Bordoni, who fulfilled in this way the double role of singer and impresario. At the age of twenty-three Farinelli already enjoyed exceptional fame, as the Abbé Conti emphasised in ironic fashion:

> The talk here is only about the operas, and people are so fascinated by Farinelli that if the Turks were in the gulf they would be left to disembark in peace, for fear of missing two ariettos. At present it is just as dangerous to speak ill of Farinelli as it must have been in the past to attack Monsieur Law's system in Paris . . .[15]

The Neapolitan castrato, who was endowed with a prodigious voice on the technical level, possessing exceptional agility and range, as well as an unusually good breathing capacity, had been a pupil of Porpora and caused a furore wherever he went, and if we are to believe the Abbé Conti, he had already earned 'more money than all the learned men of Europe of the last three centuries put together'.[16] As happened in London a few years later, the news of his imminent arrival in Venice occupied all conversation and focused all minds. People looked forward to his appearance at the Teatro Grimani and his participation, along with the castrato Senesino, in the Midnight Mass at St Mark's. The Abbé Conti, who was one of his few detractors, obviously pointed out, and on several occasions, the element that angered some people, namely the astonishing sums of money promised to the singer: 'The Teatro San Giovanni Grisostomo maintains they will be victorious, solely through Farinelli, who is costing the Grimanis immense sums of money. We shall see.'[17] Or again this determined diatribe: 'There has been no agreement with Farinelli, who passes for the greatest singer in Italy, but he is asking for one thousand five hundred sequins. These people should be punished for their insolence instead of being paid for it.'[18] It is true that these exorbitant sums seem shocking: they show in particular how salaries had become inflated during the previous century. For instance the Venetian Bonlini stated in 1730 that the sum of 2,000 ducats, which had been enough in 1637 to put on a whole opera at San Cassiano, could, a century later, barely satisfy the demands of the most mediocre singer.

Despite these criticisms, probably representative of a certain fringe opinion, Farinelli was to stay on four occasions, which were among the most triumphant of his career, so much so that our Abbé Conti no longer dared to publicise his opposition in those times when 'the constellation of musical fantasy predominates'. In the alleyways and on the piazza of St Mark's the castrato was followed at every move by several hundred admirers. When on stage he caused men and women to swoon, bewitched by that virtuoso singing that he imposed on the repertoire. He even assured the financial success of the Grimani theatre: it was victorious for a time over its rival the San Cassiano, despite the presence of Faustina Bordoni and the castrato Senesino, in addition to a very good production and superb décors.

In this way Farinelli was to sing in ten operas during four different seasons. During the winter of 1728–9 he performed in *Catone in Utica* by the Neapolitan Leo, set to a poem by Metastasio. He was accompanied on stage by the greatest castrati of his generation, Nicolino and Domenico Gizzi, as well as by the women singers Facchinelli and Negri. He sang again with the two same castrati during the two other productions of the season: *Semiramide riconosciuta* by his Neapolitan teacher Porpora and *L'Abbandono di Armida* by the Venetian Antonio Pollarolo. He returned the following year, for the 1730 carnival, to sing in two works: *Mitridate*, by the Turin composer Giai, with a libretto by the Venetian poet Zeno, in which he again sang with Nicolino and this time with Francesca Cuzzoni, who was the other *diva assoluta* of the century along with Faustina Bordoni; but also, and especially, in *Idaspe* which his brother Riccardo Broschi had written for him and in which he would be able to sing one of the most astonishing arias in his repertoire, *Son qual guerriero in campo armato* (Like an armed warrior on a field of battle): it was an incomparable example of speed and vocal agility which, through continuous virtuoso passages, intervals of an entire octave and changes of key, emphasised his amazing range (from G2 up to C5). Finally, during the two consecutive carnivals of 1733 and 1734, immediately preceding his departure for London, he appeared in five different works, all at the San Giovanni Grisostomo. In 1733 came *Nitocri*, by the Neapolitan Selliti with a libretto by Zeno, singing with the famous Antonia Merighi, and *Adriano in Siria*, by Giacomelli from Piacenza; then in 1734 there followed *Berenice* by the Neapolitan Araya, *Artaserse* by Hasse (which he would sing again in London but with additional arias by Porpora and his brother Riccardo Broschi) and finally *Merope* by Giacomelli, once again to a libretto by Apostolo Zeno.

With *Merope*, which closed the season, the Grimani family decided to celebrate and end with a real fireworks display, both vocal and scenic. Along with Farinelli was his friend and rival Caffarelli (or Caffariello), also a Neapolitan, the tenor Tolve, the excellent women singers Facchinelli and Pierri, and finally there were the décor and scenery by Alessandro Mauro. It was in this last opera that the greatest of singers was to sing one of his favourite arias, *Quell'usignolo ch'è innamorato* by Giacomelli, one of the outstanding numbers that he was to sing regularly for Philip V of Spain. Trills, torrents of notes, intervals ascending and descending, high pitched staccato notes: the entire art of this exceptional singer was there to express the warbling of the nightingale. In his manuscript chronicle of the Venetian entertainments, Benigna noted in sober fashion: '9 March 1734. Last day of the carnival. At 19 hours in the Teatro San Giovanni Grisostomo the performance of *Merope* began, which ended at midnight with the illumination of the theatre; Farinelli was there.'[19]

This list of works performed by Farinelli produces valuable information. On one hand Neapolitan operas predominated, for the singer enjoyed exporting a repertoire which he knew and liked, taking it beyond the Kingdom of Naples. On the other hand we can observe the central place given to librettos by the poet Pietro Metastasio, to which Farinelli always gave pride of place for two reasons: the absolute perfection of the texts, which were to inspire all the composers of the eighteenth and the early nineteenth centuries, from Vivaldi to Mozart and Rossini, and also his profound admiration for the poet, with whom he had made his début in Naples in 1720, and who remained his close friend, his 'dear twin', more so than can ever be imagined, for his entire life. It should be noted that this mere list of Farinelli's eight performances returns us to the stream of great names, male and female, which transformed Venice and its two prestigious theatres, San Cassiano and San Giovanni Grisostomo, into a hub of European musical theatre.

Of the sixty-seven letters written by Farinelli to his protector
Count Sicinio Pepoli – the only ones from the singer that we possess
– thirteen came from Venice: they were written between 6
December 1732, shortly after his return from Vienna, and 8 May
1734. They therefore relate to the singer's third and fourth stay in
the Republic, during two successive carnivals and immediately preceding his departure for London at the end of the summer in 1734.
Like many of his letters those sent from Venice do not always supply
the information that would have been welcome about the theatres,
the audiences, his appearances on stage and his relationships with his
employers. Many speak about details of day-to-day life, the five pairs
of socks he is sending to his Maecenas or the oysters he is having
despatched to the latter's wife, but they also mention future or
current contracts, about which he asks the opinion of his generous
protector.

The minutiae of certain details, however, are worthy of interest:
they reveal fairly clearly the stages of preparation required for a show
and the difficulties encountered by an entire team. Farinelli came to
Venice at the beginning of December 1732 during one of the worst
cold spells ever known. Many canals were frozen, both in Venice and
Mestre, and it was desperately cold in the Teatro San Giovanni
Grisostomo which struggled to sell only a hundred tickets every
evening. However, it was during this hardly favourable weather that
Farinelli, along with the entire population of Venice, attended the
ceremonial arrival of Count Amédée Pio of Savoy, ambassador of the
Holy Roman Emperor, whom he had met during his stay in Vienna.
Sumptuous boats, magnificent liveries, a great procession of riders
from all nations, applause from the Signoria and the population
after the first words in the presentation of the new ambassador: all
the splendour of ceremonial arrivals in Venice, worthy of Canaletto,
were summed up here in a few lines by Farinelli.

Although he went out as little as possible he took advantage of his
stay all the same to listen to an opera in the rival theatre of San
Angelo, to which Vivaldi was attached. It would have been interesting for us if Farinelli had at least been able to hear a work by the Red
Priest and give his impressions of it afterwards, even if he did not
meet the composer. Unfortunately this did not happen and on that
evening the castrato did not find the music he was going to hear very

interesting, apart from the performance from the woman singer Candelli. Not one mention of Vivaldi's name appears in Farinelli's thirteen letters.

Due to the persistent cold, the rehearsals and the very heavy roles that he had to perform after 26 December – no theatrical performances could take place during the two weeks preceding Christmas – Farinelli caught a 'catarrhal head infection' which tired him greatly as he fought against it. Another castrato had fallen much more gravely ill and there were fears that he might soon die. The Grimanis therefore were in dire straits and sent to Fano urgently for another singer in order to be ready for the first night of the carnival. Since the costumes worn by the castrati were usually their own responsibility Farinelli begged Count Pepoli to send the trimmings for his stage clothes, made by one Séraphin, and to send them urgently to the Grimani brothers.

At last 26 December arrived, the first day of the new carnival which was to last until Shrove Tuesday. Fortunately luck was on Farinelli's side and he was able to write the next day with his usual modesty:

> Yesterday evening we went on stage and God be praised, everything passed off well. Of myself I say nothing; I just have to convince myself that God grants me a thousand favours in exchange for my merits; thanks to the success of the opera they have sold more tickets than they did the first year [in 1728–9]. La Merighi is in very good form and everyone was distinguished in keeping with their merits.[20]

This 1733 carnival was notable for two operas already mentioned here and in which Farinelli took the principal roles, alongside La Merighi: *Nitocri* by Zeno and Selliti, and *Adriana in Siria* by Metastasio and Giacomelli, which 'sells a great number of tickets in the evening'. However, the singer remained slightly bitter about one aspect of his third stay in Venice on account of gossip that had gone around. In a city as passionately devoted to gambling as Venice, the rumour had spread that the extremely rich castrato had lost a thousand sequins in some Ridotto: the sort of gossip that was bound to horrify him, for wherever he went he led a solitary retired life, far from fashionable amusements.

After a few months of absence, shared mainly between Lucca, Florence and Bologna, Farinelli returned to Venice for the following year's carnival and began rehearsals in December. The event of the year was the arrival at his side of the other great name from the castrati planet, his rival and friend Gaetano Majorano, known as Caffarelli. In accordance with his habit of playing the star, he arrived late.

> We have begun to rehearse without the Jupiter of music and, after this letter has been written we shall have the second rehearsal, still deprived of Jupiter, the good Caffarelli. The most excellent Grimani people are extremely concerned about this, even more by the speed of time passing.[21]

Caffarelli, in order to attract more attention, arrived a week late. Was that the reason why the first opera, no doubt *Mérope*, by Zeno and Giacomelli, was a total flop, despite the presence of the two sacred monsters?

> On Saturday our opera was performed and was an utter failure. Fortunately two of my arias made a big impression, to such an extent that if these two arias had not been included the next evening, we would have performed nothing at all; for the time being we are managing, thanks to those two arias, but we are hoping to receive some publicity by staging *Artaserse* by the Saxon [Hasse] within a few days . . .

Then there follows this astonishing description, fascinating because it helps us to understand the behaviour and rivalry of the castrati when on stage.

> During the rehearsals Jupiter began to pull faces, as in Bologna, to the point that he was desperately keen to defeat Farinelli . . . and during the rehearsals in the theatre he received all the applause while Farinelli looked like a . . . On the evening of the premiere, when it was time for my two arias, I swear it without any pride, I received more indulgence from the Venetians this year than when I first came; seeing that I was going to get through this in my own way, the more I sang with Jupiter the more I felt sorry

for him, for there wasn't a soul to cheer him, except perhaps on the first evening during the first aria which he sang when I left the stage. Now this same Jupiter talks only of how bad the music is, on the first evening he didn't want to come back on stage, he was whimpering in his dressing-room that he didn't want to appear with me any more. I assure Your Excellency that it's enough to make you die laughing! The libretto contributed greatly to this setback although the music has been blamed for it. If God had not helped me, I swear to you that this year we would have lost all the fame of the past; without pride or vanity I say again that I am very pleased with the success I have had this fourth year.[22]

After this memorable duel, which demonstrates once more the appalling atmosphere that reigned in that world of operatic theatres, Farinelli was to extend his stay in Venice a little, not without suffering further calumnies about the money he was said to have lost and which, it was alleged, forced him to sell land which he owned in order to pay his debts. It was in Venice, on 8 May 1734, that Farinelli announced to Sicinio Pepoli that two days earlier he had signed a contract for his engagement in London and that he would go there in early September. He was then far from imagining that he would not see Italy again for twenty-five years.

Once Farinelli and Caffarelli had left Venice they were followed at once, as from 1735, by another wave of famous castrati who came to sing *Demofonte*: Annibale Pio Fabri, Antonio Bernacchi and Gioacchino Conti, known as Gizziello, for he was a pupil of Domenico Gizzi. In addition to the many Neapolitans there was triumph for the pupils trained in Vienna by Vittoria Tesi, in Bologna, by Pistocchi, Tosi and Bernacchi, the Milanese Appiani or again the great German tenor Anton Raaff, young at the time, who much later was to create the title role of Idomeneo for Mozart. In this first half of the eighteenth century the internationalism of the Venetian stage was becoming a reality.

Satire on behaviour in the theatres

Benedetto Marcello, born in 1686, was an original figure on the Venetian musical landscape of the early eighteenth century. He was not only a writer but also a composer, one who could be described as an 'amateur', since the practice of music for financial purposes was not a priority for him. In fact, unlike Vivaldi and most of the composers and musicians of his time, usually of modest origin, Marcello belonged to one of the greatest patrician families of La Serenissima. This family, who, together with the Capello family, were owners of the Teatro San Angelo, has already been described.

Benedetto and his brother Alessandro Marcello, who was seventeen years his senior, both belonged to the Accademia dell' Arcadia which brought together the great minds and men of letters of the time. In common with all the patricians of the city, their social status led them into having many administrative or political responsibilities and into having roles on the various councils which administered the Republic. In this way, therefore, they were dilettanti in the musical field, that is to say 'amateurs' in the best sense of the term. Benedetto notably was to become famous through his cantatas for solo voice and especially for his fifty psalms set to paraphrased Italian words and collected under the title of *Estro poetico-armonico*. Ten years before his death he considered retiring from the world, which upset many admirers, including the Abbé Conti:

> I don't know if I have told you that Monsieur Marcello has totally given up music; people are even saying that he wants to become a Jesuit or a Capuchin monk. I'm very upset about it, for his compositions had a different kind of merit, either from the impression made by their characteristics, either through their power or through the novelty of the harmonic conception.[23]

Apart from the musical works he left, it is certainly due to his famous satiric work entitled *Il teatro alla moda* (The Fashionable Theatre) that Benedetto has survived. No musicologist, no writing about behaviour in the musical world of the eighteenth century can fail to mention this pamphlet published anonymously in 1720 which remains the most famous work by this Venetian. It has not been quoted earlier because in this way the reader can distinguish more clearly what belongs to the socio-musical history of Venice proper from what remains in the first place a satire, that is to say, an exaggerated and corrosive caricature, even if it is based on perceptive observation of behaviour within the world of theatre. This vitriolic pamphlet could only have been written by a man whose social position allowed him to look down from a great height on the principal theatrical figures of his day: he watched them with irony, sometimes with jealousy and hostility, and, thanks to his remote situation, his culture and intellectual gifts, he could put his finger on everyone's faults, whether they were Venetians or not.

The *Teatro alla moda* is presented as a 'sure and simple method for composing and producing Italian operas, in accordance with modern practice'. It is all advice that was not to be followed, and in this way it presents a list of the mistakes and destructive behaviour of theatrical personalities. Twenty-eight categories of people are targeted, from composer, poets and singers down to costumiers, copyists and those who conducted a black market in admission tickets. The accumulation of these faults could almost make one despair of the theatrical world at this period: incompetent or lazy composers, vainglorious singers totally failing to live up to their own personality, unscrupulous impresarios . . . But it should not be forgotten that this is a satire and that Marcello reflects over a few pages on details noticed here and there, at different periods, in different States and theatres. The facts reported are true, for we know that such abuses existed, but it is the accumulation of them here that astonishes us. The singer, especially the castrato, comes first:

> He will sing on stage with his mouth half-closed, his teeth clenched; in short he will do his utmost to prevent anyone from understanding a single word of what he's uttering, taking care during the recitatives not to pause either at full stops or commas; when he is on stage with somebody else, while the latter addresses himself to the needs of the plot, or sings a little aria, our singer will greet the masked people in the boxes, smile at the musicians or the extras etc., so that the audience will understand clearly that he is Signor Alipio Forconi, castrato, and not Prince Zoroaster, whom he is representing. While the ritornello of the aria is being played the castrato will move away towards the wings, take snuff, tell his friends that he's not in good voice, that he has a

cold etc.; when he is ready to sing his aria, he will take good care to pause at the cadenza as long as he wants to, inventing passages and other pretentious behaviour in his own way; during this time the choir-master will remove his hands from the harpsichord and take snuff, while he waits as the singer takes his time.

Through the capricious behaviour of these performers the writer also attacks the unrealistic acting:

If the castrato is playing the part of a prisoner or a slave, he must appear with hair well powdered, his costume covered with jewellery, sporting a very tall crest on his hat, a sword and very long shiny chains, which he rattles frequently in order to win the audience's compassion . . .

Even his social behaviour outside the theatre is attacked by Marcello with colourful details:

The modern castrato will hesitate about going to sing in a private drawing-room but if it happens he will immediately stand in front of a mirror to adjust his wig, smooth his cuffs and lift up his cravat so that people can see clearly his diamond brooch, etc. Then he will play the harpsichord in a casual way, singing something by heart, beginning several times over as though he couldn't manage it; once he has finished bestowing this favour, he will begin a discussion (in order to receive applause) with some lady, recounting incidents from his travels, correspondence and political stratagems . . . Walking along with some great man of letters he will not offer him his right hand, since he thinks that as far as most men are concerned, the castrato qualifies as a 'virtuoso' while a literary man is just an ordinary man; he will even persuade a man of culture, a *philosophe*, a poet, a mathematician, an orator, etc., to become a musician for, apart from the great dignity conferred on them, they are never short of money, while most intellectuals are dying of hunger.[24]

The capricious attitudes and odd little habits of the women singers also form the subject of a fine anthology piece which is somewhat reminiscent of other behaviour in our time:*

[The modern woman singer], when the impresario approaches her by letter, must not reply at once, and in her early replies she will indicate that *she cannot settle matters so quickly, having received other offers* (although that is not true), then, when she decides, she will always demand the principal role . . . If the poet-librettist goes with the impresario to read his opera to her, she will barely listen to her part, which she claims she will re-write more to her taste, adding or subtracting lines from the recitatives, tearful scenes, madness, despair etc. She will always be late for rehearsals . . . will never sing the arias at the first rehearsal . . . will always make the orchestra go back to the beginning, alleging that the arias are being played too slowly or too quickly . . . She will miss many rehearsals and send her mother instead to make her excuses. She will always moan about her stage costume *which is a poor design, isn't fashionable, has been worn by others*, obliging Signor Procolo to have it remade, sending it back and forth constantly to the tailor, the shoemaker, the wig-maker . . . She will sing all her arias on stage keeping time with her fan or her foot, and if the singer is performing the lead-ing role, she will demand that her noble mother must have the best place in the performers' box. The leading singer will pay little attention to the second singer, and the second will behave the same way towards the third, etc.; she will not listen to the other when on stage and will stand at the side while she is singing, taking snuff offered by her protector, blowing her nose, looking at herself in a mirror, etc. Before leaving the stage she will always take snuff offered by her protector, her friends or some extra, and when she leaves the theatre, accompanied by her friends, she will ask for scarves to protect herself from the cold air . . .[25]

Throughout the pages of this bitter satire Benedetto Marcello was not satisfied by settling his scores with theatre people, sparing

*It should be emphasised that Marcello could have been surprised (and angered) by the débuts in Venice by the greatest virtuosi women of his time: the Venetian singer Faustina Bordoni in 1716, the Florentine Vittoria Tesi and Francesca Cuzzoni from Parma in 1718. All three of them therefore appeared in Venice just before the publication of *Il teatro all moda*.

nobody; he reveals a surprising attitude, for a man of the early eighteenth century, towards the weaknesses of the theatrical illusion,
dear to the baroque era. Whereas the society of his time was still
quite ready to accept the unreality of opera, that element of the marvellous, that enchanting, totally irrational quality that shone over the
drama, Marcello was already reacting against those discrepancies
that were out of keeping with the 'natural' quality of a show. The
audience was moved to tears by the heart-breaking lament of the
prisoner in chains, but Marcello could not resist attacking the contrast between the fancy costumes and the clanking chains of the
fallen hero. The audience uttered an admiring 'oh!' at the sight of
fabulous scenery which showed, in perspective, a brilliant room in a
palace, filled with majestic pillars; at this point Marcello deplores the
fact that in order to please the impresario, the designer had included
far too many pillars, so many that the singers looked twice as tall as
the pillars at the back. Long before the *philosophes* of the
Enlightenment, the *Querelle des Bouffons* and the great improve-
ments in opera performance that took place during the eighteenth
century, Marcello, through his satire, seems to anticipate those intellectuals who, in the name of 'reason' and 'truth' were to deliver a
fatal blow to the spirit of baroque.

Vivaldi's operas in their context

It was only at the age of thirty-eight that Vivaldi began to compose
operas in order to increase his fame, as his French contemporary
Jean-Philippe Rameau was to do when he was fifty. The Red Priest's
reasons, however, seem more obvious to us. From his youth until
1703 he was concentrating on the various stages of his religious
studies, which he worked through quickly. That did not prevent him
from devoting all his energy and passion to the violin, which he
played equally well within his family, with his father, as in churches.
In 1730 the priest gave way to the composer and the teacher: a new
era opened with his entry to the Pietà and his responsibilities as
teacher of the violin and the *viola inglese* and much later as master of
concerts. It was a period when Vivaldi, already prolific, began to
compose many concertos and sonatas, along with the publication in
1711 of his first cycle of concertos, *L'Estro Armonico*, dedicated to

Ferdinand III of Tuscany. If this period can be considered as gratifying for him both through this publication and the teaching results at the Pietà, it did not bring him fame and fortune. Vivaldi therefore, seeing priesthood receding rapidly, rightly wanted both: the only way he could obtain both was by turning to opera, the essential consecration for every musician. Moreover, a prodigious tidal wave of composers and works reached the city, including, in 1707, the return to the fold of Antonio Caldara, then in 1709 the immense success of *Agrippina*, the second of Handel's operas and the first written for Venice, without counting the profusion of operas by Antonio Pollarolo and Tommaso Albinoni.

Vivaldi's first master-stroke was *Ottone in Villa*, first performed in Vicenza, followed the next year by *Orlando finto pazzo*, given in Venice at the Teatro San Angelo. Seventeen-fourteen remained a very good year for him since in addition to his début as a composer of opera in his home city, he also succeeded in publishing his second cycle of concertos, *La Stravaganza*. The Red Priest's first opera clearly marks the start of his long collaboration with the Teatro San Angelo, both as composer and impresario. At this period the theatre was one of the smallest in Venice with its 129 boxes, as against the 150 or so at the Tron and Grimani theatres, but the décor was refined and famous artists were heard there. It was here that Vivaldi was to see the first performances of nineteen out of the twenty-five operas that he composed for Venice. As impresario he had to sign the performers' contracts himself without ever receiving any share in the ownership of the theatre.

Vivaldi's total opera production can be considered here. Even if he maintained that he had written ninety-four, only fifty or so operas can be attributed to him: rather fewer if the figure is limited to original creations, slightly more if we include works that were revised and produced again in a similar form, sometimes with a different name. Out of this real number we possess twenty-three works only through the scores, the others survive only through their librettos. All these scores are in the National Library of Turin, with the exception of one, *Ercole sul Termodonte*, which is in the Bibliothèque Nationale de France, in the conservatoire collection. This production can be examined from two points of view, either within the context of the Vivaldi era or from a contemporary standpoint.

At the time when Vivaldi wrote his music dramas, that is to say, between 1713 and 1739, nothing really distinguished his production from the flood of operas which invaded theatres in all the great cities, as well as the principal courts. As one of the last great representatives of the Venetian school he was subject to the normal competition from the other composers in the Republic and from the 1720s the arrival of Neapolitan production in increasingly great quantities. Since Vivaldi wanted to succeed and grow rich, both as impresario and composer, he was therefore forced to seek outlets in other Italian theatres. Practically all the cities in Venetia, from the Papal States to Tuscany were to open their doors to him during his lifetime, with the exception of the Kingdom of Naples and Piedmont. But without needing to go to all the cities where his work was produced, Vivaldi experienced a geographical spread of influence widened by performances given in Prague, Brno or Graz. Sylvie Mamy,[26] in a very detailed article where she lists all the singers who took part in Vivaldi's operas produced in Europe during his lifetime, reaches a total of nearly eighty productions, from *Ottone in Villa* of 1713 in Vicenza to a revival of *Orlando furioso* in Bassano in 1741, the year of the composer's death.

At first glance this honours list seems impressive, especially with regard to the number of productions; as far as the geographical spread of influence is concerned it remains somewhat modest compared with the works of Hasse or those from the Neapolitan school, performed from Madrid to Dresden and from London to Vienna. In spite of the real successes experienced by Vivaldi in these different States, the fact remains that his fame in the domain of opera bore no comparison to that of his concertos, published in Amsterdam, London and Paris, sold and already performed or re-transcribed across the whole of Europe.

Even in Venice, despite his undeniable success, Vivaldi had to share stardom with his more famous contemporaries. There remained a certain local fame, but it did not always equal that of other Venetians like Pollarolo, Gasparini, Lotti or Albinoni, all much sought after by the singers and the public. His operas even fared less well in comparison with those of Hasse and the Neapolitans, Porpora, Vinci or Leo who took the Venetian theatres and the whole of the Peninsula by storm as from 1725. Vivaldi, it should be remembered, worked essentially for theatres of second or third rank, such as Marcello's San Angelo or the San Samuele owned by Michele Grimani: they were less fashionable than the San Cassiano or the San Giovanni Grisostomo but also less specialised than they were in *opera seria*. Neither were their financial resources on the same scale. Vivaldi could never afford the 'stars' of the moment: neither the castrati Farinelli Caffarelli or Gizzielo, nor the divas Faustina Bordoni or Francesca Cuzzoni. That did not mean that Vivaldi had to be content with second-class singers, for the market offerings were considerable and the level sufficiently high for those taking the title roles to triumph. The performers would have infinitely varied origins, usually outside Venetia. Sylvie Mamy's study quoted above shows that out of the 220 singers, who took part in Vivaldi's operas during his lifetime only about fifty came from Venetia. They could certainly be found in Venice (and never more than two per production), but also in the most far-ranging tours, and in fairly large numbers, in Prague, Brno and Graz. Among the names which occur most often in the Vivaldi productions (Antonio Denzio, Margherita Giacomazzi, Angela Zannucchi, Elisabetta Moro . . .), none could equal the woman who was to become the 'official' performer of the Vivaldi roles: the famous singer of French origin, Anna Giraud, usually spelt Girò by her contemporaries.

What had not been written already in the eighteenth century about the woman who sang and travelled with Vivaldi and shared his life for so many years! It is clear that this close friendship, this difficult relationship, would not have been described so much if Vivaldi had not been a priest. In fact he was not spared mockery and severe criticism. The hardest blow for him was administered by Cardinal Tommaso Ruffo, papal legate at Ferrara and a great enemy of defaulting ecclesiastics: in 1738, suspecting sexual misdemeanour, he forbade Vivaldi to enter Ferrara. This threat explains the Red Priest's desire to spell out the honourable nature of his relationship with Anna and the real reasons that prevented him from saying Mass, in his letter of 16 November 1737 (quoted in Chapter 1). A few days later he again tried to justify himself, astonished that Cardinal Ruffo had shown himself so intransigent while he, Antonio Vivaldi, had been received twice by the Pope himself in his private apartment! He went on:

I never play in the orchestra, except on the night of a Premiere, for I do not condescend to work as an instrumentalist. In private life I do not live with the Girò sisters. Gossips may say what they wish, but Your Excellency knows that I have a house in Venice, which cost me 200 ducats, and the other house, a long way from mine, is the Girò house.[27]

It was probably during his three stays in Mantua, during the years 1718–20, that Vivaldi met the contralto Anna Girò and her half-sister Paolina who acted as chaperone. Anna, the daughter of a French coiffeur, immediately became his pupil and never separated from her teacher again, so much so that she was often called 'the Red Priest's little Anna' *(Annina)*. According to Goldoni she was a beauty full of grace and charm, endowed with an enchanting mouth and with eyes and hair in keeping. Her voice seems to have been rather weak, but she possessed rare gifts as an actress which were not without value at a period when great singers, especially the castrati, behaved like ham-actors when on stage. The 1724–8 seasons marked the consecration of Anna Girò on the Venetian stage, after a striking début in Albinoni's *Laodicea* in 1724. As from 1726 she began to take roles in operas by her teacher, who used his role of impresario to impose her more or less everywhere: 'Putting on an opera without La Girò is not possible,' he told the Marchese Bentivoglio. Vivaldi kept the best roles for her and made sure that she had the greatest number of appearances. Like this, in *Griselda*, Anna Girò and the castrato Valletta had four arias each, while the other singers had only three or two, the number reducing in importance. The prima donna and the *primo uomo* would never tolerate any other way of sharing the arias. Anna Girò even less so. From *Farnace* of 1726 to *Catone in Utica* given in Graz in 1740 the young woman performed fifteen major roles in twenty or so different productions, with the result that she rarely sang in the works of other composers. From long before that time, from his début in the 1720s, Vivaldi would never separate from the two sisters again, even if they did not all live under the same roof.

Then began the great period of Vivaldi's tours, usually linked to opera premieres or official invitations: these explain also the reticent attitude of the Pietà Ospedale authorities, aware of the value and reputation of their maestro, but unable to employ for any length of time a man who was constantly away over hill and dale. When he was re-integrated, as from 1735, voices were again raised against him at any election. The Girò sisters always travelled with him, on all journeys: Anna sang in the theatres but also acted as confidante and accompanist, Paolina was the ideal nurse, always ready to look after this man of frail constitution who undertook journey after journey while complaining that he could not tolerate any of them. Among all the travels that he carried out, and far beyond the value that has been attributed to his operas, three of these journeys show the degree of recognition he had earned as man, violinist and composer of instrumental music. In Rome, where he participated in three opera seasons, he was received by the Pope who asked him to play for him and showered him with compliments. In Vienna, in 1728, the Emperor Charles VI, a skilled musician, received him on several occasions during the two weeks of his stay: he gave him large sums of money, created him a knight, and gave him a gold medallion and chain. Lastly, in Amsterdam, a city which had known his instrumental work for a long time, Vivaldi was invited by the heirs of his publishers to the hundredth anniversary of the Theatre of Schouwburg, on 7 January 1738. A fourth reward could even be added to this list, without the need for any travelling: the series of orders coming from the court of Louis XV, through the intermediary of his ambassador, for celebrating various events linked to the French royal family.

Several musicologists have wondered if Vivaldi was not the principal butt of Marcello's satire in *Il Teatro alla moda*. In it the figures of composer and impresario are attacked in turn:

> [the composer] will take good care not to read the whole opera to avoid losing his way in the text, but he will set it line by line, being careful to change all the arias immediately; for these arias he will use themes already prepared during the previous year; and if the new words for these arias do not fit the notes suitably (which is usually the case), he will pester the poet again until the latter is totally satisfied with it. He won't bother to write duets or choruses, and he will even arrange for them to be removed from the opera ... When the composer is walking along with the

virtuosi, especially the castrati, he will always give them his right
hand, he will carry his hat in his hand, walking one pace behind,
remembering that in the opera the lowest-ranking of these people
is at least a general, a captain of the king or the queen . . . All the
choir-masters today will make sure that the following words are
added beneath the names of the actors: *'The music is once more by
the most celebrated Signor N.N., Master of the Singers, the Chamber,
the Ballet, Master of Arms, etc. etc. etc.'* [The impresario] will
choose a protector in the theatre with whom he will go to meet
the women singers coming from other countries; as soon as they
arrive he will hand them over to him, with their parrots, dogs,
owls, fathers, mothers, brothers, sisters, etc. . . . Most of the company is likely to consist of women; and if two women singers
demand the leading role the impresario will make the poet compose two roles made up of the same number of syllables . . . On
evenings when tickets are not selling very well the modern impresario will permit the *virtuosi* to sing half the number of arias, omit
the recitatives and laugh in the dressing-rooms, etc. . . .

Many questions have been asked about this satire, but no reliable
answer can be supplied, for Marcello left no confidential evidence
about it. Some people find it obvious that the famous pamphlet
attacks the Red Priest directly, for the clear reason that he was one of
the composers and impresarios of the Teatro San Angelo, which
belonged precisely to the Marcello and Capello families. The writer
therefore had been able to watch him with his own eyes from his
débuts there with *Orlando finto pazzo* in 1714, could introduce as
much criticism as he, wished, and even settle old scores, in this
anonymous satire.* In fact Benedetto belonged to two branches of
the Marcello and Cappello families who had no share in the ownership of the city's theatres, including the San Angelo. But the main
argument of those who reject this theory lies elsewhere. What is said
in the satire obviously applies to dozens of composers, impresarios
and singers.* Marcello speaks extensively about the musical world of

---

* The first page of Marcello's book mentions that the work had been printed by Aldiviva
Licante. Now this does seem to be an anagram of A.Vivaldi. Much other word-play can be
found on this frontispiece, mentioning the singer Anna-Maria Strada, the poet Giovanni
Palazzi, the composer Giovanni Porta, etc.

his time, in its totality, and it would be very difficult to see only Vivaldi in it, while the weaknesses described in the pamphlet have been known for centuries. Moreover, *Il Teatro alla moda* was undertaken in about 1718–19 and published in 1720: Vivaldi was still only making his début in the world of opera, beginning in Venice in 1714, and he still did not possess that impressive list of scores and contracts that were to characterise the 1730s. If there can be no doubt that Marcello had him in his sights, along with others like him, this was a time when trickery, vanity, the urge to create and the obligation to checkmate one's rivals were paramount.

Throughout all the operas that he created in Venice or abroad Vivaldi seems to have merged into the landscape of his time, without attempting to take the art of opera towards new horizons. Conventionality remained the rule, both in the choice of libretti and in a respect for form: three acts, each divided into ten or twenty scenes in which recitative and arias succeeded each other. If his libretti were mediocre or if they came from the great poets of the time, Vivaldi did not hesitate to rearrange the different moments of the action according to the diktat of the singers, for it was they who made and unmade works according to their whims. It is worth remembering the famous visit by Goldoni to Vivaldi during which the poet was to rewrite on the spot a scene from *Griselda* by Apostolo Zeno, in order to satisfy the wishes of Anna Girò. Two libretti, however, stand out from this vast production: the two very fine texts by Metastasio which were to inspire many composers of the century, the *Olimpiade*, first performed in 1734 in Venice, and *Alessandro nelle Indie*, first performed in Prato in 1736.

Neither was there any originality in the themes that were chosen or the way the work was divided between the singers. Vivaldi, faithful to tradition but also to the satisfaction of his public, chose subjects from mythology and the ancient world, or again from the tales of mediaeval chivalry drawn from Ariosto and Tasso. However, there was a small, fairly new departure towards the exotic world in *Teuzzone*, set in China, or in *Montezuma*, set in the Aztec empire. Five principal roles, and two secondary ones, following the usual

*The satire about the composer who was 'married to a *virtuosa*' is aimed in particular at the master of the chapel at St Mark's, Antonio Lotti, married to the singer Santa Stella.

arrangement of the period, expressed in turn the heartbreaking conflicts between love and honour, passion and pity, gratitude and
hatred. The Vivaldian characters (abominable tyrant, faithful abandoned wife, avenging widow, brave warrior madly in love . . .),
despite the superb arias that they give us today, remain perfect
stereotypes of their genre. Vivaldi did not try to rebel against the
smooth development of the contemporary opera, while his instrumental music, especially that of the concertos, reveals an astonish-
ingly innovative style, that would change the usual way of
composition in many countries.

There remains, therefore, the way we can look at the catalogue of
Vivaldi's operas today. At first it looks as though a certain number of
parameters have changed. We no longer live in that over-abundance
which meant that the successes or failures of the Red Priest have been
drowned or lost among so many others. The scores are there, certainly, but the performance and recordings of baroque operas which
are offered to us are merely a drop in the ocean of what the period
produced. Who today knows the operas of Alessandro Scarlatti,
Albinoni or Lotti? Where can we see or hear them? Apart from the
work of Handel, which is much more current on the stage or available in discographies, Italian *opera seria* is the poor relation among
our modern rediscoveries. It is really nobody's fault. The public is not
always ready to spend three hours immersed in these successions of
sometimes interminable arias sung by different characters which was
the main source of pleasure of Venetian or Neapolitan operas. And
then we no longer have the castrati, those outstanding, rare singers
whose penetrating voices and incredible vocal prowess were enough
to overwhelm the spectators of their time.

Today Vivaldi tends to profit rather from this rediscovery, thanks
to the fame he enjoys through his concertos. Who, even those less
well versed in the world of classical music, could fail to recognise or
simply admire the extremely famous *Four Seasons*? This is what has
led the same public to take an interest in the Red Priest's operas. Ten
or twelve of them are included in catalogues of records or compact
discs, which is still a small number compared to the twenty or so
operas by him that we know, but many when compared with the
recordings available today of works by Hasse or Porpora, much more
famous in the past among European composers. In addition there

are collections of individual arias recorded by different performers, male or female, which the exceptional singer Cecilia Bartoli had made one of her specialities. With her, as previously Marilyn Horn or others, a whole wonderful world opened for us, a world of melodic invention, with a sumptuous vocal quality and a truly amazing instrumental richness, to the point where each new recording is an event.

Vivaldi's concertos already make up a voluminous catalogue but his operatic arias continue to surprise us. Without any doubt the palm goes to those which were composed before 1725, that is to say during Vivaldi's first operatic period: the Neapolitan influence had not yet made itself felt and the maestro was not yet rushing round the theatres, risking over-production and weakening his inspiration. It is there, in his spontaneous works, that his dual talents of instrumentalist and man of the theatre blend most brilliantly. The composer of concertos is to be heard here, introducing his most varied arias and the most beautiful instrumental ritournelles. Beyond the conventional use of two horns for hunting scenes or trumpets and kettledrums for martial moments, commonly used by Handel and all the contemporary composers, Vivaldi varies the treatment of his arias and their accompaniments with infinite subtlety: sometimes two piccolos, sometimes a bassoon or a psaltery, an oboe or a solo 'cello in one place and a tenor flute in another. In each case a superb concertante prelude leads in to the entry of the singer who is then engaged in an extremely long dialogue with these instruments played *obligato*. In the aria *Di due bei rai languir costante*, published in a collection of separate pieces in 1720 without any indication of what opera it belongs to, the airy grace of two recorders, with the twists and turns of their ornamentation, form a contrast with the sober melodic line for the singer. The same enchantment can be found in *Ho nel petto un cor si forte*, an aria belonging to the title role in *Giustino*: the highly elegant and fluid timbre of the psaltery, accompanied only by the pizzicato on the strings, produces a moment of delight reminiscent of the most poetic pages of the concertos for mandolins.

Since Vivaldi often repeated passages throughout his operatic production, we should not be surprised either when extracts from certain concertos reappear in the arias. *The Four Seasons* were obviously involved in this: if the re-use of the first movement of *Spring* remains fairly banal in *Dorilla in Tempe*, the re-use of the beginning of *Winter* in Farnace's aria *Gelido in ogni vena* succeeds in creating a climate of suspense and suppressed terror which, if it is well sung, can intensify emotion to a maximum. Despite the harmonic marches and other facilities which Vivaldi sometimes over-uses, he is unique through the magic of timbre he achieves, and through this he shows that he is most of all a master of instrumental music and knew how to use this gift in creating his most beautiful operatic arias.

Vivaldi's second period, roughly from 1725–6 to 1739, differs noticeably from the first through this loss of instrumental colour in exchange for the voice alone. The arias are fewer but last longer. The Neapolitan influence has done its work and the Red Priest was to make it a duty to compete on the technical level with the most striking arias of Hasse, Porpora or Riccardo Broschi, brother of Farinelli. The orchestra, racked by tremolos or ascending or descending scales, loses its originality, but gives way to those vocal pyrotechnics of which the castrati and the great women singers possessed the secret. Idaspe's aria in *Il Tamerlano* (*Anch'il mar par che sommerga*), that of Orlando (*Nel profondo*), the astonishing hunting song (*Dopo un'orrida procella*) or the wild half-spoken aria that ends the first act of *Griselda* (*Ho il cor già lacero*), all breath-taking in their virtuosity, can rejoin without difficulty the pantheon of the most beautiful bravura arias from the end of the baroque period.

Antonio Vivaldi, who came to the opera through reason rather than personal passion, has left us a body of lyrical work that is fairly considerable but inevitably unequal: the sublime alternates with unavoidable longueurs. If this collection does not always attain the value of his 500 concertos or sinfonias or of his sacred music, it shows in any case that, through the unique character of certain pages, as well as through the time and energy devoted to this repertoire, what a hard worker he was, this tireless man who was devoured by a passion for music.

CHAPTER 6

Musical splendour of the private palazzi

Yesterday evening I went to a fête (one of the finest I have
ever attended) given by Signor Mocenigo . . .
Lady Mary Wortley Montagu

Operatic theatres, carnival, religious ceremonies and great civic festivities are by definition available to everyone. In Venice, collective
pleasures and ostentatious splendour were part of the art of living.
But the palaces, embassies, academies and other private circles none
the less overflowed with literary and musical activities. In summer, a
holiday on the banks of the river Brenta meant that princely delights
could be adapted to the joys of relaxation and 'ecological' pleasures
of a countryside that did not exist in Venice. A whole aspect of
Venetian daily life, less well known but equally resplendent was
revealed to visitors and other guests of note who were often full of
admiration for the riches of this parallel culture.

The 'academies' or music at home

During the eighteenth century the word 'academy' took on two very
different meanings. The first and more obvious of them described a
society of intellectuals, men of letters, *philosophes* or scientists, who
met regularly and exchanged literary, philosophical, aesthetic or
musical ideas, and regenerated themselves through the election of
new members, who were handpicked. The most famous of all Italian

academies was incontestably Arcadia, founded in Rome by Vincenzo
Gravina in 1690. When it started life great names from the musical
world, such as Corelli, Pasquini or Alessandro Scarlatti, father of
Domenico, belonged to it. As can be understood in a country like
Italy at that period, musicians and poets met side by side in a spirit
of mutual recognition and dignity.

The following year, the poet and future reformer of the opera,
Apostolo Zeno, founded in Venice the Academy of the *Animosi*,
which was not the first of its kind but was to become the most prestigious in the Republic. Carlo Francesco Pollarolo, but also the
brothers Alessandro and Benedetto Marcello, those famous 'amateur' musicians, also belonged to the new learned society. From 1691
to 1698 the Venetian academy existed on its own before asking to be
affiliated to the Arcadia in Rome, without losing its name. Several
academies in the Peninsula were to act in the same manner and move
closer to the famous Roman society.

As in most academies of this type the life of the *Animosi* was punc-
tuated by weekly meetings which allowed verbal jousting on suggested themes. Every Monday in spring or autumn the
academicians, who belonged essentially to the nobility, came to dis-
cuss, using poetry and music as subjects of their argument, topics
such as 'What is the greatest misfortune known to man?' or 'What
is more powerful, the love of fame or the love of beauty?'

The prestige of such gatherings soon began to flow from the
music that was heard there in addition to the vocal arguments that
the members listened to. As a rule contradictory attitudes ended
with a concert which supplied at the same time both demonstration and conclusion, as *Pallade Veneta* described: 'On Monday the
gentlemen of the *Animosi*, with all the power of their erudition
which is the rightful quality of great geniuses, resolved the problem under discussion by very fine music and rare compositions.'[1]
A few years earlier, in the Academy of the *Inetti*, three members
ended the discussion one day by performing three cantatas, each of
which took up in music the concepts expressed in the vocal argument. During the whole of the eighteenth century the excellence
of the ideas and the music, that subtle alliance between poetry and
the arts, was to motivate the spread of concerts in palaces and private homes.

Among all the academies known in the seventeenth and eighteenth centuries (the *Uniti*, the *Unisoni*, the *Rinnovati*, etc.), one of the most famous was the Philharmonic Academy of Venice. A list from 1711 mentions 192 members including fifteen procurators of St Mark's. The high-ranking nobility dominated this society that was dedicated to the amateur practice of music but also to performances of tragedies, acted or recited by the aristocrats themselves. Twice a week these nobles met in order to form an orchestra and play together, but no doubt in order to complete their number and perfect their art, they accepted professional musicians who were paid for their participation.

A very beautiful illustration of this academy is available to us thanks to the painter Gabriele Bella. The scene represented the concert given by the young girls from various *ospedali* to the Count and Countess du Nord in 1782. These names were in fact those assumed by the Grand Duke Paul Petrovitch, heir to the Russian throne, and his wife. The two of them, travelling incognito, although their identity was soon out in the open, were making a long journey through several European countries. Their stay in Venice necessarily implied some fine musical evenings, including this concert by the orphan girls. One interesting fact about this is that it did not take place in one of the *ospedali*, but in a salon of the Philharmonic Academy, situated in the Procuratie Nuove, by St Mark's square. The vast rectangular salon shown in the picture, hung with silk panels and blue draperies, is arranged like the auditorium of a theatre: seven rows of spectators face a raised platform on which the young girls were placed in three very steep tiers. As a result all the spectators to the performance could see the singers who, for once, were not concealed by grilles, but on this occasion of course they were outside the *ospedale* and it was the end of the century when the rules tended to be relaxed. Catherine II's son and his wife are seated in the back row in order to have a good view of the platform without having to raise their heads like those in the front row. Bella's painting is rich in practical information about a concert which, it should be remembered, had an unusual aspect. The young musicians, singers and instrumentalists, were not concealed, there were about eighty of them (the painting does not show them all, but this figure is authentic), which makes them more numerous than the audience, who totalled about sixty. The instrumentalists occupied the first row, while the singers were in the two rows above. As in the *ospedale* churches the young girls look down on the audience and sounds come from above. The clothes worn by the spectators are also interesting: while the Venetian aristocrats all wear their traditional black, and the men did not remove their black tricorne hats, the two foreign guests are wearing bright colours, on this occasion bright red, forming a sharp contrast to so many dark colours. This evening of 20 January 1782 at the Philharmonic Academy preceded by two days the other splendid soirée organised by the Procurator Pesaro for his Russian guests: a lavish dinner of oysters and truffles, with music, on the stage at the Teatro San Benedetto, shortly after which the tables were taken down and the stage transformed into a ballroom.

This noble Philharmonic Academy, into which other personalities would be introduced during the eighteenth century, must not be confused with the Philharmonic Society of Saint Cecilia, founded by Legrenzi in 1690. Its role in fact was quite different since it acted as a kind of 'musicians' trade union', reminiscent of the old guilds of the Middle Ages. From the beginning, out of the sixteen names listed after the founder, Legrenzi, thirteen were priests, plus two lay members, one of whom was the father of Antonio Vivaldi. Women always had the right to belong to the Society and over the years we find the names of the singers Santa Stella, the wife of Lotti, and even the famous Faustina Bordoni, wife of Hasse, in addition to 'noble ladies' such as Elisabetta Bon or Elena Soranzo. Among the men, who were much more numerous, are procurators of Saint Mark's, as well as the names of the greatest families, such as Mocenigo, Gradenigo or Pisani. The society, which at first was limited to a hundred members, would treble in numbers during the second half of the eighteenth century, but always aimed to bring together the musicians who were working in Venice as singers or instrumentalists as well as their patrons, great 'amateurs' of music.

The aim of the Society of Saint Cecilia, like all the other corporations of the period, was to protect the members during professional conflicts, help them to find engagements, arrange insurance in the event of illness and, if the family could not do so, to provide a decent funeral. Protection against illness shows the definite modernism of this society which tried to protect the individual against the main risks in life, the only condition being membership of the Society for at least a year in order to be a beneficiary.

So the sick man or woman would receive two ducats per week for three months, sometimes longer if the illness continued. Unlike the poorest socio-professional categories, who received this sum each week, the members of the Philharmonic Society received a single payment, on their recovery, proving that they did not belong to those too destitute to wait so long for what was their due.

Funerals occupied a central place in the activities of the society. When a member died, all the other members had to be present, suitably dressed, with cassock and white surplice, for the religious ceremony. Anyone who was absent without good reason was fined half a ducat. The dead man's parish would later celebrate as many masses as there were members registered at that time. On 23 November every year a Mass was said in memory of every member of the Society who had died during the year and all current members of the Society were earnestly invited to take part in them.

As for the ceremonies which marked the annual feast of Saint Cecilia in the church of San Martino, they were, as always in Venice, of exceptional lustre, if only by the gathering of so many musicians and singers, all clad in cassock and surplice. The feast of Saint Cecilia, held in a richly decorated church, with a musical programme fitting for such an assembly of professionals, could not fail to attract the entire population of Venice:

> The faithful went on Sunday to the church of San Martino where they were celebrating the feast of Saint Cecilia, patron saint of musicians; not only were all the singers from the doge's Chapel there, but also many of those who perform music in our theatres; they said a solemn Mass and vespers, piously attended by almost the entire city.[2]

The second use of the word 'academy', the one to be considered in the following pages, deals more widely with the very high-class musical soirées held in all the private circles of Venice, from the leading aristocratic palaces to the simple apartments owned by bourgeois families and professional musicians. As always in Venice, music was everywhere, and with that astonishing frequency that so amazed the

Président of the Dijon Parlement ('there is hardly an evening without an academy somewhere').

These amateur musical soirées ('amateur' in the best possible
meaning of the word) brought together people who were passionately fond of singing and instrumental music, both in their own
homes or in semi-public halls where small-scale concerts of chamber
music were given. Sometimes the music for these was composed by
the dilettanti themselves, sometimes a score had been commissioned
from one of the many composers of the city. During his stay at the
French Embassy Jean-Jacques Rousseau was amazed that making
music was so cheap: 'I hired a harpsichord, and for a mere écu I had
four or five musicians at my home with whom I practised once a
week, playing the pieces that had given me most pleasure at the
Opéra.'[3] The musical potential of Venice was inexhaustible and
everyone could find something to suit them, both in the choice of
scores they could perform and at the more or less high standard of
these soirées. Sometimes two or three academies were announced for
the same evening.

Among the most modest were the private apartments of ordinary
middle-class people who invited friends and relations merely for the
pleasure of making music together. 'My father', one of them remembered, 'occupied a very large house in the Calle Lunga at Santa
Caterina and had put aside one room just for making music. A
violin, a 'cello and a large spinet were there permanently. He had
filled it with a great deal of older and new music by the best composers and he arranged academies there from time to time.'[4] The
composers themselves received people in their houses and invited
artists to play their music and those of their colleagues. *Pallade
Veneta* described 'a superb academy of instrumentalists and voices' at
the house of the composer Legrenzi when he was chapel master at St
Mark's.

Three young Frenchwomen came, watched over by their famous
parents. These three sisters – let us call them the three graces, for
they are sisters – sang duets and trios in French, composed by
Monsieur Jean-Baptiste Lully from Paris. The eldest girl, who was
17, played the accompaniments with an inexplicable ease and
sang soprano. The second, aged 13, sang contralto and the third,

aged 10 (and that was a miracle), sang bass, as well as anyone could wish, with such a voice, that, if you heard her sing without seeing her face to face, nobody could imagine that such a sound could issue from such a chest and such a throat. We heard a concerto for strings, composed by Signore Legrenzi, whose art cannot be surpassed. Signore Pietro Bertacchini da Carpi, from Modena, played the guitar and transfixed the listeners present; this lofty genius was able to raise the guitar, in itself imperfect, to the total perfection required by the harmony of the music. He accompanied Signore Legrenzi, then, at his request, he accompanied himself alone. The most distinguished members of the aristocracy were present and everyone had the impression that these few hours passed in a single moment.[5]

Nothing however equalled the splendour and the very high musical level attained by the patrician palaces in the city. The great families, who on the outside observed a somewhat sober, almost austere lifestyle with their black gondolas and black clothes, lived in private on a scale which recalled the finest courts of Europe. In 1680 Saint-Didier was amazed that during meals the courses were announced to the music of fifes; after dinner singers were brought in who performed a few operatic arias, accompanied by a harpsichord, a theorbo, a violin or a 'cello. Concerts given in private during the eighteenth century were to reach a height of perfection and attract the admiration of visitors. They included concertos by Vivaldi or Marcello, symphonies were played and barcarolles sung, even operas were performed for the first time in the drawing-rooms of these palaces. At the homes of the Grimani, the Gritti or the Labia, to mention only a few, the quality of the performances received unanimous praise from the memoir-writers and the press of the time. In about 1780 Dr Burney was to state that the music at these private concerts in Venice was better than he had heard elsewhere in similar circumstances. In the 1770s a traveller left us an entertaining account after attending an academy at the Balbi's:

I was sitting by Signora Balbi, who would be my beauty, my siren, if I were to stay longer in Venice. In the sweetest, most seductive voice she sang to us the loveliest barcarolles, then arias, and after-

wards she told us charming stories. She persuaded the Swedish
scholar Biornhstaldt to sing, and he made us die of laughing,
especially when she told him to get himself castrated if he wanted
her to enjoy his singing.[6]

As always, music was never very far away from festivities and
dancing. Many evenings consisting of concerts ended with rejoicing
of this kind, especially if some personality was present in Venice, or
when a new procurator for St Mark's was elected. Many foreign
princes, when visiting the city, took advantage of the very special
Venetian context, where people wore masks for several months of
the year, to choose the anonymous life. The Senate then placed at
their disposal four members of the principal Venetian families,
chosen with great care. The latter were to serve as chaperones during
their outings and they had to grant their every wish. Obviously this
arrangement provided companionship as well as a form of supervision. Churches, palazzi, theatres, but also outings to the islands and
visits to the glass factories at Murano thus became the daily lifestyle
of these distinguished guests. After an evening at the opera the
august visitors were usually taken to some palace where they were
offered various games and a ball. Sometimes even a composer and a
musician were placed at their disposal, who in this way could supply
a pleasant musical background to their stay at the palace or to their
nocturnal outings along the canals.

A good example was such a visit by Frederick Augustus of Saxony
who attended the 1716 carnival in Venice and stayed there a whole
year to take advantage of this exceptional city. In addition to the parties, banquets, balls and entertainments of all kinds to which he was
taken, the German Elector decided to bring from Dresden his best
musicians – Johann Pisendel, Jan Zelenka – so that they could learn
from the Venetian masters. A good example of integration was that
of the violinist Pisendel who became so friendly with Vivaldi and
Albinoni that the latter both dedicated several of their works to him.
Pisendel was overwhelmed when he left for Dresden, where he was
to become a chapel master and in his turn was to make Venetian
sonatas and concertos known in northern Europe. The departure of
Frederick Augustus was a pretext for lavish musical homage by the
Mocenigo family, who were to invite Tartini and Veracini, while the

Pisani offered him parties, serenades and bull runs at their villa on the banks of the Brenta. Some Venetians, in their turn, obtained permission from the procurators of St Mark's to follow the Saxon prince as far as Dresden: in this way the composer Antonio Lotti, the bass singer Boschi and the double-bass player Personelli would export the musical models of Venice to the banks of the Elbe.

There was more or less the same kind of festivity to celebrate the election of a procurator at St Mark's, the highest honorary distinction after that of doge. For three successive days then his palace became the theatrical setting for celebrations during which the guests, who were always masked, divided their time between balls and feasting. Then the new procurator went to the church of San Salvatore to hear Mass, before leaving in procession towards the Merzerie, surrounded with a crowd of nobles dressed in purple, in order to visit the doge, bow before him and offer his thanks.

A party with the Contarini family

At the end of the eighteenth century many small European courts would have envied the fortune and the panache of the Contarini family. The letters of Monsieur de Vaumorière, reprinted in Paris by *Le Mercure Galant* and many writings by contemporary travellers describe the amazing celebrations of which a patrician Venetian family were capable, on this occasion that of the procurator Contarini in about 1680. These descriptions are given here because they reveal as an example the unique art possessed by a noble family, the art of receiving guests and organising festivities in a summer residence on the mainland. The Contarini's possessed at Piazzola on the Brenta, between Venice and Padua, what was modestly called at the time a 'villa', which was in fact a superb palace. It was surrounded with canals which also served as reservoirs and emptied into a gigantic circular pool, surrounded with arcades and statues. It was deep enough to receive a flotilla of sailing craft and gondolas from which serenades and small-scale concerts were given on mild summer evenings.

The caring tradition was strongly rooted in this patrician society which had already created the four *ospedali* and Marco Contarini wanted to create a small 'foundation' at his summer property, to be built round a church and to be more beautiful and larger than the one in the neighbouring town. Thirty-three poor young girls were brought up there as apprentices for various household tasks, but also, and especially, to be trained in music: the procurator Contarini reproduced here a private mini-*ospedale* from which he of course expected equally good results in the musical field. Very soon superb voices emerged from this feminine community and it was for them he built a small private theatre of exceptional splendour: it was inaugurated on 11 March 1678 with no fewer than a hundred boxes all magnificently furnished and hung with tapestries.

The connections and the fortune of the procurator also allowed him to commission specifically for this theatre a few operas from the great Venetian masters of the moment, asking them to adapt their subject for the privileged performers of Piazzola, that is for a large number of women's voices. The theatre was inaugurated with *Les Amazones dans les isles fortunées* (The Amazons of the fortunate Isles), an opera by Pallavicino revived the following year along with a second work, *Bérénice vindicatrice*, to music by Freschi.

The performances of these two entertainments, in November 1680, expressed both the refinement and the large-scale settings devised solely for the guests invited to this celebration. On the first day the opera from the previous year, *Les Amazones*, lasting three and a half hours was given again. Among the 300 performers were a hundred Amazon women, a hundred men disguised as Moors, fifty men on horseback, without counting the pages, lackeys, coachmen, etc. At the end of the performance there appeared on stage a carriage covered with gold ornamentation, drawn by frisky chargers.

The next evening was given over to a simple 'promenade' in front of the palace by more than 150 carriages, each drawn by six horses, carrying the Venetian and foreign élite, riding in state. This elegant parade was reminiscent of the carrousels organised in Paris during the youth of Louis XIV or in Rome when Christina of Sweden arrived. In short, the Venetian aristocracy, inevitably frustrated by the oligarchic ideals of the Republic, was determined to show that its members behaved like the other nobility of Europe, especially when they retired to their properties in the country. In the same way the evening ended with a ball of exceptional magnificence both in the quality of dress and the amount of precious jewellery.

Finally, on the last evening, the culminating moments of the festivities, the crowd of guests were invited to the palace theatre, lit up
for the occasion by twenty white wax torches, voluted and gilded.
That evening *Bérénice vindicatrice* was given, surpassing in magnificence everything that had been seen in the first opera. In accordance
with the rules for a baroque celebration, each evening had to be
better than the last, and bring about even more emotional shock for
the spectators; no evening should cause regret for the preceding one.
This time the show was to last five hours and include 500 performers who were to appear all together in the scene of triumph: a hundred pike-bearers, a hundred women, a hundred proud riders, sixty
halberdiers and many others still, all in costume, and with décors
completely different from those in the first opera. The procurator's
guests, who had been regaled with exquisite food throughout these
spectacles, were even taken by surprise, when they left, to find themselves presented with the furniture and tapestries from their theatre
box. As for the music, the 'special correspondent' of *Le Mercure
Galant*[7] merely noted that it 'was delightful', proving that the splendour of such a prestigious display, comparable to those of the finest
court fêtes at Versailles, had definitely outstripped the attention paid
to the music alone.

Ceremonies and receptions at the embassies

Venice, capital of an independent Republic, was as a result the seat
of several embassies and 'residencies' of the principal States of
Europe. Among the most important were those of the Austrian
emperor, the kings of France, Spain and England, situated in various
palazzi throughout the city, on purpose distant from that of the
doge. In this way 'the Palais de France' was at Cannaregio, not far
from the railway station of today.

For Venice the arrival of an ambassador was an additional occasion to display its pomp, while the people profited from extra holidays. The first day brought the ceremonial entry of the ambassador
in a luxuriously decorated boat, surrounded with a cortège of 4,000
craft and gondolas; after his craft had tied up in front of the doge's
palace, the ambassador spoke a few words and received homage and
applause from the crowd. The next day he was enthroned in the

Collegio salon inside the palace. The doge, wearing his golden cloak, was seated on the throne, flanked by his six counsellors, the three chiefs of the Quaranzia Criminale, the six Great Sages, the five Sages from Terra Ferma, the five Sages from the Orders, and by Secretaries. The ritual seemed immutable, as shown by the gentleman in waiting to the Abbé de Pomponne, who was ceremonially welcomed in 1705.

When the doge saw Monsieur the Ambassador arriving he stood up and did not remove his hat, the senators stood up and removed theirs. Monsieur the Ambassador bowed three times, once on entering, the second time in the middle of the room and the third time at the foot of the steps to the throne; then he sat down on the right of the doge, put his hat on and presented to him the letter from the King, and that from Monsieur the Dauphin. The doge handed them to the Secretary, who read them aloud, after which the Ambassador removed his hat and began his speech. Every time he mentioned the King, Monsieur the Dauphin and the Republic, he removed his hat and spoke in this way for half an hour. The doge replied to him in a few words; after which the Ambassador rose to his feet, bowed three times as he had done on entering and rejoined the knight who placed him on his right, as before.[8]

Many nobles and ladies attended this ceremony of great pomp: they were already masked, for this official occasion was the start of three feast days in Venice. One or two hours after his return to the Palais de France the ambassador received the gifts from the doge: sixteen bowls of various preserves and twenty-four bottles of white and red wine.*

During these two days the embassy was open to all masked people, who could find refreshments at two buffets served by twelve men in black coats. Doors and staircases were guarded by soldiers to prevent disorder and possible thefts of valuable objects. Outside 4,000 pounds of bread and six barrels of wine were distributed to the people. In the street, which was illuminated, twelve trumpets, eleven

*Until the seventeenth century the ambassador also received wax, hams, mortadella, salted tongues, Bologna sausages, sturgeon and two large cheeses.

oboes and twelve drums played without a pause. The four following days were given over to visits of congratulations from the Spanish ambassador, the papal nuncio, the Receiver of Malta, the Resident of Mantua of the Duke of Sforza. Those who could not come sent their compliments.

It goes without saying that ceremonies of this sort for the arrival of an ambassador initiated a display of pomp no less splendid at every moment of his stay in the Republic, especially when his country had to celebrate great events, such as the marriage of a sovereign, a royal birth, an anniversary or a victory. Life at the embassies, which was already luxurious in itself, took on a particular character in Venice. In the first place it was because the ambassadors, their families and their staff, wore the richly attractive court dress, which contrasted with the universal black clothes of the local aristocrats. Then, because of the difficulty experienced in entering into contact with the Venetian patricians, always on their guard, they were obliged to live in autarchy, arranging their own festive occasions for themselves, their compatriots and their guests from other friendly embassies:

> One meets foreign ministers from all parts of the world, [wrote Lady Montagu] and since there is no court to occupy them, they are delighted to enter into contact with foreigners of quality. Since I am the only lady in Venice at the moment I can assure you that I am toasted as if I were the only woman in the world.[9]

Lastly, all this was done because the monarchies represented by the embassies had constantly to cultivate their image as people of note in order to make a suitable impression on the Republic.

Formal embassy celebrations for which descriptions are available give a preponderant place to music and show a great awareness of the current repertoire in Venice at that period. When the Abbé de Pomponne was ambassador it was usual to meet once a week to hold an academy with instruments and voices. Ladies and knights of first rank attended, sometimes even nobles from the mainland, but never any aristocrat from the city whose appearance at an embassy would cost him his life.

Let us imagine for a moment the arrival of guests of note at the Palais de France on the evening of a reception. They would come by gondola across the lagoon and recognise the Embassy by the eight large poles, painted blue and white with fleurs de lys alongside the floating landing stage. The big garden door, surmounted with the French coat of arms, opened on to two courtyards, traversed by a path bordered by lemon and orange trees along with thirty or so statues. On reaching the top of the big staircase, where they were greeted by four Moors carrying candlesticks, the guests finally reached the series of state rooms, each one illuminated by four six-branched rock-crystal chandeliers, without counting the girandoles which ornamented the mantelpieces and the tall silver candlesticks that stood on each table. In all these salons, as in the adjoining rooms, masked visitors could help themselves to any amount of chilled water, hot or cold chocolate, tea and coffee. The most sumptuous room was the audience chamber, entirely hung with Flemish tapestries and works by master painters. This room housed the canopy of gold brocade, surmounted with a portrait of the French king: all official encounters took place by this canopy, while conversations continued between people seated in the eighteen gilt wooden armchairs upholstered in the same fabric as that used for the canopy. During the soirée the guests were invited to go down to the small private embassy theatre, where twelve candlesticks emphasised superbly the quality of the velvets and crimson damask on the walls and seats. An orchestra of fifteen or so instruments then gave a delightful concert for His Excellency and his guests. Late at night, when some people treated themselves to a last collation, some masked ladies began to go back to the landing stage to await their transport, chatting as they sat on benches covered with Turkish carpeting and velvet cushions in different colours.

Every year, the date of 25 August formed a pretext for a grand musical evening,

On Saint Louis' day, His Excellency, wishing to give a magnificent supper to Messieurs the ministers and their ladies, arranged a very fine concert at the end of the garden, which would be well illuminated. Many members of the nobility came by boat along the canal. The Electress of Bavaria also came in a gondola and the gentlemen from the court of His Excellency presented her with all kinds of gifts and refreshments. Then offerings were made politely to several ladies. This concert lasted three hours and afterwards a supper was given, including the most choice meats and game in season; all kinds of wines and liqueurs were served in quantity. In a word, no expense was spared.[10]

The opera season, starting in early October, was also the time when most official dinners were given. Florentines, people from Bologna, Bavarians, Swedes, Germans and, naturally, passing French visitors, were the usual guests of the French ambassador.

The other embassies knew an equally rich musical life. In 1748 for example Vivaldi went to the Spanish Embassy where he accompanied Anna Girò on the harpsichord until the small hours. In January 1746, when Maria-Theresa of Austria and Francis I of Lorraine came to Venice, the official ceremonies arranged in the Jesuit church were enlivened by the best musicians of the city. In the evening the Emperor's ambassador illuminated his palace as well as the Fondaco de' Tedeschi (the German trade counter) on the Grand Canal, as had been done in 1716 to celebrate the birth of the Archduke Leopold. Whatever embassy was involved, these festivities were accompanied by the same kind of rejoicing: money and bread were distributed to the poor, fireworks lit up the lagoon and the canals, while fountains of wine ran for hours on the campi.

The art of the 'serenade'

In addition to the song recitals, concertos, symphonies and sonatas that were fashionable, one of the privileged musical forms used at festivities and private soirées was the *serenata*. It was a kind of cantata which appeared in about 1660, requiring a small number of singers and musicians; it was well suited to evenings in the open air. In that way it retained the original meaning of the word, current since the fifteenth century: 'serenade', a piece played in the open air under a clear sky (*sereno*: meaning calm, clear), in a boat or beneath the windows of one's lady-love. But later it became a much more complex work, with a libretto set to music by a great composer, sometimes substituted for an opera, in both public and private theatres.

A serenade required three or four soloists, a small string orchestra sometimes augmented by wind instruments, and a choir. Unlike an opera it was an entertainment easy to organise, very well suited to the 'one-day theatres' set up in a courtyard, a garden or a small square, for the festive period. Further, many serenades included allegorical characters and events, ideal for celebrating some famous event: for the Venetians, the election of a new doge, a marriage uniting two noble families, the public reception of a procurator or an invitation to a famous visitor; for an embassy, the allegorical subject of the serenade, its gods and heroes, its nymphs and shepherds, celebrated in an ideal way the fame of the monarch, the benefits of his policy or the good fortunes of his family.

During Vivaldi's lifetime the French Embassy often found itself under the gaze of the Venetians and passing foreigners due to the frequency and splendour of the parties it gave. Several French ambassadors succeeded each other during the half-century corresponding to the last years of Louis XIV's reign and the early years of Louis XV: Joseph-Antoine Hennequin de Charmont (1701–4), Henri-Charles Arnault, the Abbé de Pomponne (1705–9), Jacques-Vincent Languet, Baron de Gergy (1723–31) and Charles-François de Froullay (1733–43).*

As from 1638 lavish fêtes had celebrated the birth of Louis XIV and later other events, accompanied by a *Te Deum* had marked the king's return to good health in 1687. Vivaldi, a young man making his débuts at La Pietà, knew in his turn the cheerful atmosphere that reigned at the French Embassy in 1704, when the Duc de Bretagne was born, 'great grandson of the very Christian Louis the Great, king of France and Navarre': the palace was illuminated and crowds of masked people hastened there to hear concerts and see the fireworks. On this occasion a *Te Deum* was sung and the composer Vinaccesi wrote the serenade *Sfoghi di giubilo* (Outbursts of joy): its success was so great that it was sent to Versailles to be performed before the court. Fame, Virtue, the Faith of the People and the Spirit of France made up the allegorical figures of this spectacle.[11]

Louis XV's youthfulness did not change the luxury of these

---

*This list corresponds to the period of Vivaldi's musical activity. There was no French ambassador in Venice for fourteen years (1709–23), due to the cooling of diplomatic relations between France and the Republic following the Treaty of Westphalia. Neither was there any ambassador between 1731 and 1733.

performances. This time Vivaldi moved from mere spectator to principal actor. By now his reputation was sufficiently established in Venice and abroad for France to order some commemorative serenades from him. One of these was given at the embassy on 12 November 1725 on the occasion of the king's marriage to Maria Lesczinska. The Red Priest was no longer a beginner in this kind of work since he had already written two serenades, one in 1708 for the departure of the governor Francesco Querini and the other in 1722 in Brescia for the visit made to the city by the Princess of Salzbach. Venice was not among the first cities to take up this form of entertainment, for the serenade remained a perfect allegory of the royal or princely court: but Venice had no court, despite the splendours of the Republic. Vivaldi profited therefore from the orders he received from other countries in order to develop this aspect of his repertoire.

This was notably the case with the very beautiful *Senna festeggiante* (The Seine *en fête*). It is not known for which real occasion Vivaldi wrote it. Was it one more commission from the ambassador Languet? Was it written for his official arrival in Venice, 4 or 5 November 1726, or for Louis XV's feast day, one 25 August? Whatever the occasion this serenade remains one of the most representative of the genre; based on a libretto by Domenico Lalli, it is written for three solo violins and a choir, along with, in homage to France, an overture in the French style at the beginning of the second part. The few directions that we possess (two or more oboes, two or more flutes . . .) might suggest that it was performed in the open air.

In this way, when Jacques-Vincent Languet was ambassador, allegorical spectacles in praise of the French royal family were to become more frequent. Venetian and French newspapers did not fail to describe these prestigious musical events. In May 1727 the minister Maurepas asked the ambassador to organise celebrations for the birth of Mesdames Royales, the king's twin daughters, 'with less pomp than if a dauphin had been born but in keeping with the king's pleasure.'[12] Vivaldi was again brought into service. He took advantage of this to compose a *Te Deum* and a serenade lasting almost two hours, entitled *L'Unione della Pace e di Morte* (The Union of Peace and Death). An artificial stage was set up on the water: the guests watched from the embassy gardens while the Venetians, both nobles and ordinary people who were not invited, admired the performance from boats on the lagoon. This at least is what can be assumed from the description given in *Le Mercure de France* a few months later:

> At about eight o'clock in the evening, all outside walls of the Palace were illuminated, as well as a kind of amphitheatre or platform set up on the lagoon on large boats. This construction was sixty feet high and fifty feet wide, representing the Palace of the Sun as described by Ovid. In the middle of this palace, standing on twelve Corinthian columns, was a statue of Apollo with his lyre, and surmounting everything were the arms of France. The edifice was completed by a brilliant image of the sun on top of a pyramid. One could also see the signs of the Zodiac, with that of the Twins in the middle of them.[13]

Two years later it was Albinoni whom the ambassador chose when the birth of the dauphin was celebrated with a sumptuous fête. On each occasion His Excellency would dutifully describe to Versailles the magnificence of the fête that was organised, the music heard on this occasion, but also the fountains of wine, the fireworks and the unique good taste of the illuminations.

The diplomatic autonomy enjoyed by the ambassadors did not prevent a strict check on their slightest activities by the secret police. The doge and the Council of Ten could know everything about the manifestations that were organised, the people invited and the extent to which these fêtes were successful. Hence this entertaining 'confidential report', which does not hesitate to give the writer's own impressions after he had spied on a French fête in August 1736:

> Yesterday evening the French ambassador gave an entertainment with an instrumental concert and supper for gentlemen and ladies, by invitation. The Papal Nuncio and the Spanish Ambassador were there, but not the Austrian Ambassador. There were eighteen people at the high table ... The supper was not very impressive: only two services of sixteen dishes and eight at the other table, where the Ambassador's son and five other guests were sitting ... There were illuminations on three levels at the end of

the garden and in each square of grass a single group of eight candles ... which were no more than candle-ends, worth possibly ten
or perhaps eight pounds each, not more ... wretched things in
fact! This celebration took place for the king's patronal festival,
Saint Louis' day.[14]

EPILOGUE

Death in . . . Vienna

List of deaths in Vienna. 28 July, in our city, the
Very Reverend Signor Antonio Vivaldi, secular
priest, in the Walleris house, near the Carinthia
Gate, aged 60.
Wiener Diarium, 2 August 1741

This brief announcement in the Viennese newspaper is the one and
only epitaph granted to the composer of *The Four Seasons*, who died
in the capital of the Holy Roman Empire, far away and forgotten by
everyone. The archives of St Stephen's Cathedral set out the (minimal) sum of money spent on the burial in the hospital cemetery,*
stating that the Red Priest's body had been accompanied by the
tolling of a single bell, that was reserved for the poor or for people
who were on their own and without any family.

'What on earth was he doing there?' as Molière would have said.
We have to look back a little. Until 1736 there was no hint of any
decline in Vivaldi's career as a composer. He was in fact at the height
of his fame and until 1740 even experienced two occasions when he
shone in the presence of eminent persons. In March 1740 Prince
Ferdinand Charles of Saxony, the king's son, went to La Pietà and
attended a concert 'with many instruments played by the young girls
of the pious ospedale', as stated by the manuscript score which is
today in Dresden. Shortly afterwards it was Ferdinand of Prussia,

---

*The cemetery lay partly below the present building of the University of Technical Sciences
and partly below the esplanade situated in front of the Karlskirche.

brother of the elector prince, who went to La Pietà and heard Vivaldi's dramatic cantata, *Mopso*, subtitled 'eclogue for fishermen in five voices'. It had a huge success. Antonio was warmly congratulated and generously rewarded.

In fact, despite these two very successful performances in Vivaldi's 'kingdom' of La Pietà, the composer had experienced many difficulties since 1737. Stormy relationships had set in between the Ferrara theatres and himself over the production of his operas. In 1738 his *Siroe*, performed in that city, had been very badly received. Even in Venice Charles de Brosses realised that the Red Priest no longer enjoyed the same reputation as in the past. *Sic transit gloria mundi*: the Venetians turned away from a composer who, both in his operas and his concertos, seemed to have renewed himself little in more than thirty years.

The operas, despite the sublime pages which stand out here and there, remained within the conventional forms of their time and never reached the two big prestigious theatres of the city. The few setbacks experienced by Vivaldi in Venice or in other capitals certainly represented nothing serious in the context of the period and it would be ridiculous to see them as the reasons for the composer's decline. To be hissed or applauded was the daily lot of those who wrote dozens of dramatic scores during the course of their life and depended more than ever on the singers available to them A star singer, man or woman, could rescue a mediocre score while a feeble one could destroy the finest creation. Disappointment may have arisen for him from the fact that his operas had always been born of a need to belong to the gratifying and lucrative world of the stage, a world for which, as Vivaldi knew, without really wanting to admit it, he was less well suited than for the world of instrumental music. His rival in Padua, the violinist Giuseppe Tartini, gave the perfect analysis of the risk taken by the Red Priest: 'Everyone must know how to limit himself to his own talent. I have been invited to work for the theatre in Venice but I have never wanted to do so, knowing very well that a throat is not the neck of a violin. Vivaldi, who wanted to be equal in both genres was always hissed in one while he succeeded well in the other.'[1] Despite this somewhat unkind exaggeration in the last sentence Tartini put his finger on Vivaldi's weak point and others repeated what he said, including Goldoni, who was to go so far as to speak of a 'mediocre composer', soon forgotten by his contemporaries.

The genius of Vivaldi therefore lies in his concertos, his sonatas and a certain number of sacred musical works. It is here therefore that his international dimension is expressed, even if only one concerto out of five was published during his lifetime. In any case there was enough here for him to acquire an 'aura' which hardly faded during his lifetime, especially abroad. But it is true that the form of his concertos went through a minimal evolution which may have reached a Venetian public who were accustomed, perhaps too much so, to hearing his work during the concerts and ceremonies at La Pietà.

In any case, the facts are there: after 1737 Vivaldi experienced serious setbacks at Ferrara, he accumulated worries, especially the criticisms of Cardinal Ruffo about his private life, and was forced to accept the loss of affection and ingratitude of the Venetians towards him. His departure for Vienna, in September 1740, indicated his desire to find new recognition in a great musical capital, along with, possibly, his secret desire to take his revenge upon Venice by taking his talent to other music-lovers who would be more receptive. When Anna Girò sang in Graz during the 1739–40 season, Antonio stopped there for a time on his way to Vienna. If one thing could have led him to attempt such an adventure that autumn, it could have been entering the service of a monarch like Charles VI, a music-lover and an excellent musician who had always given an enthusiastic welcome to great artists: Vivaldi himself in 1728 and Farinelli in 1733 had every reason to realise it.

The rest is known to us, and for those who listen to Vivaldi with delight three centuries later this story seems a shocking débâcle. He had barely arrived in Vienna when he heard that Charles VI had died on 20 October. The man who could have become his protector and ensure him of a comfortable situation, especially at a court that was dominated musically by Italians, was no more. Vivaldi did not even receive help from the Emperor Francis of Lorraine, husband of the great Maria Theresa, although he had established a privileged relationship with her. The Red Priest was certainly known in this city, as in Dresden, London or Paris, but nobody was really expecting him. Commissions and contracts became rare. Other composers occupied the terrain.

The winter of 1740–1 was to be fatal to him. Nobody knew precisely what real illness was going to kill him, unless it was the 'internal inflammation' which has been given as the official explanation. One last tangible sign of his presence in Vienna is available to us, the receipt for a sale of concertos to Count Collalto, dated 26 June 1741. The last document written in his hand is today in the Moravian museum at Brno. On 28 July, less than a year after his arrival, Vivaldi died in poverty, unknown to anyone, and was buried the same day. A funeral service of the greatest simplicity was held in St Stephen's cathedral. Among the choirboys who accompanied the Red Priest's body there was apparently a boy of nine whose name would be well known at the end of the century: it was Josef Haydn.

In Venice as in the rest of Europe Vivaldi was very quickly forgotten. We should not fail to mention that he still belonged to the baroque period, and at that time people believed that a work of art was only valid for the moment and died with its creator. A serenade vanished when the candles were put out; an opera was out of date the following year. 'Everything changes,' said Bossuet, 'everything leaves us and we ourselves come to an end.' Antonio Vivaldi suffered more or less the same fate as his contemporary Johann Sebastian Bach, one of whose sons was almost surprised, twenty years after his death, at being able, 'still' to play some works by his father in public. With the disappearance of the maestro Vivaldi his works disappeared too, and Venice was one of the first cities to forget him. The changeable nature of its people and the success of the composers who took over were sufficient reasons for finding him old fashioned. Venice, although so attached to its ancestral ceremonies, had no taste for the music of the past. During the nineteenth century many countries would come to know Vivaldi's work through transcriptions carried out here and there rather than through the original compositions.

We had to wait therefore until the end of the twentieth century not only to discover his date of birth, in 1762 actually, but also, and especially, to bring out of limbo the vast production of Vivaldi and record it. After more than two centuries in the dark this music has at last appeared in the full light of day, this music that is 'dominated from first to last by the vital solar power of rhythm'.[2]

Notes

Chapter 1: A city, its people, and music

1 C. Goldoni, *Mémoires*, Paris, 1787, vol. I, p. 280.
2 J.-J. Rousseau, *Confessions*, Everyman's Library, 1931, vol. I, pp. 286–7.
3 J.-J. Rousseau, *Dictionnaire de musique*, see *Barcarolles*.
4 J.-J. Rousseau, *Essai sur l'origine des langues* . . ., c. 1760, ch. VI.
5 *Pallade Veneta*, 18–25 July 1711, f. 4.
6 *Ibid.*, 20–7 June 1716, ff. 1–2.
7 *Guida de' Forestieri*, 1724, p. 8.
8 See in particular the many songs in manuscript preserved at the Museo Correr or at the Biblioteca Querini-Stampalia.
9 Nella Anfuso has recorded on CD (Stilnovo 8803) 'Venetian Songs', anonymous, eighteenth century.
10 Charles Burney, ed. Percy A. Scholes, *Dr. Burney's Musical Tours in Europe*, Oxford University Press, 1959, vol. I, p. 118.
11 P.-J. Grosley, *New Observations on Italy* . . ., vol. II.
12 A. Goudar, *Remarques sur la musique* . . ., pp. 20–1.
13 E. Wright, *Some Observations* . . . (1720–2), quoted by Talbot, *Sacred vocal music* . . ., p. 8.
14 A. Vivaldi, letter of 16 November 1737, published by A. Cavicchi, *Nuova Rivista Musicale Italiana*, 1967, vol. I, p. 6.
15 Ch. de Brosses, *Voyage en Italie*, letter of 29 August 1739.
16 C. Goldoni, *Mémoires*, in *Tutte le opere*, pp. 164–6.
17 Letter retranscribed by M. Rinaldo, *Il teatro musicale* . . ., p. 1.

Chapter 2: Discovering Venice in Vivaldi's day

1 M. de Silhouette, Voyage . . ., 1729–1730, pp. 150–2.
2 Cardinal de Bernis, *Mémoires*, p. 123.

3 M. Misson, *Nouveau voyage d'Italie fait en l'année 1688*, vol. I, p. 198.

4 *Ibid.*, p. 202.

5 J. Addison, *Remarques sur divers endroits d'Italie . . .*, p. 4.

6 These paintings and clock faces can be seen in E. Selfridge-Field, *Pallade Veneta*, 1985, pp. 54–5.

7 P.-J. Grosley, *New observations on Italy . . .*, vol. I, p. 248.

8 G. Commisso, *Les agents secrets de Venise au XVIIIe siècle*, denunciation of a certain Francesco Faletti, 31 August 1747.

9 Charles de Brosses, letter of 29 August 1739.

10 *Ibid.*, letter of 14 August 1739.

11 G. Baretti, *Les Italiens ou moeurs et coutumes d'Italie*, 1773, p. 183.

12 M. Misson, *op. cit.*, vol. I, p. 179.

13 Charles de Brosses, *op. cit.*, letter of 20 August 1739.

14 Cardinal de Bernis, *op. cit.*, p. 116.

15 G. Baretti, *op. cit.* pp. 182–3.

16 Abbé Chiari, *Commedia da camera*, act I, scene 3.

17 A. Conti, *Lettres à Mme de Caylus*, 13 April 1727.

18 See this poem by Barbaro in Malamani, *Il Settecento*, vol. I, p. 4.

19 Pöllnitz, *Lettres*, 15 May 1730.

20 G. Renier Michiel, *Origine delle Feste Veneziane*, 1829, new edition 1916.

21 Giovanni Battista Albrizzi, *Forestiere illuminato* 1740, p. 332.

22 Abbé Conti, *Lettres . . .*, 28 July 1727.

23 G. Casanova, *Histoire de ma vie*.

24 M. de Silhouette, *op cit.*, pp. 132–3.

25 A. Benigna, *Libro di memorie*, fo 20v and 21r.

26 G. Casanova, *Confutazione*, vol. II, p. 104.

27 M. Misson, *op. cit.*, vol. I, pp. 182–3.

28 Pöllnitz, *Lettres*, London 1741, letter of 15 May 1730, vol. II, pp. 115–16.

29 Addison, *Remarks on several parts of Italy . . .*, vol. iv, p. 4.

30 Pöllnitz, *ibid.*

31 Comte de Caylus, *Voyage d'Italie*, 1714–15, p. 112.

32 Abbé Conti, *Lettres . . .*, 27 February 1727.

33 Abbé Conti, *ibid.*

Chapter 3: The Ospedali, or the musical fame for the poorest of people

1 *Pallade Veneta*, 31 Dec.1701–7 Jan. 1702, f. 2.
2 Arch. IRE., Der. A.3, f.C. 21v.
3 For these three examples: Arch. IRE. *Nottatorio* de l'Ospedaletto (1732–48).
4 Pëtr Andreievitch Toltago, May 1698, referred to by Walter Koldener, *Nuova Rivista Musicale Italiana*, Jan.–March 1979, pp. 13-14.
5 *Pallade Veneta*, 24–31 May 1704, f. 1.
6 *Ibid.*, 9–16 November 1702, f. 3.
7 Ch. de Brosses, *Voyage en Italie (1739–40)*, letter of 29 August 1739.
8 Casotti, letter of 20 July 1713, quoted by P.G. Molmenti, *Epistolari veneziani del secolo XVIIIo*, p. 439.
9 *Guida de' Forestieri*, 1697, unpaginated.
10 Arch. IRE, Musica Der.G 1, n.48 f.v.
11 *Ibid.*, 50r.v.
12 *Pallade Veneta*, Feb. 1687, pp. 106–7.
13 Lady Mary Wortley Montagu, *Letters from the Right Honourable Lady Mary Wortley Montagu*, Everyman's Library no. 69, p. 284.
14 J.-J. Rousseau, *Confessions, op. cit.*, p. 288.
15 Arch. IRE, Musica Der G.1, n.48, f. 80r, 29 June 1717.
16 ASV, Osp. B.688, 7/G, f. 191.
17 See R. Giazotto, *Vivaldi*, pp. 383–8.
18 *Pallade Veneta*, July 1667, quoted by Talbot, *Sacred Music . . .*, pp. 108–9.
19 Version conducted by Alessandro de Marchi, with the girls' choir of the Accademia Santa Cecilia (Opus 111).
20 These manuscripts are in the Raccolta Carvalhaes at the library of the Conservatorio Santa Cecilia in Rome. See complete list in the article by G. Rostirolla, *Nuova Rivista Musicale Italiana*, Jan.–March 1979.
21 *Pallade Veneta*, 17–24 May 1704, f. 1.
22 *Ibid.*, 28 Mar. to 4 April and 25 April–2 May 1711.
23 ASV, Osp, B692, Not. Q.c. 113.
24 Ch. de Brosses, *op. cit.*, 29 Aug. 1739.

25 I. Stravinsky, *Gespräche mit Robert Craft*, Zurich, 1961, p. 103.
26 J.J. Quantz, 1714, in Marpurg, *Historisch-kritische Beitrage zur Aufnahme der Musik*, 5 vols, Berlin, 1754–60.

Chapter 4: Sacred music and religious festivals

1 G. Burnet, *Voyage de Suisse, d'Italie* ..., Rotterdam, 1690, p. 226.
2 *Ibid.*, p. 231.
3 P.-J. Grosley, *New observations* ..., vol. I, p. 257.
4 See for the one parish of S. Giacomo di Rialto the list of expenses preserved at the Museo Correr (Code Cicogna 3255).
5 Ch. de Brosses, *op. cit.*, letter of 20 August.
6 *Pallade Veneta*, September 1687, pp. 29–30.
7 A. Benigna, *Libro di Memorie*, Bibl. Marciana, Cod.It., Cl. VII–1620 (=7846).
8 See the description included in the periodical *La Galleria di Minerva*, à propos of doge Mocenigo, 6 May 1709.
9 M. Misson, vol. I, pp. 172–3.
10 V. Malamani, *Satire* ..., p. 117.
11 G. Comisso, *Les agents secrets de Venise au XVIIIe siècle*, Grasset, 1944, p. 111.
12 Abbé Conti, *Lettres à Mme de Caylus*, undated (end February or early March 1727?).
13 Bibl. Marciana, Ms. Cigogna 3118/46/7.
14 Comte de Caylus, *Voyage d'Italie, 1714–15*, p. 4.
15 M. de Silhouette, *op. cit.*, p. 148.
16 J. Addison, *Remarks on several parts of Italy, 1701-1703*.
17 Abbé Conti, *op. cit.*, letter of 3 Sept. 1727.
18 Ch. de Brosses, *op. cit.*, letter of 14 August 1739.
19 L. Bianconi, *Il seicento*, p. 134.

Chapter 5: Venetian opera and its public

1 *Pallade Veneta*, Jan. 1687, pp. 79–82.
2 See Malamani, *Satires*, p. 63.
3 Quoted by M. Rinaldi, p. 30.

4 Ch. de Brosses, *Lettres familières d'Italie (Lettre sur les spectacles, op. cit.*

5 Cardinal de Bernis, *Mémoires*, pp. 124–5.

6 M. Misson, *op. cit.*, vol. I, pp. 186–7.

7 *Gazzetta Veneta*, no. 86, 29 Nov. 1760.

8 C. Ivanovich, *op. cit.*, p. 408.

9 *Réflexions d'un patriote sur l'opéra François et sur l'opéra italien*, Lausanne, 1754, quoted by Talbot, *Vivaldi.*

10 Venise, Arch. di Stato, Notarile, Atti, box 11857, notaio, Ridelfi: 12 Mar. 1739, no. 4.

11 C. Ivanovich, *op. cit.* pp. 388–9.

12 M. de Vaumorière (d. 1693), *Lettres sur toutes sortes de sujets*, vol. II, Paris, 1714.

13 E. Wright, *op. cit.*, vol. I, pp. 84–5.

14 *Farinelli, le castrat des Lumières*, Patrick Barbier, Grasset, 1994.

15 Abbé Conti, *op. cit.*, letter of 30 Dec. 1728.

16 *Ibid.*, 4 December 1728.

17 *Ibid.* (undated letter, end Nov. or early Dec. 1728?).

18 *Ibid.*, 4 August 1728.

19 A. Benigna, *Libro di memorie*, ms. f. 52.

20 Carlo Broschi Farinelli, Bologna Arch. di Stato, Fondo Pepoli box 11 bis, letter of 27 Dec., 1732. These letters have been published by Francesca Boris and Carlo Vitali, in *La solitudine amica*, Sellerio, 2000.

21 *Ibid.*, letter of 12 December 1733.

22 *Ibid.*, letter of 2 January 1734.

23 Abbé Conti, letter of 23 September 1728.

24 B. Marcello, *Il teatro alla moda*, ed. Pizzicato, 1996, pp. 23–7 (*A' Musici*).

25 *Ibid.*, pp. 23–38 (*Alle cantatrici*).

26 S. Mamy, 'La diaspora dei cantanti veneziani', *Nuovi Studi Vivaldiani*, vol. 2, see lists pp. 596–629 etc.

27 Letter from Vivaldi to Bentivoglio, 23 Nov. in State Archives, Ferrara, *Codice di lettere di diversi del marchese Guido Bentivoglio d'Aragona*, vol. IV, ff. 476–7.

28 B. Marcello, *op. cit.*, pp. 15–22 (*A' compositori di musica*) and pp. 39–42 (*Agl'impresari*).

Chapter 6: Musical splendour of the private palazzi

1 *Pallade Veneta*, 20–27 Nov. 1698, f. 2.
2 *Ibid.*, 21–28 Nov. 1739, ff. 1–2.
3 J.-J. Rousseau, *Confessions, op, cit.*, vol. I, p. 288.
4 Foppa, *Memorie storiche*, p. 18.
5 *Pallade Veneta*, March 1688, pp. 58–60.
6 Guys, *Voyage littéraire de la Grèce*, 1776, vol. II, p. 500.
7 *Mercure Galant*, Feb. 1681, pp. 213–49.
8 Archives des Affaires Etrangères, *Mémoires et documents*, Venise 27, f. 13rv.
9 Montagu, Lady Mary Wortley, *op. cit.*, Letter of 6 Nov. 1739, p. 277 (to Lady Pomfret).
10 Archives des Affaires Etrangères, *idem*, Venise 27, f. 30r.
11 Archives des Affaires Etrangères, Correspondence Politique, Venise, vol. 139, July 1704. Includes a complete libretto of this serenade.
12 Archives des Affaires Etrangères, Correspondence Politique, Venise, vol. 180–1, letter from Maurepas to Languet, 19 August 1727.
13 *Mercure de France*, October 1727, col. 2326.
14 See G. Comisso, *Les agents secrets de Venise . . .*, *op. cit.*, report by Antonio Caimo, p. 22, 27 August 1736.

Epilogue: Death in . . . Vienna

1 Quoted by A. Capri, *G. Tartini*, Milan, 1945, p. 8.
2 M. Bontempelli, *Passione incompiuta. Scritti sulla musica*, Milan, 1958, pp. 387–8.

Bibliography and archive sources

1. Memoirs, letters, travel – seventeenth and eighteenth centuries

ADDISON, Joseph, *Remarks on several parts of Italy in the years 1701, 1702, 1703*, London, 1726.

ALBRIZZI, Giovanni Battista, *Forestiere Illuminato intorno le cose piu rare, e curiose, antiche e moderne della città di Venezia*, 1740.

BARETTI, Giuseppe, *Les Italiens ou mœurs et coutumes d'Italie*, translated from the English, Geneva-Paris, 1773.

BECKFORD, William, *Italy, with sketches of Spain and Portugal*, Paris, 1834.

BERNIS, Cardinal de, *Mémoires*, Mercure de France, 1986.

BROSSES, Charles de, *Lettres familières d'Italie (1739–1740)*, Editions Complexe, 1995.

— *Lettres d'Italie sur les spectacles et la musique* (published in 1755), Paris, La Flûte de Pan, 1980.

BURNET, Gilbert, *Voyage de Suisse, d'Italie et de quelques endroits d'Allemagne et de France, fait ès années 1685 et 1686*, Rotterdam, 1690.

CASANOVA DE SEINGALT, Giacomo, *Histoire de ma vie*, 3 vols, Bouquiras collection, Robert Laffont, 1999.

CAYLUS, Comte de, *Voyage d'Italie (1714–1715)*, 1st edition, Paris, Fischbacher, 1914.

CORONELLI, Vincenzo, *Guida de' Forestieri*, Venice, 1697 and 1724.

DOTTI, Bartolomeo, *Satire*, Geneva, 1757.

EVELYN, John, *Diary*, 1643.

GOLDONI, Carlo, *Mémoires pour servir à l'histoire de sa vie et à celle de son théâtre*, Aubier, 1992.

GOUDAR, Ange, *Le brigandage de la musique italienne*, 1777.

— *Remarques sur la musique et la danse à Milord Pembroke*, Venice, Palese, 1773.

— *Supplément aux remarques sur la musique et la danse, ou lettres de Mr G . . . à Milord Pembroke*, Venice, Palese, 1773.

GOZZI, Carlo, *Memorie inutili*, Venice, 1797.

GOZZI, Gaspare, *Gazzetta Veneta*, 1760–61.

GRETRY, *Mémoires ou essais sur la musique*, 2 vols 1789, 2nd edition 1797.

GROSLEY, Pierre-Jean, *Lettres inédites écrites de l'armée d'Italie en 1745 et 1746*, Troyes, 1897.

— *Lettres inédites écrites pendant son voyage d'Italie et de France en 1758–1759*, Troyes, 1907.

— *New observations on Italy and its inhabitants*, 2 vols, London, 1769.

GUYOT DE MERVILLE, *Voyage historique d'Italie*, 2 vols, La Haye, 1729.

IVANOVICH, Cristoforo, *Minerva al tavolino . . . nel fine Le Memorie teatrali di Venezia*, Venice, 1681.

LAMBERTI, Antonio, *Ceti e classi sociali nel '700 a Venezia*, Bologna, 1959.

MISSON, Maximilien, *Nouveau voyage d'Italie fait en l'année 1688*, La Haye, 1691.

MONTAGU, Lady Mary Wortley, *Letters, 1763–7*. Everyman's Library No. 69.

ORTES, Gimmaria, *Lettere a Francesco Algarrotti* (letters from 1746 to 1779), Venice, 1840.

— *Riflessioni sopra i drammi per musica*, Venice, 1757.

PÖLLNITZ, Baron de, *Lettres* (5 vols), London, 1741.

QUANTZ, Johann Joachim, see MARPURG, *Historisch-kritische Beiträge zur Aufnahme der Musik*, 5 vols, Berlin, 1754–60.

Racolta di cose sacre che si soglion cantare dalle pie vergini dell'Ospitale dei poveri Derelitti, rare document in the Fondazione Querini Stampalia, 1777.

ROUSSEAU, Jean-Jacques, *Confessions*, Everyman's Library 2 vols, nos 259–60.

SAINT-DIDIER, Alexandre-Toussaint de, *La Ville et la République de Venise*, La Haye, 1685.

SILHOUETTE, M. de, *Voyage de France, d'Espagne, du Portugal et d'Italie, du 22 avril 1729 au 6 février 1730*, Paris, Merlin, 1770.

THOMPSON, Charles, *The travels of the late Charles Thompson*, Reading, Newbery, 1744.

WRIGHT, Edward, *Some observations made in traveling through France, Italy etc ... in the years 1720, 1721 and 1722*, 2 vols, London, 1730.

2. Printed or written sources – nineteenth and twentieth centuries

BALDAUF-BERDES, Jane, *Women Musicians of Venice, Musical Foundations 1525–1855*, Oxford, Clarendon Press, 1993.

BASSO, Alberto, *L'età di Bach e di Haendel*, Turin, Edizioni di Torino, new ed. 1991.

BIANCONI, Lorenzo, *Il Seicento*, Turin, Edizioni di Torino, new ed. 1991.

BIANCONI, Lorenzo and MORELLI, Giovanni (editors), *Antonio Vivaldi, teatro musicale, cultura e società*, Fond. Giorgio Cini, Florence, Olschki, 1982.

BOURNET, A., *Venise, Notes prises dans la bibliothèque d'un vieux Vénitien*, Paris, Plon, 1882.

BRAUNSTEIN, P. and DELORT, R., *Venise, portrait historique d'une cité*, Paris, Coll. Points, Seuil, 1971.

BRIDGMAN, Nanie, *La musique à Venise*, PUF, Que sais-je? no. 2172.

CAFFI, Francesco, *Storia della musica sacra nella già cappella ducale di San Marco (dal 1318 al 1797)*, Fond. Giorgio Cini, Florence, Olschki, 1987.

CERESOLE, Victor, *Jean-Jacques Rousseau à Venise (1743–1744)*, Geneva-Paris, 1885.

CICOGNA, Emmanuele, *Delle inscrizioni veneziane*, vol. V, Venice, 1842.

COMISSO, Giovanni, *Les agents secrets de Venise au XVIIIe siècle*, selected and published by G.C. Paris, Grasset, 1944.

DEGRADA, Francesco (ed.), *Vivaldi veneziano europeo*, Fond. Giorgio Cini, Florence, Olschki, 1980.

DEGRADA, Francesco and MURARO, Maria Teresa (editors),

Antonio Vivaldi da Venezia all'Europa, Milan, Electa ed., 1978.

DIEHL, Charles, *Une république patricienne, Venise*, Paris, Flammarion, 1915.

FANNA, Antonio and TALBOT, Michael (editors), *Vivaldi vero o falso*, Fond. Giorgio Cini, Florence, Olschki, 1992.

FONTANA, Alessandro and SARO, Georges (anthology selected by), *Venise 1297–1797, La République des Castors*, ENS Ed., Fontenay Saint-Cloud, 1997.

HELLER, Karl, *Vivaldi, Cronologia della vita e dell'opera*, Fond. Giorgio Cini, Florence Olschki, 1991.

KOLDENER, Walter, *Antonio Vivaldi, his life and work*, Univ. of California Press, 1970.

LAINI, Marinella, *Vita musicale a Venezia durante la Repubblica, Istituzioni e mecenatismo*, Venice, Stamperia di Venezia, 1993.

LECLERC, Hélène, *Venise baroque et l'opéra*, Paris, Armand Colin, 1987.

LOGAN, Oliver, *Venezia, cultura e società, 1470–1790*, Rome, Veltro ed., 1980.

MALAMANI, Vittorio, *La satira del costume a Venezia nel secolo XVIII*, Venice, Filippi, 1886.

MAMY, Sylvie, *Les grands castrats napolitains à Venise au XVIIIe siècle*, Liège, Mardaga, 1994.

— *La musique à Venise et l'imaginaire français des Lumières*, Paris, Bibl. Nat. de France, 1996.

MOLMENTI, P.G., *La Storia di Venezia nella vita privata dalle origini alla caduta della Repubblica*, 3rd edition, Turin, 1885.

MONNIER, Philippe, *Venise au XVIIIe siècle*, Paris, Perrin, 1907.

MOORE, James H., *Vespers at St. Mark's*, 2 vols, UMI Research Press, 1981.

MURARO, Maria Teresa (editor), *Venezia e il melodramma nel Seicento*, Florence, Olschki, 1976.

— *Venezia e il melodramma nel Settecento*, Florence, Olschki, vol. 1 1978: vol. 2 1981.

RENIER MICHIEL, Giustina, *Origine delle Feste veneziane*, 1829, republished 1916.

RINALDI, Mario, *Il teatro musicale di Antonio Vivaldi*, Florence, Olschki, 1979.

ROBBINS LANDON, H.C., *Vivaldi 1678–1741*, French translation by D. Collins, Paris, J.-C. Lattès, 1994.

ROBBINS LANDON, H.C. and NORWICH, J.-J., *Cinq siècles de musique à Venise*, French translation by Béatrice Vierne, Paris, J.-C. Lattès, 1991.

SACCARDO, Rosanna, *La stampa periodica veneziana fino alla caduta della Repubblica*, Padua, 1942.

SCARPA, Jolando (editor) *Arte e Musica all'Ospedaletto, Schede d'archivio sull'attività musicale degli Ospedali dei Derelitti e dei mendicanti di Venezia (sec. XVI–XVIII)*, IRE, Stamperia di Venezia ed., 1978.

SELFRIDGE-FIELD, Eleanor, *Pallade Veneta, Writings on Music in Venetian Society 1650–1750*, Venice, Fond. Levi, 1985.

STROHM, Reinhard, *L'opera italiana nel Settecento*, Venice, Marsilio, 1991 (trans. from the German edition, Heinrichshofe Verlag, 1979).

TALBOT, Michael, *The sacred vocal music of Antonio Vivaldi*, Florence, Olschki, 1995.

— *Vivaldi*, London, Dent, 1978 (Italian trans. E.D.T., Turin 1978).

— *Vivaldi, fonti e letteratura critica*, translated by Luca Zappelli, Florence, Olschki, 1991 (original edition New York – London, Garland, 1988).

VIO, Gastone, *Giovanni Legrenzi ed il 'Sovvegno di Sta Cecilia'*, Florence, Olschki, 1994.

ZORZI, Alvise, *La République du Lion*, French translation by Jacques Roque, Paris, Perrin, 1988.

3. Articles, academic publications and encylopaedias

BRYANT, David, 'Una Cappela musicale di Stato: la basilica di S. Marco', in *La Cappela musicale nell'Italia della Contro-Riforma*, edited by O. Mischiati et P. Russo, Florence, Olschki, 1993, pp. 67–73.

CAVICCHI, Adriano, 'Inediti nell'epistolario Vivaldi-Bentivoglio', *Nuova Rivista musicale italiana*, May –June 1967, pp. 45–79.

CORTI, Gino, 'Il teatro La pergola di Firenze e la stagione d'opera per il carnevale 1726–1727: lettere di Luca Casimiro degli Albizzi a Vivaldi, Porpora ed altri', *Rivista italiana di Musicologia*, vol. XV, 1980, pp. 182–8.

DURANTE, Serge and PIPERNO, Franco, 'Cantanti settecenteschi e musicologia vivaldiana: lo stato degli studi', in *Nuovi Studi Vivaldiani*, Fond. Cini, vol. 2, 1986.

ELLERO, Giuseppe, 'Idillio all'Ospedaletto. Un documento d'archivio su Cecilia Guardi, futura sposa di Giambattista Tiepolo', *Arte/Documento* no. 10.

Encyclopedia *Storia di Venezia*, vol. VII 'La Venezia barocca', edited by G. Benzoni and G. Cozzi, Rome, 1997; vol. VIII 'L'ultima fase della Serenissima', edited by P. del Negro and P. Preto, Rome, 1998.

FABIANO, A., 'Venise, ville musicale idéale au XVIIIe siècle', in Fontana and Saro, *La République des Castors*, pp. 109–27.

GIAZOTTO, Remo, 'La Guerra dei Palchi', *Nuova Rivista musicale italiana*, July–August 1967, pp. 245–86.

GILLIO, Pier Giuseppe, 'La stagione d'oro degli Ospedali veneziani tra i dissesti del 1717 e 1777', *Rivista internazionale di musica sacra*, 1989, no. 10/3–4.

KOLDENER, Walter, 'Antonio (Lucio) Vivaldi', *Nuova Rivista musicale italiana*, January–March 1979, pp. 3–78.

LATTARICO, J.F., 'Du mécénat princier à l'entreprise commerciale, notes sur l'opéra vénitien du *Seicento*', in Fontana and Saro, *La République des Castors*, pp. 93–107.

MAMY, Sylvie, 'La diaspora dei cantanti veneziani', in *Nuovi Studi Vivaldiani*, Fond. Cini, vol. 2, 1986.

MANGINI, Nicola, 'Sui rapporti del Vivaldi col teatro di Sant'Angelo', in M.T. Muraro, *Venezia e il melodramma nel Settecento*, vol. 1, 1978.

— 'Sulla diffusione dell'opera comica nei teatri veneziani', in M.T. Muraro, *Venezia e il melodramma nel Settecento*, vol. 1, 1978.

NICOLODI, Fiamma, 'La riscoperta di Vivaldi nel Novecento', *Nuova Rivista musicale italiana*, October–December 1979.

RINALDI, Mario, 'Dati certi su Vivaldi operista', in *Nuova Rivista musicale italiana*, January–March 1979.

ROSTIROLLA, Giancarlo, 'L'organizzazione musicale nell' Ospedale veneziano della Pietà al tempo di Vivaldi', *Nuova Rivista musicale italiana*, January–March 1979, pp. 168–95.

SELFRIDGE-FIELD, Eleanor, 'Marcello, Sant'Angelo, and *Il*

Teatro alla modà', in *Antonio Vivaldi, Teatro musicale, cultura e società*, edited by L. Bianconi and G. Morelli, Florence, Olschki, 1982.

— 'Scarlatti, Gasparini, Marcello and Vivaldi', in F. Degrada, *Vivaldi veneziano europeo*.

TALBOT, Michael, 'The serenata in eighteenth-century Venice', *Research Chronicle*, 18/1982, pp. 1–50.

VIO, Gastone, 'I monasteri femminili del '600, gioie e dolori per i musici veneziani', in *Musica, scienza e idee nella Serenissima durante il Seicento*, Atti del Convegno internazionale di studi, Venice, 1993. Ed. Fond. Levi, Venice, 1996.

— 'Precisazioni sui documenti della Pietà in relazione alle *figlie del coro*', in F. Degrada, *Vivaldi veneziano europeo*.

ZORZI, Ludovico *et al.*, *I teatri pubblici di Venezia*, Exhibition catalogue, Venice, Biennale, 1971.

4. Manuscript sources

*Biblioteca Marciana

BENIGNA, Antonio, *Libro di Memorie (Memoriale di quanto accade giornalmente in Venezia dal 15 aprile 1714 al 9 marzo 1760)*, Cod. It. Cl. VII-1620 (=7846).

CAFFI, Francesco, *Materiale e carteggi per la storia della musica teatrale: spoglie e documenti*, Cod. It. Cl. IV-747 (=10462–65) and Cod. It. Cl. IV-748 (=10466).

CONTI, Antonio, *Lettres de l'abbé Antonio Conti à Mme de Caylus (1727–1729)*, Ms. Fr. App 58 (=12102).

*Archives of the IRE (Istituto Ricovero Educazione)

Archives re the music at the *Ospedale dei Derelitti (Ospedaletto)*, Music file: Musica DER G1, no. 48.

Archives re the registers at the *Ospedale dei Mendicanti*, especially file MEN B 5 (1716–32).

For archives on *La Pietà*, see the *Archivio di Stato di Venezia*, and the works of Rostirolla, Giazotto . . . for Vivaldi's period.

*Museo Correr
M. DE VAUMORIÈRE, *Lettres sur toutes sortes de sujets*, 1690, Cicogna 3282/3 (photocopies), G. Cini, MUSICA 4 VEN.

*Archives of the Ministère des Affaires Etrangères (Paris)
Mémoires et Documents Venise 27 (in particular 'Cérémonial 1705 à 1784') and Venise 35.
Correspondances Politiques, subsection Venice (by years as required).

Index

Addison, Joseph, traveller and writer 25, 47, 101

Albinoni, Tommaso, composer 3, 45,146, 148, 152, 162, 172

Alexander III, Pope 40, 97

Arnault, Henri-Charles 170

Auber, Jean, French violinist and composer 81

Bach, Johann Sebastian, composer 8, 55, 79, 81, 177

Barbarossa, Frederick, German emperor 40

Baretti, Giuseppe, writer 31, 32

Beethoven, Ludwig van, composer 81

Bella, Gabriele, painter 24, 98, 157

Bellini, Gentile, painter 98

Benedict XIV, Pope 106

Bentivoglio d'Aragona, Guido, Marchese of Ferrara 12, 125, 148

Berlioz, Hector, composer 81

Bernacchi, Antonio, castrato 139

Bernacchini da Carpi, Pietro, guitarist 161

Bianconi, Lorenzo 105

Biffi, chapel master at St Mark's 66, 94, 104

Bollani, Abbé 125

Bordoni, Faustina, singer, wife of Hasse 33, 66, 69, 132, 134, 147, 158

Bossuet, Jacques-Bénigne, writer and historian 177

Bretagne, Duc de 170

Broschi, Riccardo, composer, brother of Farinelli 134, 135, 154

Brosses, Charles de, writer, Président of Dijon Parlement 3, 15, 17, 29–30, 31, 63, 64, 72, 78, 88, 102, 117, 120, 174

Burnet, Gilbert, Bishop of Salisbury 85, 87

Burney, Charles, English musicologist 1, 7, 64, 161

Burnis, Cardinal de, French ambassador 21, 31

Caccia, Abbé 92

Caffarelli, Gaetano Majorana, known as, castrato 132, 135, 138, 139, 147

Caldara, Antonio, composer 145

Canaletto, Francesco Canal, known as, painter 20, 27, 39, 96, 98, 136

Casanova de Seingalt, Giacomo, adventurer and writer 27, 36, 41, 101–102, 106, 121

Cassanova, Zanetta, mother 121

Cassetti, Giocomo 76

Catherine II 157

Cavalli, Francesco, composer 94 97, 105, 111, 121, 129

Caylus, Comte de, writer 48, 97

Charles VI, emperor of Austria 149, 176

Chiari, Abbé Pietro, dramatist and novelist 33

Christina, Queen of Sweden 164

Contarini, Marco, procurator of St Mark's 22, 163, 164

Conti, Abbé, writer 33, 35, 39, 49, 50, 93, 101, 108, 133, 134, 140

Corelli, Archangelo, composer 156

Cornaro, Giovanni, doge 90, 98

Coyer, Abbé Gabriel-François, French traveller and writer 2

Crimarosa, Domenico, composer 82

Cuzzoni, Francesca, singer 66, 134, 147

Darmstadt, Prince of 12

Fabri, Annibale Pio, castrato 139

Falieri, Marino, doge, condemned to death 22

Farinelli (Farinello), Carlo Broschi, known as, castrato 65, 95, 132, 133, 134, 135, 136, 137, 138, 139, 147, 176
Faustina, Burnis de, Cardinal 117
Ferdinand, Charles, Prince of Saxony 174
Ferdinand, Prince of Bavaria 174
Francis I of Lorraine, emperor of Austria169, 176
Frederick Augustus, Prince Elector of Saxony 78, 162
Frederick IV, king of Denmark 37, 78
Freschi, composer 164
Froullay, Charles-François de 170

Gabrieli, Andrea and Giovanni, composers 96
Galuppi, Baldassare, composer 82
Gasparini, Francesco, choir-master at La Pietà 65, 72, 74–75, 76, 146
Gennaro, Alessandro, choir-master at La Pietà 72
Gergy, Baron de 170
Ghezzi, Pier Leone, caricaturist 15
Giacomelli, Geminiano, composer 135
Giovanelli, Count 70
Girò (or Giraud), Anne, singer, friend of Vivaldi 12, 14, 147, 148–149, 151, 169, 176
Giustinian, Leonardo, Venetian noble 4
Gizzi, Domenico, castrato 134, 139
Gizziello, Gioacchino Conti, known as, castrato 139, 147
Goethe, Wolfgang, poet 63
Goldoni, Carolo, writer and dramatist 4, 14–15, 33, 148, 151
Goudar, Ange, French adventurer and writer 8
Gravina, Vincenzo, poet, founder of the Arcadia 156
Gretry, André-Ernst-Modeste, French composer 106
Grimani, Cavaliero 105, 121
Grosley, Pierre-Jean, Swedish traveller and writer 7, 27, 87, 104
Grua, Carlo, choir-master at La Pietà 72
Guarama, Jacopo, painter 57
Guardi, Cecilia, wife of Tiepolo 69
Guardi, Domenico, painter 70

Guardi, Francesco, painter, pupil of Canaletto 20, 24, 27, 39, 102
Guyot de Merville, French writer 27

Handel, George Frederic, composer 131, 145, 152
Hasse, Johann Adolf, composer 33, 65, 104, 132, 135, 138, 146, 152, 154
Haydn, Joseph, composer 81, 177
Hennequin, Joseph-Antoine, French ambassador to Venice 170

Lalande, Jean de, writer 120
Lalli, Domenico, poet, librettist 171
Languet, Jacques-Vincent, French ambassador to Venice 170, 171
Leclair, Jean-Marie, French violinist and composer 81
Leczczynska, Marie, queen of France, wife of Louis XV 171
Legrenzi, Giovanni, composer 10, 65, 66, 94, 104, 112, 129, 158, 160, 161
Leo, Leonardo, composer 134, 146
Longhena, Baldassare, architect 57
Longhi, Pietro, painter 35, 57, 102
Lotti, Antonio, chapel master at St Mark's 65, 94, 97, 146, 152, 158, 163
Louis XIV, king of France 28, 164, 170
Louis XV, king of France 149, 170, 171
Lully, Jean-Baptiste, composer 160

Mamy, Sylvie, author 147
Manin, Ludovico, last doge of Venice 37
Marcello, Alessandro, Venetian noble, brother of the following 3, 140, 156
Marcello, Benedetto, composer and Venetian noble 139, 140, 141–142, 143, 144, 149, 150–151, 156,161
Maria-Theresa, empress of Austria 169, 176
Matteuccio, Matteo Sassano, known as, castrato 131
Mauro, Alessandro 135
Mauro, Antonio 126
Mengozzi Colonna, Agostino, painter 57
Metastasio, Pietro, poet and librettist 124, 134, 135, 137, 151
Misson, Maximilien, travel writer 47, 91, 118
Mocenigo, Alvise, doge 43

Montagu, Lady Mary Wortley, ambassador's wife, letter-writer 66, 155, 167

Montesquieu, Charles de, writer **000**

Monteverdi, Claudio, composer 3, 97, 105, 109, 111, 114, 129

Morellon La Cave, François, caricaturist 15

Mozart, Wolfgang Amadeus, composer 8, 135, 139

Nicolini, Nicolò Grimaldi, known as, castrato 131, 134

Ottoboni, Pietro, Cardinal in Rome 78, 105

Palladio, Andrea, architect 113

Pallavicino, Carlo, composer 112, 121, 129, 164

Palma il Giovane, painter 57

Pasquini, Bernardo, musician and composer 156

Pepoli, Count Sicinio 136, 137, 139

Petrovitch, Paul (Comte du Nord, future tsar of Russia) 157

Philip V, of Spain 135

Pisendel, Johann Georg, violinist 162

Pollarolo, Antonio, chapel master at St Mark's 70, 134, 145

Pollarolo, Carlo Francesco, composer 65, 112, 146, 156

Pöllnitz, Baron de 34, 47–48

Pomponne, Abbé de, French ambassador 51, 167, 170

Porpora, Nicolo, composer 65, 72, 134, 135, 152, 154

Porta, Giovanni, choir-master at La Pietà 72

Quantz, Johann Joachim, flautist and composer 81

Querini, Contessa, Caterina 99

Querini, Domenico, doge 22

Querini, Francesco 171

Raaff, Anton 139

Rameau, Jean-Philippe, composser 144

Renier Michel, Giustina, niece of the last doge 37

Robbins Landon, H.C. 73

Rossini, Gioacchino, composer 131

Rousseau, Jean-Jacques, *philosophe* and writer 4, 5, 30, 63, 67, 132, 160

Rovetta, Giovanni, composer 105

Ruffo, papal legate at Ferrara 147, 176

Sacchini, Antonio, composer 82

Saint-Didier, Alexandre-Toussaint de, traveller and writer 106, 114

Santurini, Francesco 123–124

Sarti, Giuseppe, composer 82

Scarlatti, Alessandro, composer 79, 120, 152, 156

Scarlatti, Domenico, composer, son of previous 156

Senesino, Francesco Bernardi, known as, castrato 95, 133, 134

Silhouette, Monsieur de, traveller and writer 18, 42, 100

Soranzo, Elisabetta Bon or Elena 158

Stella, Santa, singer, wife of Lotti 158

Stromba, Giacomina, violinist 65

Tartini, Giuseppe, violinist and composer 65, 175

Tiepolo, Gian Battista, painter 22, 57, 70

Traetta, Tommaso, composer 82

Uffenbach, Johann Friedrich von 16, 117, 119

Veracini, Francesco Maria, composer 162

Vinaccesi, Benedetto, composer 170

Vinci, Leonardo, composer 146

Vio, Gastone, doge 22

Vivaldi, Camilla, mother of Antonio 9

Vivaldi, Giovanni Battista, violinist, father of Antonio 9, 158

Willaert, Adrian, composer 2

Wright, Edward, writer 11, 119, 128

Zelenka, Jan, composer 162

Zeno, Apostolo, poet 134, 135, 137, 138, 151, 156

Ziani, Maria-Anna 73